DIASPORIC AGENCIES: MAPPING THE CITY OTHERWISE

# Diasporic Agencies: Mapping the City Otherwise

Nishat Awan
*University of Sheffield, UK*

ASHGATE

Published by
Ashgate Publishing Limited
Wey Court East
Union Road
Farnham
Surrey, GU9 7PT
England

Ashgate Publishing Company
110 Cherry Street
Suite 3-1
Burlington, VT 05401-3818
USA

www.ashgate.com

**British Library Cataloguing in Publication Data**
A catalogue record for this book is available from the British Library.

**Library of Congress Cataloging-in-Publication Data**
Names: Awan, Nishat, author.
Title: Diasporic agencies : mapping the city otherwise / by Nishat Awan.
Description: Burlington, VT : Ashgate Publishing Company, 2016. | Series:
  Design and the built environment | Includes bibliographical references and
  index.
Identifiers: LCCN 2015026630| ISBN 9781472433770 (hardback) |
  ISBN 9781472433787 (ebook) | ISBN 9781472433794 (epub)
Subjects: LCSH: Architecture and society--Europe--History--21st century. |
  Cultural geography--Europe--History--21st century. | Emigration and
  immigration--Social aspects. | Emigration and immigration--Psychological
  aspects. | Identity (Psychology)--Social aspects.
Classification: LCC NA2543.S6 A92 2016 | DDC 720.1/03--dc23 LC record available at
  http://lccn.loc.gov/2015026630


ISBN 9781472433770 (hbk)
ISBN 9781472433787 (ebk – PDF)
ISBN 9781472433794 (ebk – ePUB)

MIX
Paper from
responsible sources
FSC
www.fsc.org    FSC® C013985

Printed in the United Kingdom by Henry Ling Limited,
at the Dorset Press, Dorchester, DT1 1HD

# Contents

*List of Figures*                                                                                     *vii*
*Prologue*                                                                                             *xi*


Diasporas and the City                                                                                  1

## PART I  DIASPORAS AND AGENCY

Potentialities of Diasporic Space                                                                      15

1      Difference and Belonging                                                                        17
2      Diasporic Inhabitations                                                                         29

Spatial Figurations of Diasporic Agencies                                                              43

3      Trans-Local Practices: The Making of a 'Diasporic Home' in the City                             49
4      Multiplying Borders: Replicas, Imitations and Mediation                                         75
5      Diasporic Territories: Overlapping Spheres and Fragile Envelopes                                93

## PART II  MAPPING OTHERWISE

A Diasporic Spatial Imaginary                                                                         113

6      Maps and Agency                                                                                115
7      Representing the Non-Representational                                                           125
8      Diasporic Diagrams                                                                             147

A Diasporic Urbanism to Come                                                                          195


*Index*                                                                                              *199*

# List of Figures

*Trans-Local Practices: The Making of a 'Diasporic Home' in the City*

The *kahve* are spaces that rely on strong male friendships, 2009

Television plays a crucial role in the trans-local space of the *kahve*, 2009

The gesture of seed eating transposed from Turkey to a *kahve* in London, 2009

An Allegorical Map of Turkey, 2007

*Multiplying Borders: Replicas, Imitations and Mediation*

The colonial era Grand Trunk road leading to India across the Wagah border Pakistan, 2015

Shaheed Minar in Altab Ali Park, London, 2007

*Maps and Agency*

Agencies of mapping, 2010

*Representing the Non-Representational*

Map of Dreaming tracks crossing the northern end of the Canning Stock Route – surveyed in the early 1900s, the route was a source of conflict between indigenous groups and colonisers

A *dérive* with students from Sheffield School of Architecture, UK in Nowa Huta, Kraków, Poland

Walk from Dead Sea to Mediterranean Sea

*BCCI, ICIC, FAB c. 1972–91* (4th version), 1996–2000, Graphite on paper, 52 × 138 inches. Collection of The Whitney Museum of American Art, New York, NY

Gestural mimicry – 'An Eskimaux Watching a Seal'. In Parry, William Edward, 'Journal of a second voyage for the discovery of a North-West Passage … ', London: J. Murray, 1824

*Diasporic Diagrams*

A walk with a Kurdish woman involved in organising the frequent protests on the high street, 2007

Mapping of a walk with a Kurdish activist on the high street – who organised many of the protests – showing the places she frequented, 2007

Screenshots of a walk viewed in the web interface designed to explore each walk in section. The elevations at the top and bottom are used for navigation

Mapping the walks as territory, 2007

Screenshots of a walk viewed in the web interface designed to explore each walk in section. The elevations at the top and bottom are used for navigation

*Top*: The walk represented using an ANN that traces the use and

occupation of the street as intensities and rhythms, 2009; *Left*: Detail

*Kahve* network map of Beşiktas, 2008

Web interface for navigating the networks operating within the *kahve*

*Kahve* network map of Yusuf's Place (or Upstairs of Pub), 2008

*Kahve* network map of Guben, 2008

*Kahve* in Gülensu neighbourhood of Istanbul, 2009

Web interface for navigating the networks operating within the *kahve*

Kurdish woman's map drawn as a personal journey across Turkey, 2007

Diana's map was the only one that escaped the dominance of Turkey and showed a contiguous Kurdish territory, 2007

Derin's map – he could only draw Kurdistan as a narrative of the Iraq war, 2007

Yashar's map – an almost 'perfect' map from someone with a long-term involvement in the Kurdish cause, 2007

A replica of the Shaheed Minar with extracts from interviews with the Bangladeshi girls on display at the Architektur Forum, Linz, Austria, 2008

My grandfather's house in Faisalabad, 2005

# Prologue

I write these words having just returned to UK after spending a month in Pakistan. It had been eight years since I last visited and the trepidation of not recognising, of not understanding consumed me before leaving. But of course in-between the rapid changes that have occurred in the country there were also places and moments that seemed like little vignettes into the past, unchanged and available for those who needed them – I was glad of the respite. My interest in diasporas is personal, it could be considered indulgent. I began by wanting to understand my own situation and my initial exploration, through a dissertation I wrote many years ago, was of my own attempts at making a home in-between. In that work my grandfather's house in Faisalabad, Pakistan stood in for a longed for home, something so close and yet out of reach. This time around that house was one of my moments of respite. Diasporic time does that, it is cyclical, it folds in on itself and helps us out when we need it.

This book is about other people's experiences. Rather than looking inwards it looks outwards. In the many presentations I have given on this work, there have been responses around the question of introversion, of how diasporas make their own worlds and stay in them. This for me is the most fraught question. In the current context, with migrants once again in the firing line and the inexorable rise of Islamophobia, this book starts with our right as diasporic citizens to be here now – this fact is not up for negotiation. That I also go on to show how our worlds are multiple and can make all sorts of unexpected connections does not preclude the previous sentiment. I have relied on the generosity of those who let me into their worlds. I know I was a strange presence in the *kahve* and without the friendly guidance of Burak I would not have been able to negotiate that particular world. I would like to thank all those who gave their time so freely and spoke to me about their experiences.

This book started life as PhD research at the Sheffield School of Architecture and it would not have been possible without the careful guidance of Doina Petrescu who remains the person I turn to for critique, support and friendship.

My collaboration with Phil Langley was one of those amazing experiences of discovering something new together and his insights are everywhere in this book. I would also like to thank Celia Lury who gave us the opportunity to present an early version of our work together at the conference, A Topological Approach to Cultural Dynamics (University of Barcelona and Goldsmiths University, 2008). My work is also very much a product of the Sheffield environment and it has been influenced and shaped by another book – *Spatial Agency* – that I co-wrote together with Tatjana Schneider and Jeremy Till (Routledge, 2011) whilst I was completing my doctoral thesis.

I have benefitted from the generous support of the Arts and Humanities Research Council, allowing me to spend time on the initial PhD research. The maps and diagrams reproduced in this book are available to view and download in full colour alongside the code for the web interfaces at: www.openkhana.net

Parts of this book have been published elsewhere in different guises and I would like to thank the editors and reviewers for their support and comments.

N. Awan (2015) 'Diasporic Experience and the need for topological methods' in, P. Blundell Jones and M. Meagher (eds), *Architecture and Movement: The Dynamic Experience of Buildings and Landscapes*. London: Routledge, pp. 251–7

N. Awan and P. Langley (2013) 'Mapping topological deformations of space as diffused migrant territories', *Space and Culture* 16(2): 229–45. http://doi.org/10.1177/1206331213475746

N. Awan (2012) 'Re-mapping Kurdistan' in, R. Tyszczuk et al. (eds), *ATLAS: Geography, Architecture and Change*. London: Artifice, pp. 42–7.

N. Awan (2009) 'Words and objects in transposing desire and making space', *Architectural Research Quarterly*, 12(3): 263–8. http://dx.doi.org/10.1017/S135913550800119X

Finally I want to thank my parents and my husband for their patience in helping me negotiate my home in-between.

# Diasporas and the City

We live in a time of migration. The number of people moving across borders has risen exponentially since the mid-1990s, whether due to conflict, unequal global relations or the consequences of climate change. This book explores the spatial consequences of such migrations from the perspective of European cities, specifically through addressing diasporic communities in London, UK. During the time it has taken to write this book, the debate on migration across Europe has become increasingly polarised and highly toxic. In the UK the figure of the migrant has become an easy scapegoat for everything from a chronic and historic shortage of affordable housing to austerity politics. In the aftermath of September 11 and the ensuing global wars, one consequence for migrants in UK has been the rise of the problematic community cohesion agenda, alongside its highly destructive discourse on the self-segregation of Muslim communities.[1] In this context, the idea of working with and through difference seems a distant prospect, instead there is a desire to tame difference, to homogenise it, or better still to neutralise it through commodification. My aim in this book is to explore how the practices of spatial design disciplines such as architecture and urbanism can resist these impulses. I explore this question through working with and through diasporic inhabitations of space in order to reveal how diasporic agencies are produced and lived in the city.

When does a migrant become diasporic? How long before you stop being defined by the potential to move and rather by the desire to settle? The line is necessarily blurred and some have dismissed the notion of diaspora for this reason. But the diasporic condition does have relevance particularly for those populations who have been living away from their place of origin for quite some time. Second or third generation migrants do not include the place of origin within their description of home. Instead they are precursors to a new type of global citizen – not placeless yet without 'home'. Whilst many in Europe may want to 'send the immigrants back home', the populist rhetoric of such calls fails to answer the simple question – which home? The diasporas living in cities such as

London form constituent parts of a global condition where a simplistic notion of home no longer applies. Home can be many places or none. Such an urban condition is significant not only for the way in which it creates new political and social subjectivities but also for the production of corresponding spaces within the contemporary metropolis. How to include this phenomenon in the imagining of our cities has been the subject of this book.

## DESIGN-RESEARCH

Architecture and urban design have largely neglected diasporas but in associated spatial disciplines such as cultural geography and urban studies there has been a large body of work on the subject. [2] Many of the conceptualisations of diasporas that I rely upon come from cultural geography including the importance of a discourse on home. [3] Whilst these are extremely helpful what is necessarily missing from these accounts is an engagement with the field of design that is at the core of my own approach to architectural research. Urban studies on the other hand has provided many accounts of diasporic lives in cities but these rely on a comparative methodology. [4] Such approaches are embedded in what Deleuze has called a politics of re-presentation; based on ideas of fixed types and typologies the city is addressed according to the logic of the Same. [5] Unable to accommodate any real difference it is an approach that resorts to the contrasting and comparing of situations whilst keeping hegemonic assumptions on the workings of cities intact. In practice such an approach to cities combines policy concerns with project management to produce strategies of spatial planning, resulting in zoning studies, analyses of vehicle and pedestrian movements, attendance to the concerns of real estate value and the ordering of the city according to the logics of economic value and an ideal image of the city as suburb. A more recent incarnation of such an approach can be seen in the discourse around smart cities where computational advances are seen as a panacea for a range of problems in a series of diverse places. [6] As has been described by a number of commentators, it also results in the exclusion of difference and the production of docile citizens through categorising aspects of the 'good' and 'bad' city. [7]

In contrast the diasporic subject, always in-between, always becoming and heterogeneous, requires an approach to the city based in difference. Where the study of cities does not resort to already understood types and metaphors, but takes the city itself seriously as situation, subject and object of research. Here urbanism is understood not just as the study of buildings and the spaces around them, but rather as the agencies that are played out within the city; the people who occupy these spaces, their gestures and bodily practices, the networks and objects that are located within different spatio-temporalities. It is an approach that considers different scales at the same time, from the intimate scale of the body, to the planetary scale, inflected through localised practices that are often also trans-local.

Design research in architecture provides one way of resisting the comparative urge and exploring cities through the possibilities they may offer. One of the main insights of this book is that the agency of diasporic communities plays out through relational exchanges that are fine tuned to certain spaces and temporalities. To put it another way, diasporas act topologically and through these relational exchanges they make their own space-times.[8] How might one begin to represent the inhabitations of such a community? As architects we are adept at drawing spaces but how do you draw time and how do you draw relations? Specifically, how can these be represented dynamically and in a form that might be useful, for example as part of a planning process? These questions that are about the tools and methods of architectural representation, also lead to questions relating to the other understanding of representation, that is political representation and accountability. Debates surrounding the 'integration' of migrants often hinge on their (our) ability to live in multiple spaces at once, to have multiple belongings and to not always be loyal to the space-time we are supposed to inhabit. In this book I deliberately link such questions to architecture's tools of representation. Architecture, and especially its attendant practice of design research, starts at the moment of looking. What we choose to see, to notice, to draw and analyse is equally as important as what is eventually proposed, whilst proposition is conceived as an integral part of the process of drawing, representing or mapping. Sitting within a non-representational politics, the practice of 'mapping otherwise' that I describe here emphasises relations over discrete objects, subjectivities over essential identities, and a provisional politics over ideology.

Whilst in this book I argue for an approach based in design-research, it is also clear that mainstream architectural practice has remained largely unconcerned with the increasing diversity and segregation of European cities. Its complicity in the neo-liberal economy and unquestioning faith in rights of property above all others, has at best rendered it irrelevant in dealing with issues related to the fragmentation and polarisation of neighbourhoods, the decline of communal spaces, the displacement of communities and the privatisation of space and services. At worst, architectural practice is knowingly complicit in these processes. But there are a growing number of experimental practices emerging from the interstices of mainstream architecture, which contribute towards an imagining of alternative urbanisms that do not ignore these conditions but use them as a starting point.[9] As the architect, Teddy Cruz has commented, we need a different approach to architecture centred on difference and the empowerment of others.

> *Finally, in these times of crisis, empowerment also means the production of an expanded notion of practice, new ways of constructing information and conversation among ourselves, the so called "experts." ... Today, it is essential to reorient our gaze towards the drama embedded in the reality of the everyday and, in so doing, engage the shifting socio-political and economic domains that have been ungraspable by design.[10]*

This call to address larger socio-political issues, which are these days inevitably global in their scope, at the level of the local and from the vantage of everyday experience, is crucial to addressing the diasporic condition. I have translated this in my work through situating much of the research in my own neighbourhood in London, UK. Of course, everyday experience also includes the personal and my interest in migration and diasporic practices is also the result of my move to the UK from Pakistan at a relatively early age.

## DIASPORIC SUBJECTIVITY

The contested nature of the term 'diaspora' has meant that it has been the locus of a number of debates around questions of identity, home and the concept of hybridity, all of which are crucial to describing diasporic subjectivities. Associated primarily with the Jewish diaspora, the classical description of the term was sometimes extended to dislocated Armenian and Greek communities, but in contemporary understandings it has been generalised.[11] It is perhaps this flux in meaning, from the appropriation of a general verb to describe a very particular event, to its later expansion to encompass any population that has given the term such a fraught character. It has also led to conceptualisations of diasporas into ideal types and categorisations such as 'victim diasporas', 'trade diasporas' and 'cultural diasporas' to name a few.[12] Whilst conceptual clarity is useful such comparative categories and characterisations run the risk of restricting the potential of a term whose efficacy lies in its inclusivity.[13] I therefore follow a specific genealogy of thinking that takes a critical position towards fixed categories that rely on notions of identity and the relationship to an originary home, in particular the concept of return that has been so prevalent in earlier understandings of diaspora. The contemporary situation of displaced populations and their second or third generation offspring also complicates the understanding of the original meaning of diasporas as dispersion from an original homeland. Such people are 'diasporas without homeland', where the relationship to an original home is not only contested or refused but is simply not there. This radicalisation of the meaning of diaspora is especially useful for a contemporary world of increasing migration and displacement, where the fragmentation of fixed communities means that we are all tending towards the diasporic condition of 'without home'.

Being the product of displacements, diasporic subjectivities are often precarious and ambivalent. This ambivalence is seen as an important locus for diasporic agency that is able to challenge hegemonic notions, including the homogenising tendencies of national cultures. That displacement carries within it the potential for newness but can at the same time tear away at ties, relations and ways of thinking and doing, is the risk inherent within the diasporic experience. To understand how and why this happens, of how to facilitate and nurture processes of becoming and to understand what role spatial practitioners can claim in this process, was one of the underlying motivations for this book. The cultural theorist, Stuart Hall, exemplified this strand of thinking the becomings of diasporic subjects.[14] For Hall diasporas had to be defined in terms of the production of subjectivities rather than as fixed identities. Even those diasporic communities that could easily be dismissed as introverted were for him in the process of creating new subjectivities that could emerge from a dialogue with their new context. In this sense, diasporas even at their most traditional are contemporary. In many cases it is the construction of a new home elsewhere that is of bigger concern than the nostalgic act of looking backwards, but this construction cannot be based solely around similarities and must include difference. As Avtar Brah writes: 'The concept of diaspora places the discourse of 'home' and 'dispersion' in creative tension, inscribing a homing desire while simultaneously critiquing discourses of fixed origins.'[15] Thus a concept of diasporic subjectivity and temporality is required which can mediate between these different registers where 'historical and contemporary elements are understood, not in tandem, but in their dia-synchronic relationality'.[16] It is in the ambivalence of concepts such as home and the insistence on creativity and invention that diaspora culture guards against essentialised notions of the self. As Hall describes:

> The diaspora experience as I intend it here is defined, not by essence or purity, but by the recognition of a necessary heterogeneity and diversity; by a conception of "identity" which lives with and through, not despite, difference; by hybridity. Diaspora identities are those which are constantly producing and reproducing themselves anew, through transformation and difference.[17]

The concept of hybridity that is highlighted by Hall is contested within diaspora theory. Whilst Hall's own readings of the hybridity of Black diasporas were carefully crafted and historically situated accounts, often in other readings the economic, political, social, religious and gendered contexts of diasporic lives were not paid sufficient attention.[18] For this reason some prefer to use the term 'transnationalism', which deals specifically with these other flows related to the contemporary context of globalisation and advanced capitalism.[19] But it is the situated nature of diaspora theory and its explicit positioning within the everyday lived experiences of people that I find useful. Alongside this, its roots in the post-colonial experience have meant that diaspora theory is also based around a critique of the narrative of nationalism and the primacy of the nation-state. As the editors of an anthology on the subject suggest, 'theorising diaspora offers critical spaces for thinking about the discordant movements of modernity', it offers also the space to imagine the multiple, overlapping and sometimes parallel modernities in which we now live.[20] It is in the representation of and intervention within these multiple modernities and imagined worlds that diasporic agency emerges.

## DISPLACEMENTS AND RETERRITORIALISATIONS

What might be a knowledge politics particular to the diasporic condition and how might it relate to an understanding of diasporic agency? It may involve a shift from the dominant modes of explanation and explication, towards strategies of displacement and reterritorialisation, both of which emerge from the specific situation of those in the diaspora. Displacement recalls the move central to the production of diasporic subjects and as knowledge practice it is able to address topics laterally. Reterritorialisation, a concept borrowed form Deleuze and Guattari, is related to the ways in which diasporas affect space.[21] As knowledge politics it could be a way of relinquishing some of the hegemonic practices of (our own) disciplines and adapting them to the concerns of the diaspora. In my case the practice of 'mapping otherwise' was a way of working within architectural methodologies whilst at the same time supplementing and subverting them in order to represent that which architecture always expunges. In addressing those that have been excluded or marginalised from the dominant discourse I have also looked towards feminist theory and practice, whilst the approach of specifically addressing the spatial through the use of mappings has resulted in a research methodology that is related to what Jane Rendell calls a 'critical spatial practice'. She describes such practices as those that are able to 'transform rather than describe' and to 'involve social critique, self-reflection and social change'.[22] They are also practices that provoke or problematise rather than the usual mode of situating architecture and urbanism as problem solving practices, an approach that necessarily leads to a simplification and foreshortening of the complex nature of space. Instead a diasporic spatial practice uses the displacement of the diasporic subject as metonym for an appropriate way of working. Displacement becomes a methodology that valorises the tactics of looking askance, of not following given methodologies to the letter, of thinking and acting laterally.

## CONTENTS

The book is split into two main parts: the first examines the twin concepts of diasporas and agency and the second describes the practice of mapping otherwise. The first section of Part I is an exploration of the potentialities of diasporic space. It contains two chapters, the first of which is a theoretical exploration of how the concept of space can be expanded to include diasporic experience. The second chapter explores how agency is constituted through the spatial inhabitations of diasporic subjects. The second section consists of three chapters that explore three different spatial readings of diasporic agencies. These emerge through trans-local practices, in multiplying borders and as diasporic territories. Part II describes what the practice of mapping otherwise could be. It starts with a short introduction on what might be a diasporic spatial imaginary and contains three chapters. The first chapter explores the relationship between maps and the production and representation of agency. The second considers different examples of how others have attempted to represent in a non-representational mode. The last chapter relates my own practice of mapping otherwise that produced a series of diasporic diagrams. Finally, by way of a conclusion I speculate on what might be the qualities of a 'diasporic urbanism to come' that is hinted at throughout this book.

## Part I

The first chapter, *Difference and Belonging*, starts with a description of diasporic spatio-temporalities as being intimately connected to the body and to ways in which they enact a rhythmic modulation of space and time. It is a way of thinking space through the difference it embodies, a difference that plays out in degrees and intensities. It is also a way of thinking space as topological rather than topographical, foregrounding relations over static ideas of space as neutral backdrop. Space and time are therefore composed and recomposed through diasporic inhabitations and the consequences of this way of thinking are explored through an engagement with the notion of scale, perhaps the most topographic of concepts. An understanding of scale in flux also describes a different relationship to the practices of measuring and valuing, and the consequences of this are explored further through the twin notions of inclusion and belonging. What does it mean to be included and yet to not belong is a question pertinent to many in the diaspora and it leads to an exploration of time and multiplicity. The chapter concludes with a suggestion of the type of space required for accommodating difference not just through regimes of inclusion but also through practices of belonging.

The second chapter, *Diasporic Inhabitations,* explores the central role of the body in producing diasporic agencies. Ways of inhabiting space and the role of the affective body in modifying spatio-temporalities leads to an affirmative understanding of agency. For diasporas, subversive practices such as mimicry are central to these processes and also allow diasporic agency to be thought of in relation to the radically other. Following Elizabeth Grosz, I describe agency not as a fulfilling of abstract possibilities but as the production of materially real potentialities.[23] Within this relational model of agency dynamic associations are privileged over fixed properties and it is also the quality and temporality of these associations that are seen to be important. How to represent such agencies that are played out in topological modes and are embedded within spatial relations is also explored in the chapter. Here mapping emerges as a way of visualising and working with diasporic agencies, through revealing the different layers of diasporic subjectivity from the religious to the economic. The chapter ends with an introduction to the specific instances of diasporic inhabitation that will be explored in the book, that is the particulars of the areas and communities in London where the research took place.

In the third chapter, *Trans-Local Practices*, I tackle one of the most contested topics within any discussion of diasporas – the notion of home. I have already described the wider diasporic condition as that of being 'without home', where the idea of home is meant in the classical sense of an originary nation-state or cultural identity. In reality, for those in the diaspora, home is a deliberate construction that includes nostalgia for the place left behind and the need to replicate some of its customs, traditions and spaces. Knowing that an exact replication is impossible, this hybrid practice aims instead to create similar atmospheres, achieved through the deployment of souvenirs.[24] Here I discuss the creation of atmospheres at a small scale within interior spaces where the souvenirs are domestic objects – a pack of playing cards or a teapot, which combined with certain practices, rituals and gestures creates a trans-locality, a space suspended somewhere between here and there or then and now.

In the fourth chapter, *Multiplying Borders*, there is a jump in scale and site, a move out of the private sphere of the interior to the expression of diasporic urban imaginings in the public space of a park. In this instance the souvenirs become monumental, expressions of national, religious or other affiliations that represent a different culture and politics to those of the host populations. It is here that diasporic spaces become exoticised on the one hand and vilified on the other, a curry on Brick Lane is on the list of essential experiences for the savvy London tourist, whilst a mosque and its associated minar – on the same street – are too exclusive and appropriate too much public space, symbols of unwanted and inappropriate people and their practices. But at the same time there is a need for open and inclusive spaces that can accommodate different modes of inhabiting, and some diasporic spaces *are* highly exclusive. How to find a balance between the need for inclusive spaces and the inability of dominant spaces to accommodate certain traditions and behaviours, as well as handling the push and pull between the host and home cultures that never relate within an easy dialectic is a key question for a 'diasporic urbanism to come'.

The fifth chapter, *Diasporic Territories*, is the last of part one and it deals with how the concept of territory can be used to describe the production of diasporic space. The chapter explores different definitions of territory, from the geo-political to the biological, through a series of examples from contemporary art and architecture. Whilst political territory is concerned with the interplay of politics, power and space, from a biological perspective it can be construed as the primal need of all animals including humans for space and to create a distinction from their environment. This way of thinking territory moves beyond a purely anthropocentric approach towards a concern with thinking what the notion of territory would be for the radically other. In this chapter, I do this through an exploration of the worlds of ticks, trees and pigeons. Thus diasporic territory is conceptualised through what Peter Sloterdijk has referred to as 'spatial envelopes'.[25] These are made up of social, spatial and bodily relations that surround us all and are influenced by our personal circumstances, politics and practices. These personal territories become more important in the case of diasporas where the politics and concerns of elsewhere impact upon, for example where you can go and whom you can talk to.

**Part II**

In the sixth chapter, *Maps and Agency*, I explore the relationship between mapping as a practice and the representation and production of diasporic agencies. The term 'mapping otherwise' refers to a way of thinking and representing space and time as co-produced, that is through a topological sensibility. It also refers to the need for maps to mediate between the abstracted realm of representation and an embodied understanding of the world. The practice of mapping otherwise is further described as having three different modes – maps that are propositions, mediators and possibilities – each being a different way of working with diasporic agencies. Some actively generate new knowledge, whilst others are a way of intervening and facilitating situations, or are a way of imaginatively thinking of other spatial possibilities.

In the seventh chapter, *Representing the Non-Representational*, these three ways of describing mapping otherwise are illustrated through a series of examples from contemporary architecture and art. These examples cover many different topics but it is the methods of mapping and the effects that are achieved that are of relevance. They are all different ways of representing the non-representational through practices of naming and narrative, walking and wandering, tracing and drawing, collecting and curating, telling and transmitting, observing and being present. Whilst they chart a perhaps idiosyncratic route through contemporary and some historical mapping practices, they have been chosen for encapsulating modes of representation that could be useful for diasporic mapping.

The final chapter, *Diasporic Diagrams*, relates the specifics of the maps that I have produced to represent diasporic agencies. Through visually representing the relationships between the production of space, time, subjectivity and politics, the diagrams relate how diasporic agencies are constituted in the contemporary city. These maps operate in different modes that include the digital mapping of topological connections, interpretative mappings of relations, symbols and spaces, and finally, the performative mapping of gestures and embodiments. The production of these diasporic diagrams are viewed as integral to my understanding of diasporic agencies and they perform some of the discontinuities, disjunctures, displacements and dislocations that are central to any understanding of diasporas.

## DIASPORIC URBANISM

The question of agency thus emerges as being central to the practices of what could be described as a 'diasporic urbanism to come'. This book argues for an affirmative notion of agency that is attendant to both the topological nature of diasporic inhabitations and also to their marginality. The task of imagining cities has for too long been the preserve of the privileged and the powerful. As the anthropologist Arjun Appadurai writes: 'Even the poorest of the poor should have the capability, the privilege and the ability to participate in the work of the imagination.'[26] This then is the challenge set down for diasporic urbanism – how to make the conditions necessary for those other than the privileged few to participate in the imagining of our cities, and how to do this in the context of increasing heterogeneity, where there are inevitable dislocations between these different imaginings.

## NOTES

1. Samad, *Muslims and Community Cohesion in Bradford*.

2. One significant exception in architecture is the edited collection, *Drifting: Architecture and Migrancy*, which takes a much wider approach than my focus on diasporas. Cairns describes his characterisation of the engagements between architecture and migrancy as relating to: *'Architecture-by-migrants, architecture-for-migrants, and architects-as-migrants.'* Within this categorisation some of what is of interest here is covered in the first category, 'architecture-by-migrants', which includes areas in cities that have been appropriated and adapted by their migrant populations. Cairns, Markus, and King, *Drifting: Architecture and Migrancy*, 30.
   A more recent strand is work that addresses the topic of trans-local urbanism, which includes for example the architecture that has been built in migrant's home countries through the remittances they have sent back. See, Lopez, *The Remittance Landscape*; Vöckler and Zerr, 'Translocal Urbanism: The Diaspora as Urban Developer'.

3. Relevant discourses in cultural geography include those related to mobilities, transnationalism, as well as diasporas. For an overview of the interrelations between these see, Blunt, 'Cultural Geographies of Migration'. For a discussion on home in relation to diasporas see, Blunt and Dowling, *Home*.

4. See the discourse around the resurgence of 'comparative urbanism' particularly the work of Jennifer Robinson and Colin McFarlane. McFarlane and Robinson, 'Comparative Urbanism'.

5. See for example, Deleuze, *Difference and Repetition*.

6. Datta, 'India's Smart City Craze'.

7. See for example, Vanolo, 'Smartmentality'.

8. For a detailed discussion of such spatial and cultural understanding of topology see, Shields, *Spatial Questions*.

9. The book Spatial Agency collected together some of these practices. Awan, Schneider, and Till, *Spatial Agency: Other Ways of Doing Architecture*. See also, AAA and PEPRAV, *Urban/ACT*; Guidi, *Urban Makers: Parallel Narratives of Grassroots Practices and Tensions*.

10. Cruz, 'Mapping Non-Conformity: Post-Bubble Urban Strategies'.

11. Its current description: 'Any group of people who have spread or become dispersed beyond their traditional homeland or point of origin.' OED, 'Oxford English Dictionary'.

12. See for example the categorisations in Cohen, *Global Diasporas: An Introduction*.

13. For a critique of 'ideal type' diasporas see, Clifford, *Routes: Travel and Translation in the Late Twentieth Century*, 244–78.

14. Hall, 'Identity: Community, Culture and Difference', 223–37.

15. Brah, *Cartographies of Diaspora: Contesting Identities*, 192–3.

16. Ibid., 190.

17. Hall, 'Identity: Community, Culture and Difference', 235.

18. See for example Bruce Robbin's critique of several US journals publishing on issues related to the diaspora, Robbins, 'Some Versions of US Internationalism'; For a more recent publication that offers a politically inflected critique, Hutnyk, Kalra, and Kaur, *Diaspora and Hybridity*.

19.   Vertovec, *Transnationalism*.

20.   Braziel and Mannur, *Theorizing Diaspora: A Reader*, 3.

21.   Deleuze and Guattari, '1837: Of the Refrain'.

22.   Rendell, 'Critical Spatial Practice'.

23.   Grosz, 'Feminism, Materialism, and Freedom'.

24.   The use of the terms 'souvenirs' and 'atmospheres' to describe migrant space has been borrowed from Diego Barajas. *Dispersion: A Study of Global Mobility and the Dynamics of a Fictional Urbanism*.

25.   Sloterdijk and Hoban, *Bubbles*.

26.   Appadurai, 'The Right to Participate in the Work of the Imagination (Interview by Arjen Mulder)', 46.

## REFERENCES

AAA, and PEPRAV, eds. *Urban/ACT*. Montrouge: Moutot Imprimeurs, 2007.

Appadurai, Arjun. 'The Right to Participate in the Work of the Imagination (Interview by Arjen Mulder)'. In *Transurbanism*, edited by Arjen Mulder, Laura Martz, and Joke Brouwer, 33–47. Rotterdam: V2_Publishing/NAI Publishers, 2002.

Awan, Nishat, Tatjana Schneider, and Jeremy Till. *Spatial Agency: Other Ways of Doing Architecture*. London: Routledge, 2011.

Barajas, Diego. *Dispersion: A Study of Global Mobility and the Dynamics of a Fictional Urbanism*. Rotterdam: episode publishers, 2003.

Blunt, Alison. 'Cultural Geographies of Migration: Mobility, Transnationality and Diaspora'. *Progress in Human Geography* 31, no. 5 (2007): 684–94.

Blunt, Alison, and Robyn Dowling. *Home*. Abingdon: Routledge, 2006.

Brah, Avtar. *Cartographies of Diaspora: Contesting Identities*. London: Routledge, 1996.

Braziel, Jana Evans, and Anita Mannur, eds. *Theorizing Diaspora: A Reader*. Oxford: Blackwell Publishing, 2003.

Cairns, Stephen, Thomas A. Markus, and Anthony King, eds. *Drifting: Architecture and Migrancy*. London: Routledge, 2004.

Clifford, James. *Routes: Travel and Translation in the Late Twentieth Century*. Cambridge, MA: Harvard University Press, 1997.

Cohen, Robin. *Global Diasporas: An Introduction*. London: UCL Press, 1997.

Cruz, Teddy. 'Mapping Non-Conformity: Post-Bubble Urban Strategies'. *E-Misférica* 7, no. 1 (2010). http://hemisphericinstitute.org/hemi/en/e-misferica-71/cruz.

Datta, Ayona. 'India's Smart City Craze: Big, Green and Doomed from the Start?' *The Guardian*. Accessed March 27, 2015. http://www.theguardian.com/cities/2014/apr/17/india-smart-city-dholera-flood-farmers-investors.

Deleuze, Gilles. *Difference and Repetition*. London: The Athlone Press, 1994.

Deleuze, Gilles, and Félix Guattari. '1837: Of the Refrain'. In *A Thousand Plateaus: Capitalism and Schizophrenia*, 342–86. New York: Continuum, 2004.

Grosz, Elizabeth. 'Feminism, Materialism, and Freedom'. In *New Materialisms: Ontology, Agency, and Politics*, edited by Diana Cole and Samantha Frost, 139–57. Duke University Press, 2010.

Guidi, Emanuele, ed. *Urban Makers: Parallel Narratives of Grassroots Practices and Tensions*. Berlin: b_books, 2008.

Hall, Stuart. 'Identity: Community, Culture and Difference'. In *Cultural Identity and Diaspora*, Identity: Community, Culture and Difference London: 223–37. Lawrence & Wishart, 1990.

Hutnyk, John, Virinder S. Kalra, and Raminder Kaur, eds. *Diaspora and Hybridity*. London: Sage, 2005.

Lopez, Sarah Lynn. *The Remittance Landscape: Spaces of Migration in Rural Mexico and Urban USA*. University of Chicago Press, 2015.

McFarlane, Colin, and Jennifer Robinson. 'Comparative Urbanism'. *Urban Geography* 33, no. 6. Accessed September 17, 2012. http://bellwether.metapress.com/content/h1j2347 10858/?p=8b5620a363f44cf18fedc01d204e71b0&pi=0.

OED. 'Oxford English Dictionary' 2014, no. Third Edition (2007). http://www.oed.com/.

Rendell, Jane. 'Critical Spatial Practice'. In *Art Incorporated: the Role of Art in Urban Development*, edited by Sabine Nielsen and Christine Buhl Andersen. Køge: Kunstmuseet Køge Skitsesamling, 2008. http://www.janerendell.co.uk/essays/critical-spatial-practice.

Robbins, Bruce. 'Some Versions of US Internationalism'. *SText* 45 (1995): 97–123.

Samad, Yunas. *Muslims and Community Cohesion in Bradford*. Joseph Rowntree Foundation, July 2010.

Shields, Rob. *Spatial Questions: Cultural Topologies and Social Spatialisation*. SAGE, 2013.

Sloterdijk, Peter, and Wieland Hoban. *Bubbles: Spheres I – Microspherology*. Vol. 1. 3 vols. Spheres. Semiotext(e). MIT Press, 2011.

Vanolo, Alberto. 'Smartmentality: The Smart City as Disciplinary Strategy'. *Urban Studies* 51, no. 5 (April 1, 2014): 883–98. doi:10.1177/0042098013494427.

Vertovec, Steven. *Transnationalism*. London: Routledge, 2009.

Vöckler, Kai, and Irmgard Zerr. 'Translocal Urbanism: The Diaspora as Urban Developer'. In *Prishtina Is Everywhere. Turbo Urbanism: The Aftermath of a Crisis*, edited by Kai Vöckler. Amsterdam: Archis, 2008.

# PART I
# Diasporas and Agency

# Potentialities of Diasporic Space

My exploration of the potentialities of diasporic space begins with the body, which through modes of inhabitation specific to the diaspora is able to enfold multiple temporalities. What counts as being present thus emerges as an important question for those in the diaspora. For us presence as well as the present are constituted differently. These differences are related to the ways in which space, time and duration are imagined differently by us. The linearity of the modern version of time makes no sense for those whose ideas of time are interwoven with memories and nostalgias of the past that reach out to the present and beyond. At the same time the rhythms of everyday life for us are often not only tuned to the time zone that we physically inhabit, but are also attuned to other places. This connection with other places also transforms the diasporic experience of space, which is always multiple. It also confounds traditional architectural conceptions of three-dimensional space, linear time and static ideas of scale.

The diasporic figure thus challenges prevalent notions of belonging and inclusion through such dynamic understandings of space and time based in difference. Here I follow Elizabeth Grosz's conception of difference as entwined within an understanding of time as duration: 'Difference generates further difference because difference inheres the force of duration (becoming/unbecoming) in all things, in all acts of differentiation and in all things and terms thus differentiated.'[1] The potential of diasporic space thus lies in its ability to proliferate differences.

## NOTES

1.  Grosz, Elizabeth. 'Bergson, Deleuze and the Becoming of Unbecoming'. *Parallax* 11, no. 2 (2005): 4–13. doi: 10.1080/13534640500058434.

# 1

# Difference and Belonging

Certain specificities of the diasporic condition demand the conceptualisation of a different type of space than that articulated within mainstream architectural discourse. This Cartesian space dominated by the visual cannot account for the itinerant geographies of those whose lives occur in-between spaces and cultures. These require a relational approach where apparently disjointed spaces and times are connected in complex and unexpected ways through everyday interactions. But I do not want to idealise the diasporic experience of space and geography, because just as we are able to make connections we can also practice dislocations. At the same time these practices are not unique to the diasporic subject, the effects of what we have come to call globalisation mean that these qualities of diasporic space are not exclusive to it but are intensified in instances of migration.

## DIASPORIC SPATIO-TEMPORALITIES

Since the homogenising tendencies of the dominant way of articulating space cannot accommodate the difference inherent in diasporic lives, what is important in conceptualising diasporic space is not any aesthetic concern but the need to embody notions of difference including how these are accommodated in everyday life. This difference is played out in the relationships between space and time and the ways in which these are mediated through the body. A common starting point for thinking through such concerns is Henri Lefebvre's sociology of the everyday based on the seemingly simple premise: '(Social) space is a (social) product.'[1] It is useful for thinking space beyond the idealised empty container of Cartesian logic to one that is produced through the inhabitation of bodies. Whilst in the spatial discipline of architecture, as well as in related areas such as urban studies and geography, Lefebvre has been reified as *the* philosopher of space; he did not privilege space over time. In Lefebvre's schema the spatiality of the lived experience within the social realm is given a strategic place in order to critique the notion of history and the linear time of modernity. He privileged lived cyclical time influenced by memory and recollection over time measured by clocks, making a break from classical Marxist thought in its conception of history and emphasis on causality. In his theory of moments Lefebvre suggests: 'The moment has a certain specific duration.'[2] Each moment can be relived and in this repetition lies its ability to differentiate, meaning that moments embody the potential to resist the alienating tendencies of capital. If the role of the abstract notion of space is to homogenise then the element that it does not account for is the living, being, moving, gesturing body, which constantly produces difference through the way it lives in and through moments.

> The enigma of the body – its secret, at once banal and profound – is its ability, beyond "subject" and "object" (and beyond the philosophical distinction between them), to produce differences "unconsciously" out of repetitions – out of gestures (linear) or out of rhythms (cyclical). In the misapprehended space of the body, a space that is both close by and distant, this paradoxical junction of repetitive and differential – this most basic form of "production" – is forever occurring.[3]

Certain moments of everyday life play out rhythmically creating difference through repetition and with it another kind of space, what Lefebvre called a 'differential space'.[4] This entwined relationship between space, time and difference is a basis for conceptualising 'diasporic spatio-temporalities' that are produced through the displacement of bodies. They modulate space and time through memories and recollection and produce the multiple realities that are the product of the particular spatial consequences of globalisation and non-linear time.

A space-time that privileges relations and associations, that moves away from hegemonies and identity politics may require at its core a more radical shift in perspective. It would need to *start* with difference rather than ending up there. How that difference is embodied in and of space and through multiple temporalities is described in Gilles Deleuze's concept of 'becoming'. Deleuze questions the very idea of Being as a basis for thought arguing that there is no determinate foundation for knowledge, instead we should study how languages, cultures, political systems, spaces and subjectivities transform or become; the challenge is to address this becoming in all of its diversity. The feminist philosopher, Elizabeth Grosz describes the specificity of thinking such difference: 'In conceptualising a difference in and of itself, a difference which is not subordinated to identity, Deleuze and Guattari invoke notions of becoming and of multiplicity beyond the mere doubling or proliferation of singular, unified subjectivities.'[5] Difference and becoming are here central concepts for conceptualising diasporas beyond fixed notions of identity towards what Rosi Braidotti has called 'multiple ecologies of belonging'.[6] By imagining a mode of belonging that works through difference the possibility of internal contradictions and discontinuities emerges between our understandings of ourselves as diasporic subjects and the communities we inhabit, whilst at the same time opening up the possibility of constructing communities beyond for example a shared ethnicity.

Difference, normally defined in relation to what it is not, is instead defined affirmatively as the ability to transform, to *become*. Deleuze's critique of western philosophy is based in its suppression of the simulacra, which for him are the embodiment of difference; their unfaithful copy of the Form produces difference. 'If the simulacrum still has a model, it is another model, a model of the Other (*l'Autre*) from which there flows an internalized dissemblance.'[7] Unlike the Platonic copy, which still possesses a knowledge (*savoir*), the simulacrum is outside knowledge. '[T]here is in the simulacrum a becoming-mad, or a becoming unlimited … a becoming always other, a becoming subversive of the depths, able to evade the equal, the limit, the Same, or the Similar: always more and less at once, but never equal.'[8] Such a definition of difference allows us to move beyond equality as a defining factor in oppositional struggles towards notions of multiplicity.[9]

What might a corresponding space of differentiation look like? Here I turn to the difference in the understanding of space (and time) between Newton and Leibniz, a famous exchange that is one of the underlying concepts for conceptualising differential or *relational* space. Whilst for Newton objects exist independently of space and time, which provides a backdrop, an absolute frame of reference, for Leibniz space and time exist only as relations between objects and without these would not exist at all. In simple terms, this would mean that two identical objects in different locations are *not* identical because of the spatial and temporal relations of which they are a part; swapping them would also change their properties. Deleuze has written extensively on Leibniz's relational understanding of space which he calls a 'Baroque perspective': 'The new status of the object no longer refers its condition to a spatial mould – in other words, to a relation of form-matter – but to a temporal modulation that implies as much the beginnings of a continuous variation of matter as a continuous development of form.'[10] This way of apprehending the world has consequences for how space, time and subjects are conceptualised: 'The Baroque introduces a new kind of story in which … description replaces the object, the concept becomes narrative, and the subject becomes point of view or subject of expression.'[11] For spatial thinking, it is the privileging of relationalities over attributes, the topological over the topographic. Here differences are of degree and intensity (continuous variation) and there is no ideal in contrast to which others are set up as different – no ideal whiteness from which to determine others, no ideal space and no outside from which to apprehend the world. This differential space that is composed of a geography of relations is by its nature topological.

## TOPOLOGICAL SPACES

Deleuze's continuous variation is embedded in mathematical thinking and in particular in the notion of topology. In architecture we are perhaps more familiar with the word topography. The topography of a site is its contours, the way the land rises and falls and the arrangement of geographical features upon it. What becomes clear, even from this very short and partial description of topography, is its relation to the ability to measure in three dimensions. This way of thinking leads to a conceptualisation of space as territory with fixed spatial geometries. It also leads to a conceptualisation of scale as inherently stable. Whilst topography is about fixed spatial geometries topology privileges relations.

A branch of modern mathematics, topology is the study of forms under continuous deformation, one of the most cited examples of this being a coffee cup that deforms into a doughnut and vice versa. Topology is therefore concerned with the mathematics of continuity and connectivity through change. Topological thinking can be traced back to Leibniz's 'geometry of place' that, as described above, made a decisive break from the Newtonian notion of space and time as neutral backdrop. The most general version of topology, point-set theory, studies the properties of topological spaces 'reduced' to surfaces, in other words general topology could also be understood as the mathematics of the thick surface.[12] This preoccupation with the surface can also be traced in social and cultural theory, which as Celia Lury states, had already occurred in the 1920s in the sociologist Siegfried Kracauer's description of modern society. In his book, *The Mass Ornament*, Kracauer describes the appearance of masses through a reading of the Tiller Girls as ornamental phenomena.[13] 'The ornament, detached from its bearers, must be understood rationally. It consists of lines and circles like those found in text books on Euclidean geometry …'[14] It perhaps comes as no surprise that Kracauer was trained as an architect. This reductive description of the surface through recourse to three fixed co-ordinates chimed with the description of a mass society where the Tiller Girls became a 'fraction of a figure' and the audience became spectator.[15]

If in modern society the surface was Euclidean, Lury asks what model of the surface is required in a contemporary society where the lines between the spectacle and spectator are blurred and roles often reverse? Here the surface becomes folded and describes a space that is non-Euclidean, the 'turn to the surface' foregrounding questions of mediation. In diasporic relations this transformation is related most obviously to the development of cheap and immediate communication technologies. The ability to take part in social and cultural life at a distance, and to do so recursively, has transformed what it means to be a diasporic subject. My parents often recall the slightly desperate and mildly farcical telephone calls back home in the 1960s, waiting and waiting for the operator to call back, only to have the precious three minutes start even before the call was connected, and then being cut off mid-sentence … until the next time. How the politics and everyday relations of another place were experienced and understood then is rather different from now, as I follow the recent Azadi march on the various news channels and on Twitter, Pakistan and especially Lahore, are becoming more and more a part of me in London.[16] These connections that may seem immaterial at first glance also shape the material and embodied relations of those in the diaspora. My father again, recounting the story of leaving Pakistan as a young man with his own father's parting words ringing in his ears: 'Don't come back without a qualification.' In the event he came back with a qualification and a young wife, equally as qualified. The lines were clear then, you left and then you attempted to come back, but the place that you had left was not the same and you were not the same; time and space had moved on at a different pace and a different register.

In contemporary society these times and spaces may still be separated, but crucially they also intertwine and overlap, at certain moments, and through certain subjects. The diasporic subject is here key, able to mediate this topological space, a thick surface that persists through movement and change. This is Deleuze's 'fold' and one consequence of the folding in of space is for the edges to appear in the centre, not only creating unexpected connections but also disconnections and barriers. As Scott Lash states: 'The topological object is a process, a space of figuration.'[17] Within these processes of figuration, the diasporic subject can mediate the divide between the virtual and the actual, making associations not based in spatial proximity but in common properties. This has lots of consequences, for example inclusion and exclusion may not necessarily be based around territorial boundaries but could exceed them, meaning that the concept of scale in relation to space is exploded.

## Multiple Scales

Scale in architecture could be described as a certain relationship between measure and ratio that is used to index the spatial. Traditionally, scalar relations are conceived as hierarchical and have relied on a sequential mode – S, M, L, XL – and on a proportional relationship.[18] Yet when thinking about our experience of space, and especially about the diasporic experience, scale can often seem irrelevant. Intimate relations transcend the boundaries of sequential scale so that connections across distances often 'jump' scales through relations based on a shared culture, language, ideas etc. What is at stake here is not a question of scalelessness but that of a reconceptualisation of scale as folded and nested, of a complex intertwining of spaces and times that confounds architecture's usual consideration of scale as anthropometry. That is, from the Renaissance to Le Corbusier scale has usually been conceptualised in architecture as proportional to the ideal human body, or later in ergonomics to that of the statistically 'normal' body.[19]

How might a topological idea of scale transform not only our understanding of spaces, but of how we might approach them in architecture? A contemporary example of a place that has demanded a different way of being conceptualised is the Indian Ocean, which has become the site for a plethora of recent studies that have sought to understand its coming into being through a series of interactions, including migratory movements, rather than through recourse to geographical or territorial determinism. The Indian Ocean has variously been understood as a *seascape* or a shared space made up of a series of connections, trade routes, flows and currents. An interesting example is the *Folded Ocean* project by architect Lindsay Bremner, which is described as a research project on the Indian Ocean that views 'continental geographies from the perspective of the sea.'[20] This switch in perspective that privileges the edges has great significance; Bremner's careful understanding of the Indian Ocean through three specific sites along its edge redefines it as contact zone, circulator and ecology. This leads to unexpected ways of describing the ocean, from maritime and trade laws that now see it as another parcel of territory to be commoditised, to a need to understand it as a multi-scalar and relational space, to an inversion and redistribution of the traditional hierarchies of cities and spaces that global politics might point us towards.[21]

This renewed understanding of scale reveals also a different relationship between measure and value, or to put it in more expert language, between ontology and epistemology; the inescapably intertwined nature of which has long been at the core of a feminist politics of location, or what Donna Haraway named 'situated knowledges'.[22] Rather than an indexical relationship between what is measured and the way in which it is measured, reciprocal and dynamic relations emerge that can change according to different times, contexts and locations. Topology's concern with continuity and connectivity through change allows a way of understanding such relations and goes counter to the causal tendencies in architectural research and practice. These often equate the empirical with the directly quantifiable, that is recorded, known and statistical knowledge used as direct evidence for spatial, social and psychological phenomena. In order to think the empirical as part of the *practice* of architecture, an intensive relationship between *what* is measured, *how* it is measured and the ways in which this constitutes value is required. As the anthropologist, Helen Verran, claims numbers not only have the capacity to order but also to value. Verran argues that for her numbers embody 'materialised relations', forming 'an inventive frontier in social, cultural, political and moral life'.[23] Thus the process of enumeration itself is a transformative activity and numbers have an impact on that which they address. For architecture, t' e need to imagine the practices of measuring and valuing as materialised rela ions that are mediated through the different ways in which numbers perform is of importance. At the same time, the intensive relations between measure and value, or between ordering and valuing, have implications for notions of representation and foreground the need for participative methods. Lisa Adkins and Celia Lury suggest that this is resulting in new kinds of spaces that they designate, 'more-than-representational spaces', where 'the values of the "what" and the measurement of the "how" are co-produced', and where 'the indexical and the symbolic are being combined in new ways'.[24]

## Modes of Belonging

These new types of spaces embody difference; their operation renders notions of distance immaterial, while scale and measure become dependent on an index that is in flux. In such 'topological spaces' how might questions of inclusion and exclusion be considered? If the surface is continuous where does the border or the edge lie? Who and what gets included? For mathematician-philosopher, Alain Badiou, set theory provides a model for approaching these questions.[25] Interestingly, in set theory the elements of the set do not need to be defined, that is sets can be calculated without knowing their content. This reveals a very different approach to the idea of measurement. As Xin Wei Sha writes: 'Topology provides an anexact (in Deleuze's sense) mode of articulation, that does not need numerical measure, equations, exact data, statistics.'[26] It is this relation to measuring, a precision beyond numerics that is so useful in thinking new modes of belonging.

Whilst Badiou's mathematical contribution to thinking the political and the social is controversial in many aspects, his use of the still contested set theory and related areas of mathematics, point toward novel ways of thinking belonging. When we no longer have a solid boundary around us, when for example the global is inside the local, how do we belong? For some this is a question of connectedness or the openness of a set, for others it is the constitution of the set itself that is problematic, leading to the mathematics of categories.[27] For Badiou, the axioms or laws of set theory that govern the ways in which elements in a set interact, provide a framework for thinking belonging. One such axiom states that a set of all sets cannot exist because the elements of each set can be taken and reformed differently to make a set that will be larger than the original. Each set will also always contain an empty set that allows the possibility of different relations amongst elements. The existence of this empty set is key to understanding Badiou's take on inclusion and belonging in contemporary society. From this Badiou extrapolates that in any apparently totalising and complete order there is always an element that resists placing, and it is this element, the empty set, that although is present within the set does not belong to it. The distinction that Badiou draws here between belonging and inclusion is instructive for thinking the migrant position in contemporary society. 'What is included, philosophically, equals all that is possible in the world, whereas what belongs equals all that can be presented in a given worldview.'[28]

This gap between belonging and inclusion describes well the contemporary situation of many diasporic communities in Europe, and especially within the current political climate, that of Muslim communities. Often diasporic communities have lived in their 'new' home for one, two or more generations, they are included within the territory, legally speaking, they have a right to live and work there, but in a more fundamental way they cannot belong. That is to say, socially and politically they are excluded. In the UK context the increasingly toxic debate on community cohesion and its attendant ideas around the self-segregation of Muslim communities illustrates this point well.[29] At the same time for Badiou, the empty set that does not belong but is there nonetheless is the possibility of revolutionary change. In every situation there is this element that through its very presence disturbs and disrupts the status quo. It is the potential event based on this possibility that brings about revolutionary change. This affirmative agency in Badiou's thinking is the coming into existence of something new in a given situation.

## TIME AND MULTIPLICITY

The notion of the event that brings about something new, something that did not belong to a situation, is inherently linked to how we might think the future and therefore temporality. In a topological idiom, time is conceptualised very differently to the modern idea of it as an accumulation or sequential movement, the progress of time as homogenous flow. If time is not sequential, if it does not follow a steady march towards a predictable and planned for outcome, then is the future inherently unknowable? Time conceived as duration and invention in the Bergsonian sense, leads to a future that the feminist scholar Elizabeth Grosz, describes as indeterminable. It speaks to us in the future anterior as 'the openness of things (including life, texts, or matter) to what befalls them'.[30] This mode of conceptualising time does not think of the past as a template for the present or the future, instead the present is recognised as the condition of possibility of the past and the future as that which endures through processes of becoming. That is, the future is imagined not through sameness but difference, a difference conceived through divergence. Here the past 'is the virtual that coexists with the present' and the future 'is that which diverges from the present, one uncontained by and unpredicted from within the present'.[31]

Time is therefore multiple. There are many different times, from the versions of the past held within the present to the many possible futures that are divergent from this very present. Temporality then is a duration that can also conceivably allow us to think of the present as multiple, since it is co-constituted in relation to one of many pasts and to possible futures. In the diasporic experience, this multiplicity is created through the spatial and temporal dislocations that are the result of displacement. An example from my own experience illustrates this point well. My parents have just moved to Pakistan and I try to call them most weekends. This particular weekend, I was away, so I emailed and asked them to call me on the Friday. My father replied that he could not since it was Muharram.[32] At first I was surprised, 'since when did my father start observing Muharram?' But of course in Pakistan at the moment during important events, religious or otherwise, where large numbers of people might gather, mobile phone coverage in the four largest cities is blocked. This is due to the recent spate of bombings in Pakistani cities that are usually triggered using a mobile phone. Somehow what this story speaks of is another time. Although I knew that it was Muharram, I had not thought of the consequences of this in Pakistan, where another time, another calendar was in effect. Temporal dislocation is the playing out of another time, another way of measuring and valuing time between different places, in this case between my world in London and my parent's world in Lahore. Yet, as the geographer Nigel Clarke writes in response to the work of Grosz, we are resistant to the idea of temporal dislocations due to a long history of work that suggested that those living in a different place from us also inhabited a different, more primitive time. But taken carefully this notion of differing temporalities adds to the question 'Where do I belong?', the equally important 'question of the "when" of belonging and becoming'.[33] It asks the important question of how to include temporal dislocations as elements within our ways of conceptualising diasporic agencies.

## DIFFERENCE, AGENCY AND THE TOPOLOGICAL

Throughout this chapter I have explored a number of qualities that 'diasporic spatio-temporalities' might have. These have included the ability to accommodate difference in everyday life through an understanding of temporal 'moments' that differentiate through being lived differently. In this the body emerged as an important locus operating through one-to-one exchanges but also in personal relations that might span the globe. Such diasporic embodiments whilst including a type of marginality also contain the possibility of opening up a mediatory space between different times and cultures.

The important relations between notions of belonging and inclusion serve as a warning, describing how diasporic subjects come to be marginalised, whether this is through practices of differential inclusion or through not being allowed the capacity to belong. But across the trajectory of this chapter, a relational space does emerge as a place where difference can be accommodated through a mode of becoming, a process that is not constituted through identity politics but through associations. It constitutes a space that is able to mediate between the different registers of a diasporic inhabitation that can be folded across time and space. Since the processes of migration necessarily dislocate subjects and involve narratives that can span regions and borders, space becomes a contested domain full of contradictory and conflicting positions. The different concepts outlined in this chapter, allow space to unfurl and expand in order to accommodate these positionings, whilst acknowledging their entirely contingent and interdependent nature.

The topological object thus emerges as a space of figuration that sits somewhere between the virtual and the actual and it speaks to us in the future anterior. Thinking about diasporic lives as paradigmatic of contemporary topological culture also has consequences for the modes in which diasporic subjects might act. In order to think agency as topological, ideas on how power operates and how freedom is constructed in relation to it would need to be questioned. The much rehearsed divide between external structure and individual will that has shaped the discourse on agency is also elided within a topological approach, ideas that I explore further in the following chapter.

## NOTES

1.   Lefebvre, *The Production of Space*, 26.

2.   Lefebvre, *The Critique of Everyday Life: Foundations for a Sociology of the Everyday*, II: 345.

3.   Lefebvre, *The Production of Space*, 395.

4.   Ibid., 52.

5.   Grosz, *Volatile Bodies: Towards a Corporeal Feminism*, 164.

6.   Braidotti, *The Posthuman*, 193.

7. Deleuze, *The Logic of Sense*, 258.

8. Ibid.

9. Irigaray's critique of liberal notions of equality through (sexual) difference is another example of moving beyond equality towards difference, but from another starting point that is based more in deconstructing the binary relationship between the sexes. Irigaray, *An Ethics of Sexual Difference*.

10. Deleuze, *The Fold: Leibniz and the Baroque*, 19.

11. Ibid., 127.

12. Here I use 'reduced' as Deleuze would use it in his description of the fold: 'The simplest way of stating the point is by saying that to unfold is to increase, to grow; whereas to fold is to diminish, to reduce, "to withdraw into the recesses of a world"'. Ibid., 8–9. This is not a reduction in the colloquial sense but a reduction that leads to an intensity, as one might reduce a sauce to produce a more intense flavor.

13. A dancing troupe formed by John Tiller that originated the precision dancing technique. Kracauer was fascinated by the dissolving of individuals into one mass unit by the linking of arms and through a militarised aesthetic.

14. Kracauer, 'The Mass Ornament', 77.

15. Ibid., 76.

16. The Azadi march and *dharna* (sit-in) were a series of public protests across Pakistan between August 2014 and December 2014, sparked by claims of electoral fraud and governmental corruption.

17. Lash, 'Deforming the Figure', 265.

18. Here I am also referring to the eponymous book, Koolhaas and OMA, *S, M, L, XL*.

19. For a detailed discussion of scale in architecture see, Lahoud, 'The Problem of Scale: The City, the Territory, the Planetary'.

20. Bremner, 'Folded Ocean Project'.

21. Bremner, 'Folded Ocean: The Spatial Transformation of the Indian Ocean World'.

22. Haraway, 'Situated Knowledges: The Science Question in Feminism and the Privilege of Partial Perspective'.

23. Verran, 'Number as an Inventive Frontier in Knowing and Working Australia's Water Resources', 171.

24. 'Introduction: Special Measures' in Adkins and Lury, *Measure and Value*, 18 and 19.

25. Badiou, *Being and Event*.

26. Sha, 'Topology and Morphogenesis', 222–3.

27. Sha, 'Topology and Morphogenesis'; Rotman, 'Topology, Algebra, Diagrams'.

28. Van den Hemel, 'Included but Not Belonging: Badiou and Rancière on Human Rights', 23.

29. Samad, *Muslims and Community Cohesion in Bradford*.

30. Grosz, 'Histories of the Present and Future: Feminism, Power, Bodies', 16.

31. Grosz, 'Histories of a Feminist Future', 1020.

32.  Muharram is the name of the first month in the Islamic calendar. In colloquial usage in Pakistan it is often used synonymously with Ashura, which is the tenth day of Muharram and an important date in the Shia Muslim calendar.

33.  Yusoff et al., 'Geopower', 977.


## REFERENCES

Adkins, Lisa, and Celia Lury, eds. *Measure and Value*. 1st ed. Oxford: Wiley-Blackwell, 2012.

Badiou, Alain. *Being and Event*. New Ed. London: Continuum, 2011.

Braidotti, Rosi. *The Posthuman*. Oxford: Polity Press, 2011.

Bremner, Lindsay. 'Folded Ocean Project'. *GeoArchitecture*. Accessed August 6, 2014. http://geoarchitecture.wordpress.com/2013/01/22/folded-ocean-project/.

_____. 'Folded Ocean: The Spatial Transformation of the Indian Ocean World'. *Journal of the Indian Ocean Region* 10, no. 1 (2013): 18–45. doi: 10.1080/19480881.2013.847555

Deleuze, Gilles. *The Fold: Leibniz and the Baroque*. Minneapolis: University of Minnesota Press, 1993.

_____. *The Logic of Sense*. New York: Columbia University Press, 1990.

Grosz, Elizabeth. 'Histories of a Feminist Future'. *Signs* 25, no. 4 (July 2000): 1017–21.

_____. 'Histories of the Present and Future: Feminism, Power, Bodies'. In *Thinking the Limits of the Body*, edited by Jeffrey Jerome Cohen and Gail Weiss, 13–23. New York: SUNY Press, 2012.

_____. *Volatile Bodies: Towards a Corporeal Feminism*. Bloomington: Indiana University Press, 1994.

Haraway, Donna. 'Situated Knowledges: The Science Question in Feminism and the Privilege of Partial Perspective'. *Feminist Studies* 3 (1988): 575–99.

Irigaray, Luce. *An Ethics of Sexual Difference*. Ithaca, NY: Cornell University Press, 1993.

Koolhaas, Rem, and OMA. *S, M, L, XL*. Rome: The Monacelli Press, 1995.

Kracauer, Siegfried. 'The Mass Ornament'. In *The Mass Ornament : Weimar Essays*, 75–86. Cambridge, MA; London: Harvard University Press, 1995.

Lahoud, Adrian. 'The Problem of Scale: The City, the Territory, the Planetary'. PhD, University of Technology Sydney, 2012.

Lash, Scott. 'Deforming the Figure: Topology and the Social Imaginary'. *Theory, Culture & Society* 29, no. 4–5 (July 2012): 261–87. doi:10.1177/0263276412448829.

Lefebvre, Henri. *The Critique of Everyday Life: Foundations for a Sociology of the Everyday*. Vol. II. London: Verso, 2002.

_____. *The Production of Space*. Oxford: Basil Blackwell, 1991.

Rotman, Brian. 'Topology, Algebra, Diagrams'. *Theory, Culture & Society* 29, no. 4–5 (July 2012): 247–60. doi:10.1177/0263276412444472.

Samad, Yunas. *Muslims and Community Cohesion in Bradford*. Joseph Rowntree Foundation, July 2010.

Sha, Xin Wei. 'Topology and Morphogenesis'. *Theory, Culture & Society* 29, no. 4–5 (July 2012): 220–46. doi:10.1177/0263276412443570.

Van den Hemel, Ernst. 'Included but Not Belonging: Badiou and Rancière on Human Rights'. *Krisis: Journal for Contemporary Philosophy*, no. 3 (2008). www.krisis.eu.

Verran, Helen. 'Number as an Inventive Frontier in Knowing and Working Australia's Water Resources'. *Anthropological Theory* 10, no. 1–2 (March 2010): 171–8. doi:10.1177/1463499610365383.

Yusoff, Kathryn, Elizabeth Grosz, Nigel Clark, Arun Saldanha, and Catherine Nash. 'Geopower: A Panel on Elizabeth Grosz's Chaos, Territory, Art: Deleuze and the Framing of the Earth'. *Environment and Planning D: Society and Space* 30, no. 6 (2012): 971–88. doi:10.1068/d3006pan.

# 2

# Diasporic Inhabitations

Diasporas bring with them the culture and practices of another place and in this chapter I explore how this affects their inhabitation and use of city-space. A wider concern of this chapter is the connection between the inhabitation of space and the production of agency. Through exploring the specificities of the spatial inhabitations of those in the diaspora, I consider how these differ from those understood as normative within current urban approaches. If the act of displacement is seen as fundamental to the diasporic condition, then it is through practices of reterritorialisation that diasporas adapt to their new home. Reterritorialisation could also be described through the feminist concept of 'taking place', defined as a spatial politics that attends to difference whose goal is not necessarily 'to be "included" or "represented" but to participate directly from a differential position'.[1] This way of thinking imagines difference as *a tool for "taking"*[2] connecting the notion of diasporic agency directly to the inhabitation of space. It also highlights the central role of the body in producing diasporic agencies.

## MIMICRY AND THE MAKING OF DIASPORIC AGENCY

Diasporas are embedded within unequal global power relations, including a position of privilege and exploitation in relation to many in the post-colonies. Yet one of the strongest arguments for diasporic agency lies in the way that it is able to challenge hegemonic notions of the nation-state. Through multiple allegiances and complex ways of constituting the self, diasporas question the homogenising narrative of nations. As Homi Bhabha described in 'DissemiNation', the haunting return of the post-colonial migrant to the coloniser's nation disrupts the familiar through the playing out of cultural difference. But as Lily Cho states there is a limitation to locating diasporic agency merely within a ghostly haunting as it 'risks reducing [it] to something that happens only in the mind of the colonizer'.[3] Perhaps the less perfect and in some ways more problematic mode of agency described by

Bhabha, mimicry, has greater potential for thinking more affirmative instances of diasporic agencies.

Through mimicry Bhabha famously posited the possibility of resistance within the coloniser/colonised relationship. That is, the very figures that colonial authority cultivated in its self-image to lend it support became the agents of its decline. He wrote: 'The menace of mimicry is its double vision which in disclosing the ambivalence of colonial discourse also disrupts its authority.'[4] Looking at this relationship from the side of the colonised, Bhabha conceptualises it as an 'ironic compromise'; it is neither the independence that is desired nor total domination. The subversive quality of mimicry creates an excess through its unfaithful copy. 'In this comic turn from the high ideals of the colonial imagination to its low mimetic literary effects mimicry emerges as one of the most elusive and effective strategies of colonial power and knowledge.'[5] Bhabha's understanding of mimicry is based in Jacques Lacan's conceptualisation of it as camouflage, meaning that mimicry is not necessarily about blending harmoniously into the background but of keeping a distinction from it. Lacan gives the example of camouflage used in the military, where the patterned colours are simulations of only one aspect of the environment. The tank therefore does not become a bush simply by being coloured in patches of green and brown and having a few branches thrown over it; it still keeps its form and function as a tank.[6]

A slightly different definition of mimicry was put forward by the surrealist anthropologist, Roger Caillois.[7] In his seminal essay on mimicry in animals he questioned the prevalent belief that mimicry was a strategy of survival. He instead chose to conceptualise it as a certain excess in the evolution of animals and insects that had more to do with their relationship to space. Biologists usually explain mimicry in insects and animals as ornament or perhaps as coincidental similarity to an environment that is then capitalised upon in the choice of habitat. This is a version of mimicry as camouflage, whilst another type involves timid animals simulating the looks of their more aggressive counterparts in the hope that it will ward off predators. But these explanations were unsatisfactory for Caillois who stated that even animals that are not edible mimic. In fact there were specific problems associated with mimicry that led him to suggest that it was a 'dangerous luxury':

> [T]here are cases in which mimicry causes the creature to go from bad to worse: geometer-moth caterpillars simulate shoots of shrubbery so well that gardeners cut them with their pruning shears. The case of the Phyllia is even sadder: they browse among themselves, taking each other for real leaves [...] the simulation of the leaf being a provocation to cannibalism in this kind of totem feast.[8]

Caillois's explanation of mimicry instead switches the emphasis from survival to the question of an animal's relationship to space and how this produces their own sense of self. He uses the example of schizophrenics who are unable to distinguish themselves from their surroundings, and so have a sense of themselves only as one amongst many points in space, rather than as a point in space from which they reference everything around them. This failure to distinguish themselves from their environment or to become 'too similar' is what Caillois also sees in insects that mimic. He points out 'that in mimetic species the phenomenon is never carried out except in a single direction: the animal mimics the plant, leaf, flower, or thorn, and dissembles or ceases to perform its functions in relation to others. *Life takes a step backwards*.'[9] Caillois's definition reveals the dangers of mimicry; things go wrong when mimesis occurs in one direction only. In the case of diasporas, mimicry can have an emancipatory effect in relation to the host culture as Bhabha described, but the problem of becoming too similar is revealed when mimicry occurs in relation to an essentialised notion of our 'own' culture. This danger is especially prevalent in policies that seek to preserve certain aspects of a given culture, as Smaro Kamboureli describes in her appraisal of Canadian cultural policies relating to ethnic difference. 'In diasporic mimicry, mutation "enhances" the split of the ethnic subject from the dominant society, but it also reveals a split within ethnic communities.'[10]

Such a reading of mimicry that sees it as a practice with potentiality and danger is very different from the Platonic idea of mimesis as pure imitation. It is closer to that of Theodor Adorno, for whom mimesis was much more than imitation; 'In mimesis imagination is at work, and serves to reconcile the subject with the object',[11] opening the possibility of thinking mimicry as the use of the imagination in relating to the other. This creativity that may arise in a form of imitation, exceeds it to become a crucial way of gaining a sense of self through a relation to space and the corporeal. For diasporas where there is often an emphasis on rituals and tradition in how we inhabit space, our bodily gestures can become important sites for the construction of agency, if related to the imaginative use of mimesis. This opens up the possibility of imagining diasporic agencies in relation to other communities but could also be radicalised further towards animals, machines, things … Practices of naming, speaking, gestures and other bodily performances can all enact the *becoming* of diasporic subjectivities.

One way in which the body becomes central to enacting diasporic agencies starts from Michel de Certeau's critique of statistical analyses, where he writes that what should be counted are the ways of using rather than what is used. Whether it is the everyday act of walking considered as 'a spatial acting-out of the place' or speaking considered as 'an acoustic acting-out of language',[12] it is this enunciative potential latent within everyday acts that can transform them into sites of daily resistance for those in the diaspora. Walking then could be considered a tactic, manipulating space and taking advantage of a dominant spatial structure. It subverts it with reference to the walker's own personal, social and cultural desires, distorting space by fragmenting it in some places and completely skipping over it in others. These movements referred to by de Certeau as 'forests of gestures'[13] cannot be documented so easily in an image or text. They are an extra layer above the existing urban fabric, made of the countless trajectories of walkers across the city, 'a second, poetic geography on top of the geography of the literal, forbidden or permitted meaning'.[14] Since de Certeau's analysis was rooted in understanding the spatial inhabitations of those at the margins of power, it is one mode in which the mimicry described above can be understood as being enacted in the everyday spatial practices of diasporic subjects. The emphasis on mobility and temporality also resonates with aspects of diasporic culture and can be seen in the temporary adaptation of spaces meant for other uses. Whether it is the typical Victorian terrace now used as a mosque, or industrial warehouse units converted to Pentecostal churches, such enunciative practices have the ability to transform space through inhabitation. For my own purposes, the emphasis on walking as an everyday practice is especially important as it interacts directly with city-space and has a history of being adapted for use as an urban tool.

## AFFIRMATIVE AGENCIES

The diasporic subject is by condition political and one of the central questions for understanding diasporic inhabitations of space is of how people from different backgrounds and cultures can live together. This living together entails the creation and naming of a collective, the 'we' of the democratic relationship, and it also raises the question of participation within public affairs. How the collective or public is formed has been the subject of continuing debates including a concern with how to engage citizens in public processes. Traditionally, debates on participation in architecture have taken a less critical approach, especially related to the highly contested twin concepts of public space and community.[15] In architectural practice the notion of community is rarely challenged and public space is usually taken uncritically to be a space that is able to accommodate all. For a diasporic politics that deals with those who occupy the margins of society, this omission is crucial. The political philosopher, John Dewey, theorised the construction of publics around 'issues' and insisted on the participation of citizens in the democratic process. His seminal book on the subject, *The Public and its Problems*, was written at a time when it was becoming clear that technological advances would mean that the containment of public issues within the bounds of existing communities was increasingly unlikely.[16] This, of course, is a fundamental issue for contemporary politics and one that gains even greater importance in the diasporic context.

Contemporary theory has dealt with this problem of making meaningful democratic relationships at a distance – the issue of scale – in a number of different guises, including how to bring together a public or a community through identifying common concerns. For Dewey and also for Bruno Latour, a public is assembled around issues that are not addressed in the current system, and in the process of finding this common ground with others a democratic process is initiated.[17] This relational model of democracy that works with a logic of equivalence over that of equality is highly useful for a diasporic politics.[18] The condition of the migrant is such that frictions around social, cultural and religious issues, to name only a few, are inevitable. Sometimes these occur around differences in opinion, other times they are the result of misunderstandings of cultural and social codes. These frictions require a space for discussion without the pressure of a final consensus. In this, the traditional

African *palaver* is an interesting model where the object of the discussions is not to impose a certain point of view on people who would not normally share it. Instead the *palaver* provides a space where everyone's opinion can be heard and a position constructed that has been contributed to by all.[19] The definition of the word 'palaver' is given variously as, 'talk intended to cajole, flatter, or wheedle; unnecessary, profuse, or idle talk; chatter' or 'a talk, a discussion, a dialogue; (spec. in early use) a conference between African tribespeople and traders or travellers'.[20] This word although originating in traditional West African practices is steeped in the unequal power dynamics of the colonial encounter. As Chikwenye Okonjo Ogunyemi writes of the palaver, in comparison to European norms perhaps it seemed unnecessarily protracted and the value of time spent not fully appreciated but even so the 'palaver emerges as critical discourse – serious as well as trifling, logical and rambling, orderly and haphazard, written and spoken, a celebration of the contradictions of life with the principled use of word power for communal good'.[21] At its best, then, the palaver can be all of these things but it does not always work this way; if dictated from above, rather than below through self-organising mechanisms, it loses its power. There is therefore no given time or frequency to this event rather it happens as and when needed, mobilised by the collective passions of the people. Traditionally there is a given space for it in every village, a certain tree is known to be the 'palaver tree' under which to gather when the time comes. The tree is thus a sign and a spatial organiser, the presence of a group gathering underneath it could provoke a meeting.[22]

Collective passions are at stake in the palaver, its indeterminate nature meaning that the system can respond to the desires of the group rather than waiting for the political system to reach its cycle of change. To be able to exercise and follow these desires is what Arjun Appadurai has called, 'the right to participate in the work of the imagination'.[23] What form of agency allows such a right to be exercised? Traditionally, oppositional struggles related to feminist or migrant causes have been based in more prosaic demands that conceive power in the mode of interdiction and so find agency in the freedom from oppressive structures.[24] At the other end of the scale is the question of individual will, where agency is conceived as the freedom to act in other ways. If we take seriously the notion of the topological in our conceptualisation of diasporic spatio-temporalities, then a different mode of agency is required, one that is not embedded in traditional ideas of space as container, in the linearity of time, or in the causality of the universe. We need instead a mode of agency that is able to encompass the indeterminate nature of the mimetic effect, the discontinuity and disjuncture of the diasporic experience.

Elizabeth Grosz describes another genealogy of thinking freedom and its relation to subjectivity that starts from the writings of Henri Bergson, who did not rely on the western philosophical tradition of setting up binary distinctions. For Bergson the freedom to act was neither confined to the subjectivity of individuals nor to the structural conditions of society, instead he posited that acts themselves are free. '[F]ree acts are those that spring from the subject alone (and not from any psychical state of the subject or any manipulated behavior around the subject); they not only originate in or through a subject, they express all of that subject'.[25] Combined with Bergson's privileging of time as duration, free acts are conceived as those that take part in the becoming of the subject, that is they express the subject in transformation. In couching free acts as such Bergson's concept of agency is affirmative, it is embedded within actions, in their possibility and in their performance. As Grosz makes clear in her appraisal of Bergson, neither the determinist position of structural conditions that will only allow one choice to be made, nor the libertarian position that allows a choice of a number of outcomes that are equally possible and remain available to the free will of the individual, acknowledge that the different outcomes were never equal in the first place. This is because they are not abstract possibilities but materially real potentialities.

In thinking about the agency of diasporic subjects, this notion of free acts that are embedded in the becoming of the subject is key. At the same time, as an architect I am interested in the spatiality of such acts and the ways in which the becoming of subjects could be apprehended spatially. In the book *Spatial Agency*,[26] we were concerned with a human centred notion of agency based on the definition of agency provided by Anthony Giddens, as the 'capability of acting otherwise'.[27] Giddens works with the classical concept of agency that sees it as emerging through a negotiation between the free will of the individual and the constraints of social structures. The difference in Grosz's definition is that agency is no longer centred around the human subject, instead it emerges from an assemblage of relations between humans, objects, systems; a vision of a relational world that is less stable and more distributed. It is a world where architectural acts may well have agency – including the objects of architecture considered alongside the exchanges that form around them, but perhaps not so the architect as individual subject. What is being described here is a culture that is topological. It privileges dynamic associations over fixed properties. It is a question of how to imagine agency in a time of flux, in a time of crisis, when things are constantly changing. When the temporality is different, when what you can do, the acts that you can make have very different potential to more stable times. Of course, it is not only a question of privileging relations in this more distributed model of agency. It is also about the quality of the connections that are made, their temporal dimensions and historical reach. How and when are relations made, what stresses do they come under and how are they mediated? The question of mediation is in fact crucial to thinking diasporic agencies.

## REPRESENTING AGENCIES

The performative role of the body is central to such processes of mediation as Brian Massumi relates in an example of a ball in a football game.[28] The ball moving around the field arranges the players in space: 'The ball is the subject of the play. … The player is the object of the ball.' In the kicking of the ball, 'human physicality transduces into the insubstantiality of an event, releasing a potential that reorganises the entire field of potential movement.'[29] This way of thinking the relationships between the ball, the players and the field conceptualises reality in flux, a field of potentialities. 'The player's subjectivity is disconnected as he enters the field of potential in and as sensation. ... Sensation is the mode in which potential is present in the perceiving body.'[30] This example takes the notion of agency described above as an assemblage of relations and places the body at its centre. Thus it is not the individual will of the subject played out through social structures, but the affective body and its sensations that allow us to access the field of potentiality. The spatial practices I refer to in this book try to capture some of this quality of the body as transducer, converting physicality into events or the modification of spatio-temporalities.

If diasporic agencies reside in the inhabitations of space and in the ways of doing, then the question of representation takes on a crucial role. How to capture these modes in which diasporic bodies function? In recent years, mapping has emerged as an important representational practice within architecture, referred to in the adjective to denote a process over a finished product. These mapping practices acknowledge the dynamic nature of the world in which we live and the critical changes that cities are undergoing. They attempt to deal with such complexities through showing the same situation or space from many different perspectives and representing those aspects not previously thought important. Mapping as practice is described as 'the conceptual glue linking the tangible world of buildings, cities and landscapes with the intangible world of social networks and electronic communications'.[31] It is in this sense described by Abrams and Hall that I am using mapping as a way of working with diasporic agencies. In this newly emerging practice of mapping there is a different focus from traditional cartographic practices; rather than re-presenting an already 'known' situation, contemporary maps are taking on new agencies, they are more propositional in nature, imagine other possibilities and play mediatory roles.[32]

In my own mapping practice I develop 'diasporic diagrams' that ask what might be the essential elements of a practice of mapping that does not place primary importance on buildings, streets and developments but instead on the constitution of diasporic agency. How might such modes of representation affect the way in which we conceive cities, beyond essentialised notions of property and land ownership? As will hopefully emerge over the course of this book, a way of mapping the city that foregrounds diasporic agencies, brings with it also new concerns for architecture and urbanism. Rather than walls, buildings, pavements and city blocks, we might consider trans-localities, networks, bodily gestures and postures, borders and territories. Whilst not eliding the former, these do emerge as the primary elements in a different practice of architecture. In trying to map beyond the solely physical, I have used techniques that are not associated with traditional cartography and I have attempted always to make situated maps that are embodied and performed. Practices such as walking, speaking and drawing have been used, sometimes alone and sometimes together to try to articulate beyond the dominant and easily visible modes of inhabiting space. Here maps are used as a way of uncovering another narrative in order to understand how diasporic agencies emerge in the city.

The mappings have exposed layers of diasporic spatiality, which include the political, religious, ethnic, gendered and economic all working in parallel, creating frictions as well as connections on a personal and collective level. The negotiations and playing out of these sometimes conflicting positions is what I try to map in the following chapters. It is the process of space-making through subjectivation, which embodies the 'agonistic' dimension that Chantal Mouffe has called for.[33] These mappings also foreground a particular way of thinking about place that Doreen Massey has described as moments of 'intersecting social relations, nets of which have over time been constructed, laid down, interacted with one another, decayed and renewed'.[34] The points of intersection, the 'nodes' at certain moments in time constitute place. The temporal nature and sheer number of relations is what gives places their multiple and layered character and defines their history as a layering of these complex relations. Since these relations do not always remain within the geographical bounds of any particular place, such a conceptualisation breaks down essential categories for a more open and inviting way of thinking place. Here globalisation, which is often seen as a homogenising force, helps to create the specificity of a place through the intersection of local and global relations. For diasporic subjects such a networked understanding of place is almost intuitive, we feel it in the way we inhabit the world. To make faithful representations of such ways of inhabiting and apprehending cities is one of the main challenges this book has attempted to tackle. Thus the maps and writings described here ask the question; within the networked, global condition of the diasporic citizen, what objects, subjects and processes can play the role of mediation that is required between here and there, or between the layers of this multiple subject? Language, personal idioms and gestures all play an important role, are subject to translations and can become mediators. I have carried out my research through mapping small-scale, localised examples of such conditions in the everyday diasporic inhabitation of the city.

### Figurations of Diasporas in London

The following section, 'Spatial Figurations of Diasporic Agencies', takes as its site of study different situations in London but the main site has been a single street in north-east London – Stoke Newington High Street that is renamed southwards as Dalston Kingsland Road in the London Borough of Hackney. It is the everyday shopping area for the local neighbourhood and has a concentrated population of Turkish and Kurdish migrants. Although the street has been used as the site for most of the research this is not an ethnographic study into the Kurdish and Turkish community. Instead I use the insights I gain from this and my exploration of the Bangladeshi diaspora in one of the chapters to interrogate the (non)engagement of architectural and urban practice with diasporas. The two chapters, *Trans-Local Practices* and *Diasporic Territories* both use the street as context. Here I have explored the geopolitics of the 'Kurdish question' and how this affects the highly localised and specific space of the street. Through going for walks with people from the two communities, I explore how it provides both a conflictual space of protest and also a place for everyday interactions between the two intertwined communities. The exploration of the private space of the *kahve* (Turkish and Kurdish social clubs or cafés) and their distribution on the street adds another intimate layer of interaction.[35]

The remaining chapter in the section is called *Multiplying Borders* and it uses a different context of the Bangladeshi community of Spitalfields and Whitechapel in East London, but the research interest remains the same. Interviews with teenage Bengali girls on the subject of language are combined with an exploration of how certain objects within public space take on forms of political agency. The Bangladeshi community of East London has been the subject of countless books and articles, but the juxtaposition of this established community with the newer Kurdish community brings interesting insights. Both communities are majority Muslim but the Kurds of course have a rich diversity of religious practices, and their relationship to Islam is very different to that of Bangladeshis. The dynamics within Muslim communities themselves and the general relationship of the West with the Muslim world also appears in both these cases. The relationship between the host and home culture is also at issue, as is the often quoted observation that the preservation of traditions within migrant communities is far greater than those in the country of origin. Within all these examples the fact of there being no originary nation-state as homeland for the Kurds upsets the balance and disallows easy generalisations in both cases.

The places I have chosen to study are also those that I have close contact with, at the time I worked in one and lived in another. This was important as a way of knowing the area, 'being there' is an important part of the type of urban practice I am interested in. As the group Stalker writes: 'Being "present" is often necessary … To be present means to observe sympathetically, to suspend judgement, to pay attention to the process.'[36] It also allows a 'way in' that is not demanding and gives that which is hardest to give – time. My way of working therefore actively includes the possibility of chance encounters, informal conversations and quiet observation and an acknowledgement of my own positioning. This has also meant that the decision to base the research in neighbourhoods that I was familiar with and spent time in was crucial, allowing a relationship with the area and inhabitants that is very difficult to replicate otherwise.

## Topological Readings of Diasporic Agencies

The specific spaces that I have chosen to study operate at different scales and between different registers of the public and the private. These spaces range from the domesticated interiors of Turkish and Kurdish *kahve* that are highly gendered male spaces, to the public nature of a street whose physicality forces a certain visibility on to those who traverse it (and which also makes it an ideal space of protest), to a park in East London that through being claimed by one diasporic group has come to symbolise wider notions of political agency. All these situations also address the question of diasporic agency as the reterritorialisation of space through the specific modalities of inhabitation that diasporic subjects produce.

For example, the *kahve* space revealed how such agencies are constituted through actively constructing a 'home' in the city that is the product of certain embodiments and gestures arising from a place of tension in-between tradition, ritual and habit. The mapping of Kurdistan in the chapter, *Multiplying Borders*, was a way of inscribing diasporic agency as inextricably entwined to wider geo-political concerns, whilst sometimes also remaining in thrall to them:

> *... if they create a Kurdish country there, US will want to put all the soldiers there, they are going to have a new base and Kurdish people are going to be rich, day-by-day rich, and one day they want from us the east part from my country. That's why we never allow that and now it is going to start a war because our soldiers are now in the area but I don't think it is in the English newspaper ...* [37]

The quote above is from an interview with a young Turkish man and it shows how his experience of London is inextricably linked to the political situation in his home country. For him the stories and events that he considered crucial to his view of the world were not being given enough visibility in the UK. Questions of visibility and of mediation are absolutely central to diasporic experiences and to the construction of a home in a new place. In the case of the Kurds it is the fraught relationship with the place left behind that influences what home could be here and now. As one Kurdish woman I interviewed explained to me: 'You know, I am from Turkey but I don't know anything about Turkey except for the system and you know the poverty. ... we don't know what do [sic] we have in Turkey except for from the books and on the TV.'[38] The popular construction or image of Turkey as a country is not her experience and yet at the same time is an inextricable part of it.

> *Kurdish, even Turkish people, they came recently, they have been here about 10 to 15 years, children who are here who have been born in this country, they are mixed, they have like kind of three different identity [sic], Kurdish, Turkish and British identity and sometimes they mix up, some of them they are lost but it is not stable at the moment because Kurdish people, I mean even Turkish, when they came to this country, they were hoping that one day they will go back to their country.* [39]

Articulating a relation to a place is fraught with questions of identity within the diaspora, questions that continually animate the ways in which we see our place in the world. In choosing to go for walks with Turks and Kurds I was attempting to find ways of negotiating this terrain with them, and in so doing to relate how the space of a European metropolis is inscribed by the regional affinities of elsewhere. This diasporic confidence in taking public space is not quite unique to London, but is certainly more pronounced here in comparison to many other European cities. The multicultural politics of Britain that are now so contested, ensured that diasporic agencies here can be played out in explicit ways of taking space in the city. Finally, the park in East London and the Bengali girls I interviewed also display some of this confidence in their inhabitation of the city. The park as political space of assembly and encounter, a place for a politics of proximity, highlights how diasporic agencies can unfurl outward towards a more generalised notion of the city as emancipatory space. This space is produced through the creative act of mixing languages, bodily practices and through the appropriation of nationalistic symbols for a transversal politics.

## AGENCY IN/AS DIASPORIC INHABITATIONS

The displacement of bodies produces a special kind of space that is related to the cyclical time of everyday life – to its rhythms and modulations. Diasporic inhabitations are thus necessarily non-linear and they open possibilities of operating tactically in everyday life through privileging experience. The creativity of such approaches lies in the 'how' rather than the 'what' of an action, which has the potential to resist the homogenising tendencies of capitalist society. One mode in which diasporas do this is through the risky practice of mimicry, which on the one hand holds the potential to resist a dominant culture, but on the other hand could be deployed as a preservation of an essentialist and exoticised notion of our own culture. But mimicry's most precious subversive gift is the promise of a creative relating to the radically other that emerges through Caillois's idiosyncratic reading of mimicry in insects.

The notion of agency embedded in free acts describes what might emerge through a diasporic politics of affinity based around collective passions. Here the notion of mediation that is played out through the body acting as transducer gives a glimpse into the exploration of the spatial figurations of diasporic agencies that follows in the next section. The second half of this chapter introduced the context in which I will explore these figurations and described the central place that mapping holds within this process.

## NOTES

1.  Hoskyns and Petrescu, 'Taking Place and Altering It', 23. This could be considered a spatial appropriation of Giorgio Agamben's work; 'Taking Place' in, Agamben, *The Coming Community*, 13–16.

2.  Hoskyns and Petrescu, 'Taking Place and Altering It', 23.

3.  Cho, 41.

4.  Bhabha, *The Location of Culture*, 88.

5.  Ibid., 85.

6.  For an extended discussion on this see, Leach, *Camouflage*.

7.  Caillois, 'Mimicry and Legendary Psychasthenia'.

8.  Ibid., 25.

9.  Ibid., 30.

10. Kamboureli, *Scandalous Bodies*, 112.

11.  Leach, *Camouflage*, 22.

12.  de Certeau, *The Practice of Everyday Life*, 98.

13.  Ibid., 102.

14.  Ibid., 105.

15.  For an alternative history of the more critical debates on architecture and participation (containing historical and contemporary examples) see, Blundell Jones, Petrescu, and Till, *Architecture and Participation*.

16.  Dewey, *The Public and Its Problems*.

17.  Latour, 'From Realpolitik to Dingpolitik or How to Make Things Public'.

18.  For more on this see, Laclau and Mouffe, *Hegemony & Socialist Strategy: Towards a Radical Democratic Politics*.

19.  For more on the Palaver (tree) see, Edwards, 'A Palaver at Tutuila Samoa, 1883. Two Photographs by Captain William A.D. Acland'; See also, Petrescu, 'Life Matters Making Place'.

20.  OED, 'Oxford English Dictionary'.

21.  Ogunyemi, *Africa Wo/Man Palava: The Nigerian Novel by Women*, 98.

22.  In some ways the Shaheed Minar discussed in the chapter *Multiplying Borders* functions as a contemporary palaver tree.

23.  Appadurai, 'The Right to Participate in the Work of the Imagination (Interview by Arjen Mulder)'.

24.  Foucault's conceptualisation of power as being dispersed in society through space and institutions is based in this positive understanding of power. The intensive nature of a topological culture supports a mode of thinking power and freedom in the way that Foucault has described it.

25.  Elizabeth Grosz, 'Feminism, Materialism, and Freedom', in New Materialisms: Ontology, Agency, and Politics, ed. Diana Cole and Samantha Frost (Duke University Press, 2010), 144.

26.  Awan, Schneider, and Till, *Spatial Agency: Other Ways of Doing Architecture*.

27.  Giddens, *Social Theory and Modern Sociology*, 216.

28.  Massumi, *Parables for the Virtual: Movement, Affect, Sensation*.

29.  Ibid., 73–4.

30.  Ibid., 75.

31.  Abrams and Hall, *Else/Where: Mapping New Cartographies of Networks and Territories*, 12.

32.  For a full discussion on this see the chapter, *Mapping Otherwise*.

33.  Mouffe, 'Some Reflections on an Agonistic Approach to the Public'.

34.  Massey, *Space, Place and Gender*, 120.

35.  The choice of basing the majority of the research around the Kurdish and Turkish community was strategic. The Kurdish situation is paradigmatic of the diasporic condition; Kurds are the largest stateless group in the world, their position being a direct consequence of British colonial decisions. The relationship between the Kurds

and the Turks can also be said to be similar to the relationship between the peoples of the nation-states of the Indian Subcontinent or some of the nation states of the African continent. Colonial practices of splitting regions with no understanding of the cultures and histories involved has reproduced a similar situation in many of the post-colonies: much similarity in culture and a shared history, yet the present situation is riven with antagonism played out along nationalistic lines. The notion of conflict is also important, the Kurds have been in an almost constant struggle for a homeland and the prevalence of conflict around the globe, especially in the post-colonies, seems only to be growing. Turkey's geographical and cultural place as the edge of Europe also makes it of interest, as well as its long-promised inclusion within the European Union.

36. Stalker, 'Stalker and the Big Game of Campo Boario', 231.

37. From interview I carried out with a Turkish waiter who worked in a local café on the high street.

38. From an interview I carried out as a walk along the high street with a local Kurdish activist.

39. From an interview I carried out with a Kurdish woman who works at a local community centre.

## REFERENCES

Abrams, Janet, and Peter Hall, eds. *Else/Where: Mapping New Cartographies of Networks and Territories*. Minneapolis: University of Minnesota Design Institute, 2006.

Agamben, Giorgio. *The Coming Community*. Minneapolis: University of Minnesota Press, 1993.

Appadurai, Arjun. 'The Right to Participate in the Work of the Imagination (Interview by Arjen Mulder)'. In *Transurbanism*, edited by Arjen Mulder, Laura Martz, and Joke Brouwer, 33–47. Rotterdam: V2_Publishing/NAI Publishers, 2002.

Awan, Nishat, Tatjana Schneider, and Jeremy Till. *Spatial Agency: Other Ways of Doing Architecture*. London: Routledge, 2011.

Bhabha, Homi. *The Location of Culture*. London: Routledge, 1994.

Blundell Jones, Peter Blundell-Jones, Doina Petrescu, and Jeremy Till, eds. *Architecture and Participation*. Abingdon: Spon Press, 2007.

Caillois, Roger. 'Mimicry and Legendary Psychasthenia'. *October* 31 01622870 (Winter 1984): 16–32.

Cho, Lily. 'On Eating Chinese: Diasporic Agency and the Chinese Canadian Restauran Menu'. In *Reading Chinese Transnationalisms: Society, Literature, Film*, edited by Maria N. Ng and Philip Holden, 37–62. Hong Kong: Hong Kong University Press, 2006.

De Certeau, Michel. *The Practice of Everyday Life*. Berkeley: University of California Press, 1984.

Dewey, John. *The Public and Its Problems*. Chicago: Swallow Press/Ohio University Press, 1927.

Edwards, Elizabeth. 'A Palaver at Tutuila Samoa, 1883. Two Photographs by Captain William A.D. Acland'. In *Making Things Public: Atmospheres of Democracy*, edited by Bruno Latour and Peter Weibel, 48–53. Cambridge, MA: The MIT Press, 2005.

Giddens, Anthony. *Social Theory and Modern Sociology*. Cambridge: Polity Press, 1987.

Hoskyns, Teresa, and Doina Petrescu. 'Taking Place and Altering It'. In *Altering Practices: Feminist Politics and Poetics of Space*, edited by Doina Petrescu. London: Routledge, 2007.

Kamboureli, Smaro. *Scandalous Bodies: Diasporic Literature in English Canada*. Waterloo, ON: Wilfrid Laurier University Press, 2009.

Laclau, Ernesto, and Chantal Mouffe. *Hegemony & Socialist Strategy: Towards a Radical Democratic Politics*. London: Verso, 1985.

Latour, Bruno. 'From Realpolitik to Dingpolitik or How to Make Things Public'. In *Some Reflections on an Agonistic Approach to the Public*, Making Things Public: Atmospheres of Democracy: 14–41. Karlsruhe/Cambridge MA: ZKM/MIT Press, 2005.

Leach, Neil. *Camouflage*. Cambridge MA: The MIT Press, 2006.

Massey, Doreen. *Space, Place and Gender*. Cambridge: Polity Press, 1994.

Massumi, Brian. *Parables for the Virtual: Movement, Affect, Sensation*. Durham, NC: Duke University Press, 2002.

Mouffe, Chantal. 'Some Reflections on an Agonistic Approach to the Public'. In *Making Things Public: Atmospheres of Democracy*, 804–7. ZKM/MIT Press, 2005.

OED. 'Oxford English Dictionary' 2014. Third Edition (2007). http://www.oed.com/.

Ogunyemi, Chikwenye Okonjo. *Africa Wo/Man Palava: The Nigerian Novel by Women*. Chicago: University of Chicago Press, 1996.

Petrescu, Doina. 'Life Matters Making Place'. In *Material Matters: Architecture and Material Practice*, edited by Katie Lloyd Thomas, 225–36. London: Routledge, 2007.

Stalker. 'Stalker and the Big Game of Campo Boario'. In *Architecture and Participation*, edited by Peter Blundell Jones, Doina Petrescu, and Jeremy Till, 249–56. Abingdon: Spon Press, 2007.

# Spatial Figurations of Diasporic Agencies

How might a diasporic inhabitation of space signal new modes of acting in the urban realm? What are the different ways in which such inhabitations are made manifest and what do they tell us about the contemporary city? In this section I explore the use, transformation, adaptation and appropriation of city-space by its diasporic inhabitants as specific elements of the urban landscape. This means that such uses of the city are seen in relation to and often opposing modern European versions of urbanity. The diasporic urban experience also does not stand in straightforward opposition to the neo-liberal city; it has a more complex relationship to it, as do diasporas in general. In this section, I relate *spatial* figurations of diasporic agencies that are based in particular modes of acting. I follow here Rosi Braidotti's definition of figuration as 'forms of literal expression that bring into representation that which the system has declared off-limits'.[1]

Mediation is once such mode, playing an important part in diasporic lives whether through the communication technologies that connect us 'back home', or through signs and symbols that facilitate different ways of inhabiting and allow objects to take on specific meaning and importance. In my case, certain ornaments such as a lamp brought over from our house in Lahore, plays just as important a part in my construction of a 'diasporic home' as do the frequent phone calls to my family in Pakistan. In this sense the diasporic experience is at times incredibly dependent on a material culture, whilst at others times it is completely dematerialised. How to create figurations that can accommodate such contradictions is also a concern of this section.

## NOTES

1.  Braidotti, 'Nomadism: Against Methodological Nationalism', 410.

*Kahve* – Beşiktaş

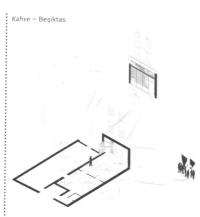

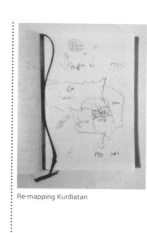

Re-mapping Kurdistan

# 3

# Trans-Local Practices: The Making of a 'Diasporic Home' in the City

Certain semi-private spaces, the deployment of particular signs and various practices play an important role in the making of a 'diasporic home' in the city. In this chapter I construct a figuration of such a home through interrogating a series of spaces and practices. In my attempts to understand the role of these spaces, I have tried to move away from the twin caricatures often found in mainstream discourse, of either portraying such spaces as being too introverted, or of regarding them as exoticised markers of culturally interesting neighbourhoods.[1] My interest lies in understanding how they facilitate a living between places and cultures for their diasporic users. How do they function spatially and socially? They are at times a means of support and comfort in their emulation of a place left behind, but at other times they can be restrictive, often becoming places that embody a very specific strand of national culture and value. Although these are social spaces, borne specifically out of the need to be with similar others, they are not public spaces that can make the claim of being open to all. Usually found in private or semi-private locations, they operate sometimes strict exclusions, but what makes them interesting is that very often they host activities that in the place of origin would have occurred in public. They therefore hold a potential for becoming public and the move to more private settings is perhaps an inevitable consequence of displacement, as what were once mainstream activities become marginal.

## PARALLEL WORLDS AND ALLEGORICAL MAPS

In the novel, *The City and the City*, China Miéville writes of two cities that occupy the same space and yet are separated, perhaps occupying different times.[2] Read by some as a parable for class, it could equally be seen as a more general metaphor for the stratification of contemporary society. Often diasporic communities are described similarly, as occupying parallel worlds, whether this occurs through the replication of shops and services that serve particular cultural needs, or through a way of inhabiting the city that does not exclusively rely on proximate social relations. How do these inhabitations transform our understanding of the city and what types of maps do we require to negotiate such urban experiences?

Walking along Stoke Newington High Street one could easily miss the many Turkish and Kurdish cafés that used to proliferate in this area of North London. They were versions of the traditional Turkish coffeehouses or *kahve*, spaces that could easily be conceptualised as constituting 'parallel worlds', a phrase used by Mörtenböck and Mooshammer to describe one aspect of the networked logic of contemporary European cities.[3] In their description of such spaces, they use the example of the twin areas of Highbury and Finsbury Park in North London, where football fans intersect with a migrant Muslim population. They place an emphasis on the juxtaposition of difference and their analysis rests on the commodification of football as spectator sport against the backdrop of a less than interested migrant population. Whilst the essay is interspersed with images of the controversial Finsbury Park Mosque, there is no mention of religion as another organising logic within this particular urban setting.[4] Instead the rather sensational image of Arsenal fans walking past the prostrate bodies of Muslims praying in the street is used as an example of worlds that pass each other by, and yet never meet. The problem thus defined through an extreme and highly unique example, a networked logic is offered as the possibility for transcending the social atomisation described in these parallel worlds. In comparison to the sensational narrative surrounding the Finsbury Park Mosque the *kahve* are nondescript spaces, they neither offer any particular image of difference nor do they advertise their religious or political affiliations – although they do often advertise their sporting allegiances. They prove useful as an example through which to interrogate the specificities of a particular strand of diasporic urban experience in which religion, gender and the political mix alongside an economic logic that often transcends the monetary.

When I first started researching the *kahve*, an architect familiar with the area related to me a story she was told by a Turkish acquaintance who insisted that if someone were to map all the *kahve* on the high street they would end up with an almost perfect map of Turkey down to the smallest village. This was due to the fact that each of them had a strong regional affiliation to a certain area or a local football team. It was often the names of the *kahve* that gave an indication to their loyalties, which were usually those of the owner. In the space of the street there was an overlapping of the physical location of the *kahve* with their toponymic distribution that alluded to regional affinities elsewhere. This other geography that was overlaid onto the physical space of the street formed an allegorical map of Turkey that was performed daily in the everyday comings and goings of the *kahve's* diasporic users.

The naming of the *kahve* thus functioned metonymically, folding space and linking a locality in London to a specific place in Turkey. This practice of naming reterritorialised space and produced invisible borders related to the regional and political conflicts, solidarities and nostalgias of another place. Whilst not all *kahve* were named after areas or regions in Turkey, having heard the claim of the existence of this other map, I was intrigued to test it, sketching out a map of the street and overlaying it with a Turkey that was deformed according to the regional affinities and the location on the street of each *kahve*. But whether described in words or drawings the map that I produced was always already out-dated, because the allegorical map I have alluded to is not static, it is in constant flux, shifting and changing as the *kahve* open and close, change names or proprietors. This allegorical map operates through the names on the signage, the colours used and the objects that are displayed, but also through word-of-mouth. Irit Rogoff has written of the importance of gossip, rumours and word-of-mouth within a feminist practice of counter-narration as 'gossip turns the tables on conventions of "history" and "truth" by externalising and making overt its relations to subjectivity, voyeuristic pleasure and the communicative circularity of story-telling'.[5] It perhaps did not matter that some of the *kahve* were named otherwise or that the map of Turkey that I overlaid on top of the *kahve* locations did not fit properly.[6] What seemed important to me was the affective force of this invisible geography and how it influenced the spatial politics of those who could apprehend it. Rogoff describes one of the important functions of gossip as 'an area for the cathexis of phantasmic projections by audiences which can alert us to the way in which we shape narratives through our own desire'.[7] Here I would also add that it alerts us to the way in which we shape space because this other map of the street was overlaid onto the physical structure, causing topological deformations to the actual, lived space. This may well have been intangible to those who had no knowledge of Turkey, but for others it ranged from a background low-level reality to a kind of territory that had to be negotiated daily.

This underlying territory did sometimes make itself felt in the consciousness of the other users of the street. A major event in Turkey, which at the time included the incursion of Turkish forces into the Kurdish controlled areas of Iraq and a hunger strike by Kurdish political prisoners in Turkey, meant the organisation of a protest along the street. At those moments the two worlds would collide, if only for a voyeuristic 10 minutes or so, as the protesters walked past whichever shop or café. The manipulation of space in this way, whether it was through the subtle, sometimes subversive naming practice of the *kahve* or the eruption of the protest into people's daily reality happened in an affective register that was produced through the interplay of signs and subjectivity in urban space.

Whilst some *kahve* names referred to Turkey, others did not have a formal name and no signage to announce their presence. Their names and their very existence functioned through word-of-mouth. Other places took on the signage and so by default the names of the business from which they had taken over their premises; for example the signage of one of the places I visited read 'Guben' and it also proclaimed the existence of an internet café – neither was true. The place had a number of different names, some called it Guben but most used the name of the proprietor. This familiar way of naming a place is passed on from person-to-person and can be seen as a collective performance of social knowledge. The lack of signage or the use of old signage was also a kind of camouflage that allowed these places to recede from the everyday experience of those users of the street who would never visit a *kahve*.

## *KAHVE* AS 'DIASPORIC HOME'

The signage, if indeed there was any, announced the presence of member's only sports or social clubs, but in reality no-one who used the *kahve* referred to them as such. Their status as member's only clubs was merely a way of negotiating British planning law, as this meant they were subject to different and generally more lenient rules than a coffee shop that was assumed to be open to the general public. At first glance and from the outside, the *kahve* seemed like nondescript spaces, usually situated within an old shop-front with obscured glass. Their presence on the street was generally quite inconspicuous, and although people were aware of their existence, they tended to fade into the background. Some had been established for over 10 years and had not changed much in the intervening period, whereas others were more contemporary with new backlit signage and satellite television. Often they occupied what had become desirable commercial units but were mostly in a bad state of repair. This particular area of North London was at the time in the beginning of what is now considered to be an instance of 'super-gentrification' and during the time I was mapping the high street many *kahve* closed down to make way for upmarket coffee shops.[8] Others, generally the more popular places and those with a younger clientele, were refurbished and managed to reinforce their presence on the street with new shop-fronts and signage.

There was a definite typology to the buildings that the *kahve* occupied, which was linked to the need for cheap space that had a degree of privacy. The majority occupied shop units on the high street and the surrounding area, having the advantage of a prominent location but the disadvantage of being highly visible with transparent façades. A fine balance was sought between the level of obscurity and the traditional open invitation that the *kahve* as guesthouse embodies.[9] This was achieved through layers of adjustable screening such as net curtains, whilst the door was usually left ajar – it was always possible to look inside. On one of my many trips in and around the high street with my Turkish guide, I asked him to accompany me to a *kahve* a few streets away that I had walked past several times. It interested me because the sign announced that it had been established since 1997, over 10 years ago at the time, and it always seemed quite busy with men chatting and smoking outside or sitting outdoors on chairs if the weather permitted. On that day it seemed quiet with no-one outside and although my guide was interested when he saw it at a distance, he did not feel comfortable going inside. He told me there was a social protocol to entering a new *kahve*; the door should be open so you can look in, maybe exchange a greeting or two before deciding to enter. Screening and the details of interior decoration may at first seem superficial, but in the economy of sign and bodily gesture they play an important role as mediators between the inside world of the *kahve* and the outside. A number of different methods of screening were used: some just kept their roller shutters down to about halfway, others use net curtains or obscured glass, whilst others still had built a kind of shelf in their window that acted as both a partial screen and a display for various objects from Turkey.

Since these businesses were not very lucrative, cheap space was a priority and the *kahve* that were located in shop units were generally the older ones that were acquired when the area was less expensive. For newer places there were other options, such as the basements of buildings (usually shops) on the high street. Although the quality of space was lower due to the lack of windows, these spaces had the advantage of being well screened from the busy street whilst also being able to keep their doors open. Only partial views were afforded of the steps leading down to a group of men sitting around a table. Some *kahve* were also located in industrial buildings, but these were quite rare and in these situations they occupied a small out-of-the-way corner.

In many ways the function of the *kahve* in London is similar to those in Turkey, a part of everyday life, they are themselves modernised versions of traditional guesthouses, which were rooms or even a small building in each village associated with an important family. The guesthouses were central to village life and were 'the forum for business transactions, exchanges of gossip, and discussions of communal problems'.[10] They also functioned as short-term lodging for any visitors to the village. Physically the *kahve* in London that I visited appeared to be very similar to those in many parts of Turkey, containing the same type of furniture and objects, but their transposition to another culture had changed their character.[11] Their role as spaces that facilitated a crucial connection to a home left behind gave them a special status in the lives of their diasporic users since they often functioned as places of support. But unlike many *kahve* in Turkey that hold a high status for their important role as social and political hubs, the *kahve* in London are marginalised places. As a minority often the spaces we are obliged to rely upon are at the edges, but as bell hooks has described these can also be transformed into a home of sorts, a place of nurture and rejuvenation.[12] This process can lead to the construction of a 'diasporic home' that can begin in certain locations such as the *kahve* but also includes a process of re-subjectivation, which for those in the diaspora consists of acknowledging our marginal positioning, and of finding a way of telling our own stories and our own histories. This could be in the form of autobiography, which as Trinh T. Min-ha writes, acts 'both as singularity and as collectivity, a way of making history and of rewriting cultures'.[13] Autobiography in the collective mode was present in the *kahve*, a space that allowed for the recalling of past lives as well as for the construction of new ones that emerged in dialogue with the other place left behind. The phrase, '*kahve* talk', often used disparagingly within the Turkish-speaking community to dismiss the types of discussions that occur in a *kahve* as cyclical and never-ending, could also be the key to the functioning of the *kahve* as 'diasporic home'. They can sometimes act as surrogate homes, emulating a certain domesticity, whilst at other times they are more public in nature. They operate within a hybrid logic, filtering and making relations between a home here and a home there. The multiplicity of the *kahve* space gives an indication to the different functions that these places perform, of their highly specialised nature, each serving a specific network of people and places. It is this combination of extreme specificity in the atmosphere and social relations contained within the space, combined with what may seem like a highly banal physical space, that makes them so interesting yet overlooked – on the surface they can appear quite boring.

**Affinity Networks and 'Diasporic Domesticity'**

Whilst the names of the *kahve* hint at their affiliations, the *kahve* space itself sits within a network of trans-local relations that facilitate a crucial connection to 'home' for their users. But the *kahve* are undoubtedly gendered, they are male spaces where women enter rarely and if they do it is usually as waitresses. Corresponding spaces in Turkey, especially in and around Istanbul are becoming mixed but this is a fairly new phenomenon, although women are never stopped from entering they rarely do. Social life for men revolves around the *kahve* whereas for women it circulates within domestic space, in the homes of friends and family. A recent, largely middle-class alternative to the *kahve* for women is 'gold parties', gatherings organised in turn by different members of the social group where women eat, chat and play board games. Since these are organised at a large scale they can become quite expensive, so the hostess is presented with a piece of gold as a way of thanking her for her effort, as well as contributing financially towards the gathering. The important role that gold plays in Turkish daily life and economy is apparent through the presence of gold-merchants in the bazaars of even the smallest towns in Turkey, and similarly in the presence of jewellers who also trade in small quantities of gold in th Turkish neighbourhoods of London.[14] But gold is also crucial in a feminine everyday economy both in contemporary Turkish society and traditionally: women accumulate gold on marriage, at the birth of their children and other special occasions. As Julie Marcus notes: 'This gold is not consumed except in emergencies; instead, it is a durable asset in a fluctuating economic world, an asset which is both portable and convertible on demand.'[15] The tiny bits of gold and gold jewellery are accumulated and passed down from mother-to-daughter; they are a mode of social exchange that creates a type of saving for women who may not be in a position to have a formal pension or savings account. It is also a traditional mechanism for passing wealth through the maternal line of the family.

Gold mediates between two different value systems, economic and symbolic, giving women a way of entering an economic system to which they may not have easy access. The *kahve* also operate within this other sphere, the activities and exchange they sustain is predicated on their value within a symbolic realm that mediates between cultures, places and economies. A large proportion of the men who used the *kahve* moved to London on their own, whether as asylum seekers (in the case of the Kurds in particular) or as economic migrants whose families were still in Turkey. In these cases the *kahve* performed a vital function of support and sociability, especially for those who could not speak English. Some of the *kahve* even re-appropriated the traditional role of the guesthouse as a place of informal lodging for visitors. The logic of visitors from other villages who were connected through kinship ties worked here too and there was an exchange of favours that could span distance and cross generations. One of the *kahve* I visited, called Beşiktas after a Turkish football team, seemed to be used as lodging from time-to-time. The owner, with some irony, likened it to a community service that takes people in when they are having difficulties. These were people with whom he had some link, usually through a convoluted social network of acquaintances with some connection back to his village in Northern Cyprus. This practice of hosting visitors in places that have the legal status of private social clubs, combined with the sometimes precarious immigration status of the visitors, gave these activities a clandestine nature. Although I met one of the people sleeping at Beşiktas, I was not allowed to take any photos or given too much detailed information.

There are in fact conflicting accounts of why people stay in the *kahve* overnight. A young Kurdish woman working in a local cultural centre viewed the *kahve* with disdain, which in her view were no more than illegal gambling dens. She told me that many of the men who stayed at the *kahve* overnight did so after arguments with their families, alluding to the high incidence of domestic violence in the lives of the people she dealt with day-to-day. Others have spoken of the *kahve* as places where 'illegal immigrants' stay and still others view them as crucibles of 'anti-Turkish' activities. I have no way of knowing for sure why the man I met was sleeping in Beşiktas and perhaps it is not so important for this discussion. It is possible that there is a degree of truth in at least some of these accounts, but what does remain true is that the *kahve* can act as a place of support that is accessed through social networks of family, kinship and strong male friendships. What I find interesting is the way in which the *kahve* creates an atmosphere of 'diasporic domesticity'; activities that usually take place in the home, such as sleeping, eating and chatting are transposed here to create something close to a domestic atmosphere. It

The *kahve* are spaces that rely on strong male friendships, 2009

becomes a living room of sorts that for at least some of the users of the *kahve* stands in for a settled home life.

## Languages of Practice

The dispersed, informal networks that constituted the space of the *kahve* required constant work to sustain and nurture them. This work included the making of trans-local connections and whilst some of this could occur through face-to-face interactions much was mediated through technology. As with any other network the distance between nodes, people and places collapsed within the *kahve*'s networks, whilst anyone or anyplace outside seemed infinitely far away. This made them extremely difficult to just walk into – none of the places I visited had any passing trade, customers were friends-of-friends and the regulars brought their family, friends and acquaintances. In fact, one of the owners I interviewed spoke of having to wait a few years after moving to London before he opened his place. Although he knew this was the business he wanted to start, he needed to establish a network of people who would become his first customers. This reliance on a close network is based on a pattern of reciprocal exchange that can be seen in other instances of close community relations, for example in a study of women in Tunis, the author relates the crucial role that visiting each other's homes played in maintaining the network of support that the women relied on. She remarks that this is 'serious and costly work: creating and maintaining the critical ties of exchange and support ... upon which they can count to survive in an increasingly impersonal and unpredictable urbanising nation'.[16] A similar reliance on close networks allowed the men who used the *kahve* to negotiate an often unfamiliar and sometimes hostile city. It also meant that the *kahve* were thoroughly embroiled in the wider politics of Turkey, as well as the local concerns of the particular region of the country that they were associated with. In fact, '*kahve* talk' also referred to this essential function of the *kahve* as a place where politics was played out through discussion, sometimes heated, sometimes earnest, sometimes detached that was also replenished through the news and atmosphere facilitated by satellite television, in particular 'DigiTurk', the satellite provider of choice in the *kahve* I visited.

One of the most obvious distinctions between the various *kahve* was that of generation. The more established places, which also had the least intrusive presence on the street, were occupied by the older generation, Turkish or Turkish-Cypriots who moved to London in the 1970s and mostly worked in the garment factories of East London. These tended to have positions on the street that were quite desirable now as commercial units, but of course when they first opened this was not the case. These older *kahve* were quieter places and were more regional in nature. Although most did have satellite television, they did not advertise this and the television occupied an inconspicuous corner. These *kahve* called themselves 'social clubs' in English. A second *kahve* type was the 'sports club', places that were more geared towards the younger generation and were normally named after a football team supported by the owner. The presence of DigiTurk was advertised

Television plays a crucial role in the trans-local space of the *kahve*, 2009

and seen as an asset and the television occupied a privileged position. They were also louder places, the young men who used these types of *kahve* were a mixture of first and second-generation migrants and the majority had strong ties to Turkey. The last type called themselves 'sports and social clubs' and they had a more family oriented atmosphere where fathers often brought their teenage sons.

## THE BODILY PRODUCTION OF LOCALITY

The *kahve* can be described as a type of trans-local space that mediates in the assemblage of relations between the local and the global, or between a number of different localities.[17] They are a type of mobile space each one being a node in a net of relations over space and time, a figuration of place in a globalised world that I have borrowed from Doreen Massey.[18] The specific entanglements of social, economic and political relations that each *kahve* sits within produces its own spatio-temporalities that at times folds together distant localities and at other times stretches distances. In this sense the *kahve* space is paradoxical, while these could be considered highly contemporary spaces that are the product of large-scale migration, they are at the same time traditional spaces that emulate the form and function of their counterparts in Turkey. Macgregor Wise describes the types of processes that the *kahve* space produces as instances of cultural territorialisation. He writes: 'Cultural territorialization of whatever scale (region, nation, group, individual) is always permeable, formed in relation to and flow with elsewheres and elsewhens, though the borders at times become hardened by habit, fear, and weaponry.'[19] Considering the *kahve* as a mobile space of cultural territorialisation also challenges the prevalent notion of globality in a city like London. Rather than thinking of globality as being produced solely through the 'space of flows' of financial capital, the global can also be *experienced* as connections to other spaces through the networks and ties described above, something that has very little to do with the global circuits of power and wealth.[20] Diasporic inhabitations thus challenge Castell's classic description of the network society. The anthropologist, Arjun Appadurai also describes something similar in his renewed definition of locality, which responds to the inadequacy of the original definition that was used to describe people's lives beyond the closed concept of community.[21] His re-working of locality is based in the anthropological notion that locality in indigenous communities was not a given but was instead the product of hard work, an insight that resonates with the example of women in Tunis described earlier. For Appadurai this material labour constitutes 'complex social techniques for the inscription of locality onto bodies' and he describes naming, circumcision and segregation as 'ways to embody locality as well as to locate bodies in socially and spatially defined communities'.[22] Thus in older societies locality is not seen as a given but is viewed as the result of 'hard and regular work' which enables it to 'maintain its materiality'.[23]

A contemporary example of this embodied production of locality that also leaves a concrete physical residue is the subject of a video installation by Mieke Bal and Shahram Entekhabi called, *Glub*.[24] The work is based around the everyday ritual of seed-eating that is prevalent in most Arab societies; the word '*glub*' means 'heart' or 'kernel' in Arabic and is used to denote the seeds as well as the act of consuming them. The video is an example of what Bal calls 'cultural analysis', a way of viewing the subject from different angles and perspectives without claiming authority or reducing it to an instance.[25] It investigates the habit of eating seeds in public as a performative inhabiting of the city that produces its own locality through the bodily postures of eating: the gesture of hand-to-bag, the shaping of the mouth just so to extricate the seed from its shell, the waste that is produced and shed on to the street. Bal writes about this unconscious act of eating that is at the heart of the project: 'This function of seed as unofficial food connects seed to invisibility and formlessness, but its constant consumption, which produces cracking sounds, smells of roasting, and waste that changes the feel of the street and the sound of walking, makes it at the same time hyper-visible.'[26]

The eating of *glub* on the streets of Kreuzberg in Berlin transformed them, making them dirtier and giving them a special atmosphere that derives from the act of communal, convivial eating. The seed-eating habit was also passed on from the migrants to some of the local population, and Bal contrasts this to the touristic consumption of food in exoticised ethnic restaurants. The video focuses on this smallest of gestures that recurs and multiplies in the everyday practice of the former guest workers of Berlin and creates a continuous cultural territory of sorts from the Middle East through Turkey to Berlin. This process of territorialisation occurs through the bodily inscription of locality as described by Appadurai. The poignancy of this observation that the film makes reveals itself in the context of the conditions that the guest workers had to endure in Germany as hired workforce, never allowed to settle and make a home in their new country. Murat Aydemir, commenting on *Glub*, writes:

*The images of people consuming the seeds on the streets of Berlin can be seen to portray guest workers and their descendants enjoying a leisure time that they were never supposed to have in the first place, and inhabiting a public sphere in which their presence should have been temporary and ephemeral.[27]*

bell hooks writes on the establishment of hegemonic power through a refusal to allow people to create a 'homeplace' for themselves, a place of nurture where they can regain their sense of self.[28] The practice described in *Glub* is one way of making homeplace through a simple everyday act carried out in difficult conditions that becomes a form of resistance.

Seed-eating also occurs in the *kahve* but here always combined with the drinking of tea or coffee and the playing of cards – languages of practice that are crucial to this work of constructing trans-localities. These are communal activities that often occur in public in Turkey, outside on the pavement or in the square, but in London they are contained physically within the interior space of the *kahve* and its immediate vicinity. These semi-private gestures and rituals, although screened from the street outside, make other connections to various regions in Turkey. The specific way of making tea in a samovar, the playing of certain card games and seed-eating itself are all instances of ways in which diasporic communities carry out the work of producing maps that locate them within an unfamiliar and shifting context. It is perhaps only the host society that can navigate without such maps, but with increasingly heterogeneous communities this is now also a challenge.

That bodily postures somehow manage to create a 'diasporic home' in another location is also the subject of an installation and article by the artist Simon Leung, 'Squatting through Violence'.[29] However, he addresses the topic from the other side, of how a home or a locality is purged from unwanted, foreign bodies through

The gesture of seed eating transposed from Turkey to a *kahve* in London, 2009

a process of assimilation. Using the example of the Vietnamese 'boat people' of the 1980s who waited at a bus stop squatting, or that of the Latin American migrant workers who squat daily, waiting for work in San Jose, California, Leung remarks that squatting as a bodily posture is not considered acceptable in suburban USA. Referring to Marcel Mauss's observation from the 1930s that 'humanity can be divided into those who squat and those who sit', Leung writes that Mauss was describing 'the ways in which bodies are themselves instruments used in an acculturated, mechanical process, constrained by social traditions and utility'.[30] Bodily postures, gestures and techniques are thus continually learnt and relearned, breaking and remaking habits, but problems arise when just one type of technique is considered acceptable over others, interfering in the important work of the production of locality.

**Mapping Trans-Localities as Performative Networks**

In trying to understand these different habits and gestures that produce the locality of the *kahve*, I have used certain techniques of mapping as they privilege the spatial, whilst also acknowledging that a number of intricate and overlapping processes play themselves out in this one place. These interpretative maps, described further in the chapter *Diasporic Diagrams*, represent the different networks that the *kahve* are a part of and also inscribe these within physical space. This tracing of networks in order to describe a 'state of affairs' takes its reference from Actor-Network Theory (ANT) as a method of revealing the relations and associations between people, objects and places.[31] Whilst ANT as a method of analysis is very good at tracing relations, it has been criticised for being less specific about the nature of those relations. How are they constituted and what mode do they operate in? Seen in this way it is perhaps the performative dimensions of network behaviour and its consequent tracing that ANT neglects. The work of French psychoanalyst, Fernand Deligny, attends to this omission. At his residential centre Deligny and his colleagues lived alongside autistic children who were deemed too difficult by mainstream practice. Whilst the children could not communicate in language, Deligny and his colleagues followed them, their movements and gestures, producing a series of overlaid tracings. Deligny describes the act of making the tracings as sharing a place. In her commentary on Deligny's drawing practice as a new mode of mapping for architecture and urbanism, Doina Petrescu writes:

> This geo-analysis is not merely pedagogy or therapy but an attempt to invent through mapping ways of being and sharing with "the other", the radically other, the one who does not live in the same manner, who does not have the same means of communication, the same logics, the same gestures: the autistic, the idiot, the fool ... There where nothing is common, instead of language, what is shared is the "place" and its occupation – and this place together with its different activities, gestures, incidents and presences is drawn on the map with different lines and signs. The drawing act is a "tracing", tracer.[32]

My drawings of the *kahve* space were an attempt to combine the different modes of tracing as sharing space (Deligny) and as describing a state of affairs (ANT). I did this through frequent visits to the *kahve*, meeting with people who spent time there and through creating maps that allowed for multiple ways of apprehending the same space. The maps overlaid a number of different attributes: physical space, trans-local connections, mental spaces and their affects. Whilst such a method of representation is useful for any space, in the context of diasporic subjects and the multiplicity of the spaces they produce, it could be a necessity.

## TRANS-LOCAL PRACTICES

The starting point for this chapter was my own experience of viewing certain types of places, rituals and ways of inhabiting as essential to the diasporic experience; beyond the triggering of memories they enable the construction of a place that could be called home. This seemingly simple understanding is complicated as soon as the construction of home is moved out of the confines of domestic interior spaces and into the public and semi-public realm. What were comforting smells and familiar gestures become part of another discussion altogether around exoticised locales, assimilated bodies and introverted gazes. Of course this contrast is stark for its over simplification, decades of ethnographic and anthropological research into diasporas, has at least taught us that the clear-cut lines and simple dichotomies between the host and home culture are misleading, and that domestic and familiar spaces are not always as comforting as they might at first seem. But starting with this binary is an acknowledgment of the positioning from which I started and much of this chapter has been a complicating and testing of this easy assumption for a better understanding of what I felt myself and have seen in others.

This essential work of creating home occurs through trans-local practices and I have explored a number of different instances of this related to the Turkish and Kurdish *kahve*: from bodily postures to affinity networks and the role of gossip and word-of-mouth. The aporia of hospitality as Derrida described it is present here in the workings of the *kahve*, many of whom are thoroughly embroiled in the regional politics of Turkey, making them inviting places for some and excluding others.[33] But these spaces that are so easily condemned for their introspection, also hold out a promise of another kind of space through their functioning within a value system alien to capitalist logic. Operating within sprawling networks of family and friendship they engage within a reciprocal economy based on symbolic rather than monetary value. The role that gold plays is telling, sitting between these two value systems, it can be used subversively as women across the East have done and known for centuries. Gold, upon whose value the wealth of nations is based, also teaches us about another kind of value system, and about the merits of subverting the dominant order from within.

Bodily gestures and subversions of one kind or another and a networked logic reveal the crucial role of performativity within the construction of diasporic spatio-temporalities. This chapter ends with speculation on how particular instances of these could be represented through a practice of mapping that moves back and forth between the sharing of a place and a mode of tracing as abstraction. This way of approaching the question of representation also has repercussions for the way in which the original question of living together is framed. The negotiation of a place together moves the discussion away from questions around public and private space towards the sharing of a space, while the necessity of forms of abstraction in the visual representation of space is acknowledged and worked through.

## NOTES

1. The area around Brick Lane in East London is a good example of such reactions towards diasporic communities who are exhorted upon to integrate, but just enough so that London's hip fashion district can keep its 'exotic' feel and the hordes can keep eating curry. The council, never far behind in such matters, was only too happy to package the whole thing up for touristic consumption as Bangla Town.

2. Miéville, *The City and the City*.

3. Mooshammer and Mörtenböck, *Networked Cultures: Parallel Architectures and the Politics of Space*, 232–55.

4. Between 1997 and 2003, the mosque became a centre for Islamic extremism whilst under the leadership of the radical cleric Abu Hamza al-Masri. After being removed from his role at the mosque, for several months he continued preaching to his supporters on the road outside. For more information see, 'Abu Hamza Profile'.

5. Rogoff, 'The Feminism and Visual Culture Reader', 268.

6. On the map one outline of Turkey is elongated with Cyprus moving up to the middle, whilst the other outlines remains much closer to the original.

7. Rogoff, 'The Feminism and Visual Culture Reader', 273.

8. 'Super-gentrification' is a term coined by Loretta Lees in relation to areas of New York and London. 'A Reappraisal of Gentrification'.

9. The traditional guesthouse was the precursor to *kahve* in rural Turkey, serving as the social hub of the village: 'No one is denied admittance, but the clientele tends to be regular except when there is a need to conduct special business or to entertain the infrequent visitor in the village.' Beeley, 'The Turkish Village Coffeehouse as a Social Institution', 479.

10. Ibid., 481.

11. A description of coffeehouses in rural Turkey from the early 1970s was very similar to the social clubs I visited in London, apart from obvious differences that were the result of technological advances: 'The main part of the room contains wooden tables and chairs, a transistor radio, some decks of cards and a chess or backgammon board, and a lantern (electric light in rare instances). The walls display a variety of posters, pictures, and announcements; included among these might be lists of village men to be drafted into the armed forces, for-sale notices relating to land, farm implements, and animals, and other items of public concern such as the village tax assessment.' Ibid., 482.

12. hooks, 'Choosing the Margin'.

13.   Min-ha, *When the Moon Waxes Red: Representation, Gender and Cultural Politics*, 191.

14.   'The importance of gold in the economy of daily life can be seen in the markets. The bazaars of even small Turkish towns contain large numbers of gold-merchants. Gold coins and jewellery are bought and sold there at a daily fluctuating rate which relates to the international gold market. Certain objects are of standard quality and weight – bracelets, for example, are manufactured and sold in this way so that they carry regular and known values within marriage exchanges. The customers in the gold markets are almost exclusively women, all of whom have some knowledge of the qualities, weights and age of gold. The predominantly male goldsmith's guild is a large and powerful commercial organisation and in the seventeenth century it was the same'. Marcus, 'History, Anthropology and Gender: Turkish Women Past and Present', 157.

15.   Ibid.

16.   Holmes-Eber, *Daughters of Tunis: Women, Family, and Networks in a Muslim City*, 33.

17.   The classic mode of describing the relations between the local and the global is based on the concept of flows. A well known example of a global-to-local flow is the process of 'McDonaldisation': the imposition of a set of hegemonic and stabilised spatial practices to a new location that crosses national and cultural boundaries. Examples of local-to-global flows are given as migrations across borders or cultural tourism; in both cases localised and marginal practices take on a global dimension through the movement of people across national borders but the circumstances and means of movement in the two examples could not be more different. Another major difference in these two versions of local-to-global flow is the networks that they produce. Whilst migration produces dispersed diasporic networks that hold great importance in the lives of those who are a part of them, cultural tourism does not usually sustain such interaction, it takes the form of serial exchanges. The last type of flow is between distinct localities and usually takes the form of subculture, where a number of localities across the globe are connected through a shared interest in a particular cultural or religious practice. Whilst describing flows in this way brings a degree of analytical clarity, it also serves to mask their multiple, overlapping and sometimes disjointed nature.

18.   Massey describes place in a globalised world as: '… particular moments in intersecting social relations, nets of which have over time been constructed, laid down, interacted with one another, decayed and renewed. Some of these relations will be, as it were, contained within the place; others will stretch beyond it, tying any particular locality into wider relations and processes in which other places are implicated too.' *Space, Place and Gender*, 120.

19.   Wise, *Cultural Globalization*, 150.

20.   Such circuits form the classic description of the network society and its attendant 'space of flows' that was first identified by Manuel Castells in the 1980s. See, *The Rise of the Network Society*.

21.   Appadurai, *Modernity at Large: Cultural Dimensions of Globalisation*.

22.   Ibid., 179.

23.   Ibid., 180–81.

24.   Bal and Entekhabi, 'Glub (Hearts)'.

25.   See, Bal, *Double Exposures: The Subject of Cultural Analysis*.

26.   Bal, 'GLUB (Hearts)', 2.

27.  Aydemir, 'Piecemeal Translation', 316.

28.  hooks, 'Homeplace: A Site of Resistance'.

29.  Leung, 'Squatting Through Violence'.

30.  Ibid., 308.

31.  See, Latour, *Reassembling the Social: An Introduction to Actor-Network Theory*; Law and Hassard, *Actor-Network Theory and After*.

32.  Petrescu, 'The Indeterminate Mapping of the Common', 90–91.

33.  Derrida, *Of Hospitality: Anne Dufourmantelle Invites Jacques Derrida to Respond*.

## REFERENCES

'Abu Hamza Profile'. *BBC News*. January 9, 2015. http://www.bbc.co.uk/news/uk-11701269.

Appadurai, Arjun. *Modernity at Large: Cultural Dimensions of Globalisation*. Minneapolis: University of Minnesota Press, 1996.

Aydemir, Murat. 'Piecemeal Translation'. *Art History* 30, no. 3 (2007): 307–25.

Bal, Mieke. *Double Exposures: The Subject of Cultural Analysis*. New York: Routledge, 1996.

_____. 'GLUB (Hearts)'. *Transit* 1, no. 1 (2005): 1–4.

Bal, Mieke, and Shahram Entekhabi. 'Glub (Hearts)'. *Mixed Media & Video + Photo Installation* 29:00 min (2003).

Beeley, Brian W. 'The Turkish Village Coffeehouse as a Social Institution'. *Geographical Review* 60, no. 4 (1970): 475–93.

Castells, Manuel. *The Rise of the Network Society*. Vol. 1. Cambridge, MA: Blackwell, 1996.

Derrida, Jacques. *Of Hospitality: Anne Dufourmantelle Invites Jacques Derrida to Respond*. Stanford, CA: Stanford University Press, 2000.

Holmes-Eber, Paula. *Daughters of Tunis: Women, Family, and Networks in a Muslim City*. Boulder, CO: Westview Press, 2003.

hooks, bell. 'Choosing the Margin'. In *Yearning: Race, Gender and Cultural Politics*, 145–54. London: Turnaround, 1991.

_____. 'Homeplace: A Site of Resistance'. In *Yearning: Race, Gender and Cultural Politics*, 41–50. London: Turnaround, 1991.

Latour, Bruno. *Reassembling the Social: An Introduction to Actor-Network Theory*. Oxford: Oxford University Press, 2005.

Law, John, and John Hassard. *Actor-Network Theory and After*. Oxford: Blackwell, 1999.

Lees, Loretta. 'A Reappraisal of Gentrification: Towards a 'geography of Gentrification''. *Progress in Human Geography* 24, no. 3 (September 2000): 389–408. doi:10.1191/030913200701540483.

Leung, Simon. 'Squatting Through Violence'. In *Radio Temporaire*, edited by Sylvie Desroches Zeigam Azizov, 307–18. Grenoble: National Centre for Contemporary Arts, 1998.

Marcus, Julie. 'History, Anthropology and Gender: Turkish Women Past and Present'. *Gender and History* 4, no. 2 (1992): 147–74.

Massey, Doreen. *Space, Place and Gender*. Cambridge: Polity Press, 1994.

Miéville, China. *The City and the City*. London: Pan, 2011.

Min-ha, Trinh T. *When the Moon Waxes Red: Representation, Gender and Cultural Politics*. London: Routledge, 1991.

Mooshammer, Helge, and Peter Mörtenböck. *Networked Cultures: Parallel Architectures and the Politics of Space*. Rotterdam: NAi Publishers, 2008.

Petrescu, Doina. 'The Indeterminate Mapping of the Common'. *Field:* 1, no. 1 (2007): 88–96.

Rogoff, Irit. 'The Feminism and Visual Culture Reader'. In *Gossip as Testimony: A Postmodern Signature*, The Feminism and Visual Culture Reader, 268–76. London: Routledge, 2003.

Wise, J. MacGregor. *Cultural Globalization: A User's Guide*. 1 edition. Malden, MA: Wiley-Blackwell, 2008.

18

19

21

23

20

22

25

24

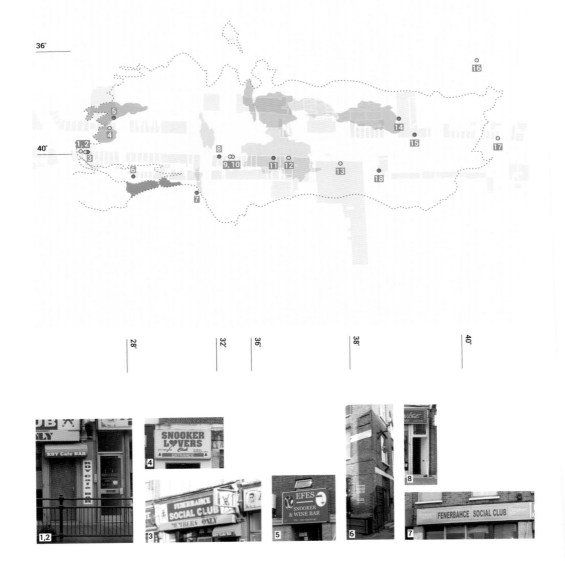

An Allegorical Map of Turkey, 2007

A combination
of curtains,
roller shutters
and shelves
provide partial
screening, 2009

Doors are kept ajar
for the traditional
open invitation of
the *kahve*, 2009

*Kahve*

Azizye Masjiid
An important hub for the local Muslim community

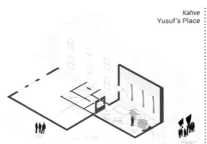

*Kahve*
Yusuf's Place

**4**

## Multiplying Borders: Replicas, Imitations and Mediation

We live in a world where borders have become paradoxical; on the one hand, they are hardening through the building of walls and fences, and on the other they are becoming increasingly dispersed. In this chapter, I explore the manifestation of displaced borders at different sites in London, in order to understand how these complex spaces and their attendant conflicts affect the lives of those in the diaspora. I argue that the multiplication and diffusion of borders is intimately connected to the movement of bodies, and is affected by the way in which contemporary border regimes carry out an evermore sophisticated filtering of unwanted people. Whilst people may find it difficult to cross borders, images are able to move across effortlessly and through their replication and imitation objects also do the same, taking on new and often surprising meanings. It thus becomes clear that it is not necessarily the provenance of images that is of significance but the stories that they can tell (of) us.

This chapter is therefore concerned with what diasporic subjects transpose across borders, a topic related to the increasingly fraught debate on migration in Europe. There is an unspoken assumption that the peacefulness and prosperity of Europe is being threatened by the presence of migrants, whether it is through the trope of the Muslim terrorist, or the undeserving economic migrant-cum-criminal. Such thinking is based in an understanding of Europe as a separate entity, sealed and immune from the rest of the world. This narrative of European space might be considered a triumph of the Enlightenment ideal, built on the exclusion and expulsion of all that is Other, projecting a kind of false peace based on a finely tuned balance between sameness and difference. The presence and visibility of migrants and diasporic subjects shatters this illusion, leading to reactionary responses. It is therefore an urgent task for architects and urbanists to give detailed and nuanced accounts of the use and production of space by those in the diaspora.

As Stephen Lanz has noted, the secular gaze of European urbanism creates a bias in the Marxist analysis of cities that privileges a political-economic analysis above all other factors.[1] In such thinking religion hardly features, although there is a belated but growing body of work that focuses on the role of religion, political movements and their often-intertwining nature in the study of cities.[2] In the occupation and use of space by the diasporic subject both borders and religion reassert themselves within European space. Here, I interrogate how they manifest in particular areas and within certain communities in London. Neither function quite as expected, challenging ideas of space within the European city, in particular the emphasis on public space, a type of space thoroughly embedded in Enlightenment ideals and one that is utterly inadequate for describing diasporic inhabitations and uses. Instead, other spaces emerge, not just the in-between spaces of the semi-public or the semi-private that are tending towards one or the other, but more nuanced spaces such as private spaces that are open to a very select public, such as the *kahve* described in the previous chapter, or open spaces such as parks that are temporally occupied by a select public and hold symbolic value for them. These then are the elusive and temporal arenas for the production of diasporic agency and they are often overlooked in critical urban theory.

## BORDERS

Whilst the word 'border' brings with it images of physical barriers, the vast fence built at the US/Mexico border, the Berlin wall, or the more recent walls built in Baghdad, I am referring to a more ephemeral understanding of borders. I am interested in how such contested borders manifest themselves in the lives of people far from territory's edge. The ways in which borders map themselves onto the intimate topology of bodies no longer at the border is affected by the paradoxical nature of contemporary borders. The flows that characterise globalisation and the neo-liberal economy produce many borders, meaning that they not only describe the edges of nations and regions but are dispersed throughout, wherever there is an overlapping of the flows of people, goods, data or capital. In the case of European space, the attempt to expunge borders through the outsourcing of border security to Europe's edge has only served to fold and disperse the border further inside. For example, for the many who fit a certain profile immigration and visa checks no longer occur solely at the physical border.

Contemporary conceptualisations of the border vary from an artificial divide that only manifests itself in the act of crossing, to a borderzone as a thickening of the area around the border where its influence ranges. The border in relation to the boundary is seen as less rigid, allowing for some permeability and exchange, having the potential to turn a site of division and containment into a fertile plain where subjectivities could slip and new cultures may form. But the rich potential of the border is always mediated by the risk of transgression, whether spatial, cultural, political or otherwise, meaning that the border can also function as a set of internalised limits. In the following examples, I explore these limits and opportunities of the border, not on a national or continental scale, but through their production and reproduction at a local or micro-scale in the city. What are the shifts that occur in this switching of scales and what are the consequences of the prominence of these sites in the lives of an increasing number of people?

## The Impossibility of Mapping Borders

The border as a demarcation that limits, contains and bounds, has been questioned consistently by those who live near, work on or around borders. Yet, the physical manifestation of the border as exactly such a device of division between 'us and them' has proliferated. Bequeathed as colonial exports to their former subjects, borders continue their practice of separation and division in the former colonies. For my younger self living in Pakistan, one part of the now partitioned Indian Subcontinent, the line was the India/Pakistan border, drawn over 60 years ago in violence and maintained ever since in the threat of it. I lived in Lahore, the historical heart of the once unified Punjab province, and for me the border manifested itself only when transgressed, for example, in the very occasional sighting of a Sikh turban.[3] For a child not yet fully aware of history, the turban signified the not-quite-other. This dispersal of the border also manifested itself in the radio waves and television signals that managed to melt through physical barriers and deployed armies. Although we did not watch Indian television in our home, it was always a background humming presence at my aunt's house that reminded us of our shared histories across the border. These dispersed presences were perhaps more poignant for us (the younger generation) who had not lived through Partition, than the Grand Trunk Road that leads from the heart of old Lahore to Amritsar across the border in India. The television's images travelled effortlessly.

The colonial era Grand Trunk road leading to India across the Wagah border Pakistan, 2015

The arbitrariness of the border that divided Lahore from Amritsar is related in Saadat Hasan Manto's celebrated short story, *Toba Tek Singh*. The lunatics described in the story were the only people able to recognise what the leaders of either side could not, that their well-intentioned division had left their citizens in limbo.[4] As one patient insistently and with growing urgency inquired as to the whereabouts of Toba Tek Singh, the answers of those deemed sane began to sound mad:

> *If they tried to tell him, they themselves were caught up in the perplexity that Sialkot used to be in Hindustan, but now it was said to be in Pakistan. Who knew whether Lahore, which now is in Pakistan, tomorrow might go off to Hindustan?*[5]

In other times and in other cultures the border has not always been a line drawn as such. It has instead been conceptualised as a zone but one that is very different from the buffer zone of contemporary geo-politics, such as the area between North and South Korea, or the deliberate wilderness at the eastern edge of Finland that marks Europe's edge with Russia. Instead the border as zone could be considered a productive area that is shared by those on either side. This then, is the border constituted as resource rather than divide. In his book, *Siam Mapped*, Thongchai Winichakul has traced the misunderstandings that arose from this difference in attitude between the Siamese and the British, who in the first half of the nineteenth century were busy annexing parts of present day Burma.[6] Whilst the British were keen to adopt a borderline, for the Siamese the question of the border was far more complex. Each town had jurisdiction over the areas around it but these did not always meet, there could be neutral zones in between. The Siamese concept of territory was of a heterogeneous patchwork rather than a continuous appropriated territory. It meant that the patrolling of the boundary was a local affair and the border itself was not a line but a place, or *places*. Whilst watchtowers marked the boundary it was the patrol and the inhabitants that demarcated the locally maintained and negotiated borders. This concept of the border functioned much like a set of nested dolls, boundaries sat within boundaries, having different levels of sovereignty, together constituting what we might call a border. As Winichakul points out: 'Sovereignty and borders were not coterminous.'[7] Thus there was not only an indeterminacy to the concept of the border, but also discrepancies within the actual physical borders whose edges were fuzzy and imprecise. Of course this was also related to the question of scale and of how space was conceptualised differently by them: for the Siamese it was still related to experience and lived reality, whereas for the British it had already been abstracted into the flattened representations of maps. But the conceptualisation of the border as zone is not completely alien to Western thinking; instead it has been systematically expunged from it. As Richard Sennett's description of the Athenian agora shows, there were spaces within it that blurred the notion of the border and created a kind of liminal zone between public and private – a zone of possibility rather than a line of separation.[8]

In contrast, where national borders have not yet been drawn and are still actively contested the question of their representation becomes even more fraught. I have explored this subject in the context of Kurdistan, a nation-state that does not yet exist and perhaps never will. Kurdistan is a demand for another politics that could be met with another way of representing that is able to embody shifting and internalised borders. Yet the question of representation itself is fraught, as has been proven by much recent critical theory that has addressed this question through a dialectical discussion around what can or cannot be represented. In contrast, Hito Steyerl uses the concept of 'presencing', in reference to an early article by Walter Benjamin that introduces the idea of a 'language of things'.[9] When speaking of language in this article, Benjamin is not referring to the spoken languages of humans but to the silent languages of objects. This seemingly strange concept is reinterpreted by Steyerl to provide a way of thinking representation beyond its current impasse: the translation inherent in representation occurs not in the written words of national languages nor in the visual vocabulary of art, but instead at the level of practice and through the objects of everyday use. The power of such languages is perhaps most obvious in situations of oppression, for example, under General Zia-ul-Haq's dictatorship of Pakistan in the 1980s, the most vocal critic on state television was the satirical Uncle Sargam – a puppet. Translated into a language of practice through the skill of the puppeteer the non-threatening everyday object that was a puppet managed to say for a while what no person could.

**Bodies (Re)Drawing Borders**

In the chapter, *Diasporic Diagrams*, I relate how I have used mapping as a way of representing Kurdistan and its contested borders through the experiences of the Kurdish and Turkish diaspora in London. Whilst the maps used drawing and narrative to describe borders as mental constructions, the same borders also manifested themselves in the physical space of the street through the movement of diasporic bodies. Stoke Newington High Street/Kingsland Road in the London Borough of Hackney was, at the time, the site of regular demonstrations by Kurds against events in Turkey. The protests were organised by a number of cultural and community centres working together with the reason for the march governing which groups chose to participate. Since the protests were happening so regularly the community had an understanding with the police and their applications were usually processed quickly so that they could be granted licences for marches at short notice.

Protests are often described as having certain characteristics that include the contestation of and resistance to power, the bringing together of a certain community, and of course they are public in nature. In his appraisal of the role of protest in creating a form of community, Michael Hirsch states that the 'most important aspect is the de-functionalisation of urban space: the interruption of the usual order of business, transport, work and specialisation. But it is also the interruption of the stratified, hierarchical order of a class society: the positions individuals inhabit in the social order are suspended'.[10] In the context of these particular protests these comments need further exploration, because the protest did not really disturb the order of business on the high street, nor did it have much impact on the class relations between these diasporic bodies and their hosts. In fact, the size of the protest was considered small – insignificantly small as one local councillor laughed off my description of the marches as protest; 'they just have a few banners'.[11] But perhaps the significance of this act was lost on him. It was not the size of the marches that gives them an importance, nor even the disruption and de-functionalisation of space they did or did not cause. After all the protests covered a relatively small stretch of road and occupied only a small portion of a wide street so that traffic could continue flowing. What made the impact was of course, as always, the audience. These marches, the ones that happened on a local, neighbourhood level, were not directed at a government or a state but were instead directed at the other users of the street. The borders that were drawn and redrawn through this intermittent practice hardly registered in the lives of those who did not have a connection to Turkey, but for those who did they were highly significant.

The protests were called peace marches by one of the women involved in organising them, which for her was another way of limiting their antagonistic dimension. But the march, or protest, did actively increase the territory of the group within public space. It created a kind of corridor that at those moments of protest embodied the idea of Kurdistan and became a territorial and symbolic figuration of it. The form of the street, its linear nature and the proximity of Turks and Kurds living and working there made it an ideal space of protest. As the people carrying banners moved down the street, they affected the spaces around them. At the edges where this dynamic corridor met other spaces, for example the open doors of shops or the pavement where people were walking or sitting outside a café, there were inevitably people of Turkish origin. I witnessed many of these events and like others I would turn around to watch both the protest itself and the reactions of others. There would be blank faces from those who could not read the banners; those who could were Turkish or Kurdish. I could not read most of the banners but I did recognise the name and face of Abdullah Ocalan, the PKK (Kurdistan Worker's Party) leader on a number of the banners.[12] The remarkable thing about these protests was that they were very quiet; they had none of the loudness, music and chatter of other protests I had witnessed. Perhaps it was their small size that made them quiet, but they also seemed to be an essential part of everyday life for those who protested in order to claim the right to exist. They were therefore not really moments of spontaneous expression or rupture but they were a form of the political territorialisation of space through a performative enacting of contested borders.

## The Instability of Meaning Across Borders

The protest is an example of the active (re)production of borders by diasporic bodies, supported by symbols and images that together created a figuration of Kurdistan on a street in London. This is a form of diasporic agency that relies on the particular quality of diasporic subjectivities and symbols to move across an often fluid boundary, allowing zones of possibility to be created as certain spaces and objects take on multiple and changing meanings. Arjun Appadurai describes these as 'diasporic public spaces' that are created when 'moving images meet deterritorialised viewers'.[13] This proliferation and movement of images across borders is also described by filmmaker and writer, Hito Steyerl. In the film *November*, she traces the image of her friend Andrea Wolf, her life and subsequent death as Sehit Ronahi and the identity she adopted as part of her role in the Kurdish resistance. After her reported assassination at the hands of the Turkish military her image became a powerful symbol of martyrdom, carried in demonstrations through the streets of Berlin. Steyerl's film tells the story of what she calls the 'travelling images' of Andrea/Ronahi, from her role in a feminist martial arts movie that Steyerl directed in the 1980s, where she played the part of the tough heroine, to her transformation into the image of Ronahi as martyr.[14] As Steyerl narrates in the film, 'Andrea became herself a travelling image, wandering over the globe, an image passed on from hand-to-hand, copied and reproduced by printing presses, video recorders, and the Internet'.[15]

The film's title, *November*, comments on the state of politics and the role of images today. Referring to Sergei Eisenstein's film, *October* about the Russian Revolution, *November* is a comment on contemporary politics, where nothing is clear-cut and where collective struggles are no longer able to transcend lines of ethnicity and nationalism. Instead, there is as TJ Demos writes, 'unaccountable government power (the kind that allegedly killed Ronahi), fragmented oppositional struggles (in which Ronahi willingly participated), and representational instability (signalled by Wolf's proliferating identities)'.[16] In the historical time of November there is a fragmentation of struggle that is reflected in the ways in which signs and images take agency, adopting new meanings as they travel and constitute their own space-times. It is a time that demands self-reflexivity, as Steyerl reminds us. 'None of us found our way out of the labyrinth of travelling images. In November we are all part of the story, and not I am telling the story, but the story tells me'.[17]

It seems to me that Steyerl is advocating an uncertainty, an openness to the provenance of images and their meaning, a concern with their repetition and iteration, their incessant reproduction and loss of resolution, which allows images to be imbued with meaning over and over again. Here I would like to relate a similar repetition of image at the scale of object, within a particular diaspora spread across many cities around the globe, a 'travelling image' that has become an ambivalent and often surprising carrier of meaning in its different locations.

## REPLICAS AND IMITATIONS

### The Travelling Shaheed Minar

Whilst I was working at the art and architecture practice, muf, we were invited to participate in an exhibition that re-presented a series of public spaces in London.[18] Each participant was asked to choose a space they liked or that had particular significance for them and to interpret it in a new and personal way for the exhibition. The space that I looked at was a small urban park in East London that was chosen by an anthropologist from the local Bengali community. He dropped out at the last minute, leaving me to come up with a reading of a space that I knew vaguely from my visits to the nearby Whitechapel Art Gallery and to Brick Lane. The history of the park revealed that it was the site of the White Chapel after which the area was named and which was destroyed in the Second World War. Its current name, Altab Ali Park, revealed another strand of its history; the park was named after a local Bengali resident who had been killed in a racist attack in the 1970s, around the time of the notorious race riots in that area of London. But I was also aware of the park's role in recent politics; in 2003 a large demonstration against the Iraq War had started at the park and marched to Whitehall.

I began to think of the connection between this small inconspicuous pocket of land and the agency of the local community. This thinking was reinforced by a conversation with a local community leader, who told me about the significance of what looked to me like a strange sculpture in one corner of the park. The Shaheed Minar, which translates as *Martyr's Monument*, was built in commemoration of students killed in the Language Movement Day riots in Bangladesh, fighting for the right to have Bengali as a national language alongside Urdu in what was then East Pakistan. The original Shaheed Minar was a small stone monument that was destroyed by the Pakistani army in the Bangladeshi independence struggle; it was later replaced by a large-scale monument designed by the sculptor, Hamidur Rahman. The cubist sculpture made of white marble denotes a mother protecting her children with a red disc in the background representing the blood that was spilled during the independence/language struggles. What stands in Altab Ali Park is a 1:5 scale replica of that monument and it is not the only one. There is another Shaheed Minar in the UK in Oldham, near Manchester, others are in Tokyo and in Sydney and there is one planned for Toronto, as well as many other versions in Bangladesh itself. What did this proliferation of monuments, wherever there was a critical mass of the Bengali population, tell me about the public space I was trying to reinterpret?

One of my colleagues found the whole idea of the monument difficult. He was disturbed by the claiming of public space by what for him was essentially a manifestation of a nationalistic struggle for independence. But for me there was something more interesting at work here in the repetition at different scales of the same monument, where it seemed to me that repetition did indeed produce alteration.[19] This included variations in construction that responded to the specific weather conditions or security concerns at the different sites as well as personalised interpretations of the design. The original monument was made of white marble while the one in the park was made of mild steel, painted white. Other versions neither replicated the material nor the exact design. The minar as image had travelled alongside the Bengali diaspora but in this travelling it had taken on an agency of its own. Its status as a replica and an imitation allowed it to be appropriated. Whilst it contained echoes of the original Shaheed Minar, it

Shaheed Minar
in Altab Ali Park,
London, 2007

also underwent surprising transformations that were beyond the control of the Bengali community that commissioned the monument in the first place.

## The Agency of the Shaheed Minar

Interrogating the Shaheed Minar not as mute object that at best represents the nostalgia for home or a commemoration of past struggles, but as a 'quasi-object' in the sense that Bruno Latour has described it, reveals its agential potential. For Latour a quasi-object works across the false divides of modernism, between nature and culture, or between east and west. In order for this illusory divide to be kept intact, hybrids are needed to mediate in-between. These are what Latour calls, 'quasi-objects/quasi-subjects'.[20] The minar's status as a replica that is to be imbued with meaning allows it to act as such a mediator between different cultures and places. This way of thinking the minar and the diasporic communities involved, not just as hybrids but as mediators also implies a way of conceptualising difference that retains the possibility of being in common. In a recent book, *Differences in Common*, the editors state: '*Community does not fill the gap between subjects but places itself in this gap or void.*'[21] Both the minar and the community it gathers around it are able to fill such a gap through their ability to mediate. As Latour describes:

> There are no more naked truths, but there are no more naked citizens, either. The mediators have the whole space to themselves. [...] The imbroglios and networks that had no place now have the whole place to themselves. They are the ones that have to be represented; it is around them that the Parliament of Things gathers henceforth.[22]

The diasporic subject is thus placed at the centre, part of an intricate network that reaches across space-times. Returning to the exhibition itself, I had heard that there was a lot of interest in the language that teenagers from this community were speaking, mixing English and Sylheti. I arranged to meet with a group of teenage girls at a local youth centre. Immediately I was struck by their acute self-awareness. They had lived through an almost constant interest in their community, both from academia and governmental institutions and they could perform for their audience, in this case myself as the naïve researcher. 'Was I not aware that there was a name for the way they spoke, 'Benglish' they were calling it and no it wasn't making new words, just mixing English and Sylheti phrases'.[23] They looked at me pityingly, 'do you not speak your own language, what is it anyway?' 'Urdu', I say guiltily and 'yes I do speak it', acutely aware of my country's diabolical past regarding language and the fate of East Pakistan. They proceed to tell me of how they speak another language, b-language or back slang, the practice of adding a letter in this case 'b' after every letter you speak – something that I remember trying to do as a child but never quite managing.

In my conversation with the girls I was aware of the long networks that they were a part of and the places that they were mediating between. Their conversation skipped from talk of events in their locality, a murder of a young woman and her children, the father who had disappeared, perhaps to Bangladesh, their articulation of UK politics and the role of the police. Would they bother going after the man if he had fled back home? Then teenage talk of boys, the b-language, discussions of school, another research project they were involved in, this time an oral history project, giggling amongst each other, talking about friends and then about politics in Bangladesh and visiting there. It occurred to me that this was exactly what was so difficult to represent, this skipping from one place to the other, the networks these girls were tracing, the merry dance their subjectivity was leading you through. In Latour's terms the girls became quasi-subjects, able to mediate between here and there, not just belonging to one place or another. This promiscuity and lack of care for static ideas of culture perhaps had much to do with their age, their subjectivities allowed for new forms of culture to emerge, whether it was the b-language or some other way of doing that I was not witness to.

In some ways the Shaheed Minar also acted in similar ways. As I have mentioned earlier, the park had been used as a gathering point for a demonstration against the Iraq war, a protest that included not just Bengalis but many others from the local community. It had also been used as a place to gather when the Bengali community was rallying together for help during the collapse of a money transfer business that many of them used.[24] As such the park represented not only the agency of the Bangladeshi community but was also in the process of becoming an active place of protest, of meeting, of gathering for all sorts of other people. As a public space it had the dimension of agonism that Chantal Mouffe has called for, whilst the Shaheed Minar itself embodied a sophisticated form of agency that was able to create a meaningful set of associations across people who perhaps shared a present but had diverse pasts. [25] It is the negotiation of this shared present that many commentators have identified as the biggest challenge facing society today and the diasporic agency described here has the potential to do just this. Through the intricate network that they were able to convene, the park and the minar brought together a series of disparate and overlapping claims to an inconspicuous pocket of land in East London. Most people who gathered in the park to protest were not really aware of the exact history of the minar; they just knew that the park was somewhere you came to when something needed to be said. The Shaheed Minar itself was therefore subject to transposition – it altered as it moved across borders.[26] An account of the minar in Toronto or Sydney could tell a very different story, but in East London, it meant that the park could indeed become a site, alongside many others for what Latour has called a 'Parliament of Things'.[27]

Such a reading of the diasporic subject and the objects that form part of the network of meaning around them allows for a new conception of space that places an emphasis on relations and associations. It inherently privileges a fluid and dynamic understanding, which acknowledges that although particular nodes (subjects or objects) may appear static at certain times, the way that they are connected is always in flux and always has an impact on them. It also emphasises the instability of meaning across borders that is often outside our control, but which in turn shapes our own narratives and understandings of space. The story of the travelling Shaheed Minar and its attendant diasporas is of a topological object that through crossing borders also constituted them.

## MEDIATING A SHARED PRESENT

This chapter started with a desire to understand diasporic space and its habit of transposing distant geo-political borders to European urban space. Through describing different instances of dispersed and multiplied borders I related how diasporic and migrant bodies are key to the production and (re)production of displaced borders. Contemporary border regimes allow everything but bodies to move across freely and the mobile images described in this chapter are key to understanding the production of diasporic agency in these circumstances. Through an exploration of the travelling Shaheed Minar and the manifestation of Kurdistan in a London street, I described how images and their meanings become unstable as they cross borders. That none of us are really in control of this process brings the notion of the replica and the imitation that allows, through its own ambiguity, to be imbued with different meanings. Such subjects and objects play the role of mediators and are key actors in the process of negotiating our shared present that is perhaps the most challenging consequence of what is termed globalisation.

## NOTES

1.  Becker et al., *Global Prayers*, 21–2.

2.  See for example, Beaumont, *Postsecular Cities*.

3.  The Punjab is an area with many important Sikh and Sufi shrines, and at the time I lived there during the 1980s, pilgrims of either faith were the only ones allowed to cross the border on a strict quota system.

4.  Manto, 'Toba Tek Singh', 2010.

5.  Manto, 'Toba Tek Singh'.

6.  Winichakul, *Siam Mapped: A History of the Geo-Body of a Nation*.

7.  Ibid., 77.

8.  Sennett, 'Democratic Spaces'.

9.  Steyerl, 'The Language of Things'.

10. Hirsch, 'The Space of Community: Between Culture and Politics', 291.

11. A comment made in an informal conversation following a chance meeting.

12. The Kurdistan Worker's Party or *Partiya Karkerên Kurdistan* (PKK) is a group established in 1978 who 'from 1984 to 2013 fought an armed struggle against the Turkish state for cultural and political rights and self-determination for the Kurds in Turkey'. 'Kurdistan Workers' Party'.

13. Appadurai, *Modernity at Large: Cultural Dimensions of Globalisation*, 22.

14. Steyerl, *November*.

15. Ibid.

16. Demos, 'Traveling Images'.

17. Steyerl, *November*.

18. muf architecture/art is a practice based in London that specialises in design in the public realm. For more information see, www.muf.co.uk. The exhibition, *Revisit: Urbanism Made in London*, was curated by Peter Arlt and shown at Architekturforum Oberosterreich, Linz (2 February–3 March 2007) and Haus der Architektur, Graz, (19 June–24 July 2008) Austria.

19. I am referring here to Derrida's concept of 'iterability'. He writes: 'Iterability alters, contaminating parasitically what it identifies and enables to repeat 'itself.' Derrida, *Limited Inc*, 62.

20. Latour, *We Have Never Been Modern*.

21. Sabadell-Nieto and Segarra, *Differences in Common. Gender, Vulnerability and Community*, 8.

22. Latour, *We Have Never Been Modern*, 144.

23. All quotes in this paragraph are from an interview I carried out with teenage Bengali girls at a youth centre in East London in 2007.

24. In June 2007, the First Solution money transfer business collapsed. It had a branch in East London, which was used almost exclusively by Bengalis to send money to their relatives in Bangladesh. Most of these people were not very well off themselves

and some lost their life savings. A rally was held in Altab Ali Park to persuade the government to offer an aid package.

25.    Mouffe, *The Democratic Paradox*; Mouffe, 'Some Reflections on an Agonistic Approach to the Public'.

26.    I am referring to Rosi Braidotti's concept of 'transposition', which she defines as: 'The term 'transpositions' has a double source of inspiration: from music and from genetics. It indicates an intertextual, cross-boundary or transversal transfer, in the sense of a leap from one code, field or axis into another, not merely in the quantitative mode of plural multiplication, but rather in the qualitative sense of complex multiplicities.' Braidotti, *Transpositions: On Nomadic Ethics*, 5.

27.    See, Latour, 'From Realpolitik to Dingpolitik or How to Make Things Public'.

## REFERENCES

Appadurai, Arjun. *Modernity at Large: Cultural Dimensions of Globalisation*. Minneapolis: University of Minnesota Press, 1996.

Beaumont, Justin. *Postsecular Cities: Space, Theory and Practice*. New York: Continuum, 2011.

Becker, Jochen, Katrin Klingan, Stephen Lanz, and Katnhrin Wildner. *Global Prayers: Contemporary Manifestations of the Religious in the City*. Zürich: Lars Muller Publishers, 2013.

Braidotti, Rosi. *Transpositions: On Nomadic Ethics*. Oxford: Polity Press, 2006.

Demos, T.J. 'Traveling Images'. *Artforum International*, June 22, 2008.

Derrida, Jacques. *Limited Inc*. Northwestern University Press, 1977.

Hirsch, Michael. 'The Space of Community: Between Culture and Politics'. In *Did Someone Say Participate?: An Atlas of Spatial Practice*, edited by Markus Miessen and Shumon Basar. London: MIT Press, 2006.

'Kurdistan Workers' Party'. *Wikipedia, the Free Encyclopedia*, January 21, 2015. http://en.wikipedia.org/w/index.php?title=Kurdistan_Workers%27_Party&oldid=643436925.

Landry, Donna, and Gerald Maclean, eds. *The Spivak Reader*. New York: Routledge, 1996.

Latour, Bruno. 'From Realpolitik to Dingpolitik or How to Make Things Public'. In *Some Reflections on an Agonistic Approach to the Public*, Making Things Public: Atmospheres of Democracy Karlsruhe/Cambridge MA:14–41. ZKM/MIT Press, 2005.

_____. *We Have Never Been Modern*. Cambridge, MA: Harvard University Press, 1993.

Manto, Saadat Hasan. 'Toba Tek Singh'. In *Saadat Hasan Manto: Kingdom's End*, 9–17. New Delhi: Penguin Classics, 2010.

_____. 'Toba Tek Singh'. Translated by Frances W. Pritchett. Accessed January 8, 2015. http://www.columbia.edu/itc/mealac/pritchett/00urdu/tobateksingh/translation.html.

Mouffe, Chantal. 'Some Reflections on an Agonistic Approach to the Public'. In *Making Things Public: Atmospheres of Democracy*, 804–7. ZKM/MIT Press, 2005.

_____. *The Democratic Paradox*. London: Verso, 2000.

Sabadell-Nieto, Joana, and Segarra, eds. *Differences in Common. Gender, Vulnerability and Community*. Amsterdam/New York: Rodopi, 2014.

Sennett, Richard. 'Democratic Spaces'. *Hunch* 9 (Autumn 2005): 40–47.

Steyerl, Hito. *November*. DV, 2004.

_____. 'The Language of Things'. *Under Translation*, 2006. http://translate.eipcp.net/transversal/0606/steyerl/en.

Winichakul, Thongchai. *Siam Mapped: A History of the Geo-Body of a Nation*. Chiang Mai: Silkworm Books, 1994.

Certain shops were important nodes within the
diasporic space of the high street

Anatolian Cultural Centre is an important node for
Kurdish activism in the area

# 5

# Diasporic Territories: Overlapping Spheres and Fragile Envelopes

How might the concept of territories be used to describe the production of diasporic space? In this chapter I approach the figuring of diasporic territories from two distinct angles, from the geopolitical perspective of territories seen as the product of the interplay of politics, power and space, and from the biological perspective of territories seen as the primal need of all animals, including humans, for space and a certain distinction from their environment and from others. Theoretically, the notion of territory is constructed as *'umwelt'* and 'the refrain', as well as through referring to contemporary art and spatial practices.[1] This chapter was written in close conjunction with the mapping of diasporic territories along the high street that is related in the chapter, *Diasporic Diagrams*, and in this sense it is also about the relationship between power, bodies and the diasporic experience of urban space. The theoretical understandings of this chapter are therefore supplemented with the embodied spatial practice of walking in order to understand how our bodily practices affect the local space of a city, creating micro-territories related to the social, the political or to everyday life.

Territory as a concept has a number of overlapping meanings, from a geo-political construct relating to the power and influence of sovereign states, to territoriality as a social phenomenon that describes the relationships between societies and their understandings of space and time. Delaney states the contemporary role that the concept plays; '… territory is commonly understood as a device for simplifying and clarifying something else, such as political authority, cultural identity, individual autonomy, or rights. In order to have this effect territory itself has to be taken as a relatively simple and clear phenomenon.'[2] Yet, territory is anything but simple. The common etymology of the word links it to 'territorium', but going further back it relates to both 'terra', meaning earth or 'terrere', meaning to terrorise or frighten.[3] This contradiction in the meaning of the word is still present in its use today, where territory is either constructed as a natural urge, a way of connecting back to Nature, or as a patch of land to defend against outsiders. Whilst these definitions relate to human ideas of territories, territoriality is also a powerful construct for animals, but the classic geographical text on the subject, *Human Territoriality,* made a sharp distinction between what territoriality could mean for humans and animals: 'For humans, territoriality is not an instinct or drive, but rather a complex strategy to affect, influence, and control access to people, things, and relationships.'[4] In this chapter, I argue that this distinction between conceptualising territory as human or animal is restrictive and through looking for overlaps and continuities between human and animal territories, the prevalence of territory as violence in human history could be countered towards a richer and more intense conceptualisation. Such a conception of territory also proves to be more helpful in thinking about the production of diasporic agencies, as well as providing important ways of thinking our long-term relationship to the planet – to imagining our planetary future.

## TERRITORY

### The Archipelago as Geo-Political Territory

The migrant is by condition political, both due to past events and present realities. Any figuration of diasporic territory therefore needs to engage with the ways in which the geopolitical realities of other places are inscribed on to the bodily practices of the migrant. I start this chapter with an analysis of a number of contemporary territorial projects within art and architectural practice that seek to interrogate the relationships between power, politics and space. They reveal how the representation of space motivated by politics is used as a means of exerting power and hint at the possibility of counter-power, of how a counter production of space could also be possible.[5]

On a global and political scale territory cannot be uncoupled from the representation of it, whether it is the historic use of maps and their role in constructing a world, or the numerous examples where communities that have not been included in official maps are considered to not exist at all. In the case of territorial research then, there is a fundamental connection between our understanding of territory and conflict as a base condition. That in many cases this conflict has been borne out as violence serves to underline this connection. Much of the work is predicated on the fragmentation of the notion of territory – with the slow demise of the nation-state, globalised power structures and the state of constant war in which we now live, territory as a self-contained, discrete entity has fragmented into what has been referred to as an 'archipelago'.[6] The analogy of the archipelago is useful as it keeps the notion of a level of containment and isolation whilst adding to it connections and relations that are the result of exterior power applied from above without the knowledge or consent of the majority. The archipelago as territory includes instances such as refugee camps, prisons, the factory and other spaces that are not under the control and jurisdiction of sovereign states but are serving private interests, usually corporate. The concept of archipelago thus refers to a dual condition, the fragmentation of sovereign power and the rise of extra-territorial powers. Whilst classic geo-political territories relied on the policing of strict borders, these fragmented islands of territory have fluid and temporal boundaries.

The mapping of the West Bank produced by Eyal Weizman in collaboration with the Israeli human rights organisation B'Tselem, is an example of empirical territorial research in an environment where space is highly contested, and the practice of cartography has been used overtly and consistently as a political bargaining chip and as a means of changing the facts on the ground.[7] As Weizman writes: 'Whatever the nature of Palestinian spatiality, it was subordinated to Israeli cartography. Whatever was unnamed on the map ceased to exist as a part of the political realm.'[8] In this context the mapping of the numerous Palestinian villages left unrecorded in Israeli maps was imperative, but Weizman et al. also mapped Israel's territorial strategy of the deployment of settlements, as well as the network of bypass roads and tunnels that were constructed in parallel. This mapping tells a very different story from the official Israeli line. The map reveals the role of infrastructure in not only connecting the settlements to the rest of Israel but also their strategic placement as a means of fragmenting Palestinian territory, creating isolated pockets of land. Added to this already complex situation is the presence of precious underground water sources and Israel's desire to keep control of the skies above the whole of the West Bank. This has meant that unlike a normal territorial map where the lines and boundaries drawn on the horizontal plane can be extended above and below ground, in the West Bank the control over these artificially separated planes does not correspond. The effects of this three-dimensional strategy of control have been named the 'politics of verticality' by Weizman.[9]

One of the major consequences of conducting research on geopolitical territories is that it creates opportunities for intervention at a regional and sometimes national level by non-governmental actors, and allows for some power to be shifted from the state. Its success relies on dealing not with the source of power, which in the end is too powerful anyway, but instead by intervening in localised power relations it leads to an understanding of the processes through which power functions. This way of operating relates to Michel Foucault's description of power as being dispersed through society through space.[10] In order to understand how these territories operate there is a need to comprehend the shifting power relations that constitute them. Foucault describes power as something 'beyond interdiction'; he calls it a performative act that takes place in the everyday interactions of society.[11] As Weizman has commented, in the case of the West Bank these dispersed forms of power are exercised through the act of building itself that is used to fragment Palestinian territory, or through the strategic placement of settlements on hilltops that act as fortresses to survey the Palestinian villages below. Through such moves the practice of architecture itself is deployed as a weapon. The strategic occupation of land reveals the need to conceptualise space as territorialised within such situations of conflict.

The discussion on territory defined as archipelago and the 'politics of verticality' provides a framework for the conceptualisation of diasporic territories through foregrounding the relationship between the representation of space and the production of power. Even in the fraught geo-political context of Israel/Palestine power is exercised through concrete and localised relations, opening up the possibility of a space of resistance at the micro level. Whilst the fragmentation of territory is being used as a powerful device of oppression, diasporic territories could also be conceptualised as fragmented and extra-territorial in their spanning across national spaces. Just as diasporic trans–localities have the potential to subvert the workings of the network society through making connections across networks based on affinity rather than capital, diasporic territories could work with the fluid and temporal nature of territory as defined above so that a notion of diasporic territory could be used to make connections of solidarity.[12]

## Trajectories of a Bodily Networked Territory

The importance of territories as a concept also reveals itself in other situations where conflict is present, but where it does not necessarily manifest itself in the violence of war. The video artist, Ursula Biemann, has carried out a large body of research on such extraterritorial spaces that are the product of militarised borders, unequal economic relations and post-colonial geographies. In particular her work focuses on gender and mobility, places of transit, border areas, refugee camps, free trade zones and along the routes of major infrastructure.[13] This type of research-based artistic practice is especially useful for this discussion as it focuses on the biopolitics of these spaces understood as territorial assemblages and on how their production is performed socially through the politics of labour, gender and mobility. In Biemann's work the question of territory is explicitly linked to the corporeal, a quality that is less apparent in the empirical mappings of Israel/Palestine discussed earlier. The location of most of the sites outside of or on the edge of Europe is also important, as is Biemann's description of her work as a 'postcolonial representative practice' foregrounding the role of colonial attitudes and practices in constructing the relations her work exposes.[14]

In the video essay, *Sahara Chronicle*, Biemann follows the journey that thousands of Africans take through sub-Saharan Africa to the Maghreb in the hope of a passage to Europe. Biemann has commented that her work is an attempt to show the other side of this journey than the usual story seen in Europe of failed passage and capsized boats. In contrast, the beginning of the journey is full of hope and a sense of excitement. Her video traces the network of people and places that allow this passage to occur, and Biemann describes her work as a recasting of Castells's concept of the 'network society' from the capitalistic world of global finance to the tribal structures of the nomadic Tuareg of the Sahara.[15] It is also a reaction against the isolated event-based take of the popular media to an understanding of the condition of migration.

The video reveals the different ways of conceptualising territory; from the boundedness it is afforded in the West, to the right to pan-African mobility that the continent's inhabitants enjoyed until recently. Biemann makes the point that the Schengen Agreement that made possible a Europe without borders was also what curtailed free movement in Africa by outsourcing European border security to the Maghreb.[16] The construction of territory in Africa is therefore intimately connected to European power, but this power is also subverted and deterritorialised to some extent by the mobility of the Tuareg. They have historically been the natural passage providers between the southern and northern parts of Africa, and the artificial split of their territory across four different countries by the former colonial powers has left them in a state of limbo. As Biemann points out, they are by condition transnational and this makes their position ideal for facilitating the transit across the Sahara. In the clandestine movement of people criss-crossing the vast desert political territories are made and remade, and the unsympathetic borders drawn by the receding European powers are rendered at least momentarily ineffectual. Biemann relates the deals that are struck for this passage, whether it is the money handed over to the Tuareg by the would-be migrants, or the diesel bought by local authorities in exchange for returning the unsuccessful migrants back across the desert. There is a parallel economic network shadowing the movement of bodies across distances, and together these different networks constitute what could be characterised as a shifting migrant territory.

Biemann's particular take on territories as intimately related to social constructions of gender and to bodily practices provides an important point of departure for thinking diasporic territories. The localised power relations on which diasporic territories are constructed are played out in everyday relations of regional politics and gender, for example in the male *kahve* space that also excludes according to political affiliation.[17] Other ways of imagining territory than the dominant Western account of it, such as those of the Tuareg whose conception of territory is related to acts of transit and passage, are also useful for thinking diasporic territories as related to movement and the becomings of the diasporic subject.

## Conceptualising Bio-Political Territories

How can these two very different ways of conceptualising political territories – archipelago and trajectory – become useful in an understanding of a rather nondescript London street? Whilst it is easy to see the formidable workings of political power in places like Palestine, it is harder to imagine its work in a placid street where everyone seems to be able to go quietly about their business. It is therefore a matter of trying to unravel the intricate network of people and places that lead to power and the formation of political territories. Biemann's approach is useful here as it emphasises the way in which state and extraterritorial powers can affect the lives of those caught in their wake. In my walks with Kurds and Turks along the same high street I became acutely aware of how different their experiences of it were, where one saw a building that housed a community organisation another saw a hotbed of 'terrorist activity'.[18] Both these people worked yards away from each other, had almost definitely passed by each other, each walking a different street. In this sense, the concept of the fragmentation of territories becomes useful in analysing geo–political relations being enacted on a London street.

This fragmentation of territories is often described in contemporary theory as a return to pre-Westphalian realities, a reference to the Peace of Westphalia that in 1648 through a series of peace treaties ended decades of war in central Europe. Crucially for this discussion, it is regarded as the birth of the modern (European) nation-state and the concept of 'sovereignty' that it rests upon.[19] So, whilst trying to conceptualise these fragmented territories and the return to 'pre-Westphalian' realities as this process has been described, I keep in mind Gayatri Spivak's comment on the formation of modern nation-states: 'Westphalia belongs to European history. In the 18th century it was thought that it opened a world for Europe, but we are now in the 21st century. It's just an incident in European history.'[20] The post-colonies in fact owe their nationhood not to Westphalia but the politics of decolonisation and the partitioning of territories. Therefore, I want to think fragmented territories not as something new but as the state of being for many of the people and situations that I write about (including myself). This altered perspective has concrete consequences when the discourse on territories is moved back to European city-space as I intend it to. In particular it has consequences for the way in which the shadows of these fragmented territories are cast upon Europe and the way that they are interpreted differently by those who could claim Westphalia within their historical perspective and those who could not. In fact, the way political territories affect the personal territories of those in the diaspora is through this always already fragmented point of view. The place from which the Kurds especially spoke was never a bounded, secure place, never a nation-state, and so I am aware that my attempts to conceptualise diasporic territory should account for this other perspective. In this attempt, the mapping of diasporic space as territories that I relate in the chapter, *Diasporic Diagrams*, uses the body itself as a tool to try to narrate the street. It is therefore a corporeal mapping of what could be called personal territories, a kind of space or sphere in which we all live and that is affected by our surroundings and our personal politics.

## 'SCAPES', 'SPHERES' AND *UMWELT*

Traditionally notions of territory are inextricably linked to the bounds of the nation-state, yet the very nature of diasporic relations contests those boundaries. To be able to participate in the democratic processes of the nation-state requires a mode of citizenship usually linked to birth right and ethnicity, where the public sphere is the space of communication for the citizens of a sovereign (Westphalian) state. The diasporic subject's transgression of territorial boundaries challenges Habermas's conception of the public sphere, which is predicated on the idea that communication within such a sphere contributes towards the democratic process.[21] As Nancy Fraser states 'it matters who participates and on what terms'.[22] The fact that this participation may *only* take place in the national language, with the help of the national media, and for the reproduction of the imagined community of the nation-state becomes profoundly problematic in a globalised world. Of the many critiques of public sphere theory, one strand describes the birth of 'multiple modernities' that are the product of the realities of globalisation such as mass migration and communication. It is the uneven spread of the spoils of modernity (from industrialisation to bureaucratisation and secularisation), their encounter with different cultural forms, the legacy of colonialism and the contemporary reality of imperialism that produces such 'multiple modernities'.[23] It is an account of the heterogeneous ways in which the global meets the local.

Arjun Appadurai's 'scapes' provides a conceptual framework for understanding such processes, from the role of different forms of media to politically and economically striated global spaces. He also uses the term 'diasporic public sphere' to describe the sorts of spaces that are proliferating in most major cities around the world, springing up around their diasporic populations and fulfilling particular cultural and social needs.[24] He gives examples of Turkish guest workers watching Turkish films in Germany, or Pakistani cab drivers in Chicago listening to sermons recorded in mosques in Pakistan and Iran. Through these examples Appadurai is writing of the particular types of spaces that are associated with diasporic populations. It is interesting that both these examples occur in enclosed spaces, whether it is the domestic space of the home or its extension within the private car. How can these types of spaces be re-conceptualised and represented in the space of a street beyond enclosed walls, where there is the opportunity for an active overlapping of appropriated space? What possibilities for interaction between diverse groups can this provide? Can we as diasporic subjects speak and be heard in the types of spaces described by Appadurai, which are often characterised as introverted? Or do we require a different conceptualisation of public spheres, one that is more inclusive and therefore, necessarily, more conflictual.

Peter Sloterdijk's 'spherology' provides one such opportunity for rethinking the notion of the public sphere.[25] Using Lacanian psychoanalysis as a starting point he traces a Heideggerian 'Being-in-the-world' that concentrates on the exact nature of the 'in' within that phrase; a concern that is traced at different scales in his trilogy, from the pre-natal to the global. The three scales also correspond to the three phases of globalisation, from the metaphysical to the terrestrial, and finally, to the contemporary epoch. The first volume of the trilogy, *Bubbles*, sets up Sloterdijk's thesis of human existence as a thoroughly spatial process that is described as the making of spheres from within. Spheres are spaces of inhabitation, which at their most basic are the result of two elements working in relation. These structures, therefore, begin with the dyad as opposed to the Leibnizian monad. Here Heidegger's 'being in' is reimagined as a 'being together'. Sloterdijk has called his spherology, 'a general theory of the structures that allow couplings'.[26] The exploration of these structures begins with the pre-natal (the womb) and ends with the atmospheric. It is a way of thinking inhabitation as negotiation, and crucially, for Sloterdijk 'being together' or 'being with' is also a being inside. *The Spheres Trilogy* is an exploration of the interior. Human history is here explored through asking what kinds of spheres or interiors have been built and inhabited. Sloterdijk's 'spheres' provide a framework for thinking contemporary reality in the time of the interior; for a conceptualisation of diasporic inhabitation that seeks to move out of enclosed spaces to the space of the street, it provides an interesting paradox. If all space is interior, how might the interior also provide possibilities for encounter?

In the second volume of the trilogy, *Globes*, Sloterdijk describes a spatial imaginary of the sphere or globe – a move from the micro to the macro. In his description of the image of the globe combined with its geometric representation, is an account of the process of globalisation that starts much earlier than the standard description of it as communication and connection. For Sloterdijk, the process of creating the multiple modernities described by Appadurai begins much earlier through the mathematisation of the globe, by for example the geographic system of latitude. As Sloterdijk states: 'Mathematical globalization proceeds terrestrial globalization by more than two thousand years.'[27] The importance of conceptualising globalisation as inextricably linked to representation and therefore to power is invaluable. If the imaginary of the globe as a singular entity that could be traversed and appropriated (conquered) started the process of globalisation (colonisation), how might a different imaginary allow for more equitable relations to distant others? What type of imaginary would allow a move beyond the Cartesian logic of three dimensions towards a more dynamic and relational understanding?

The final volume of the trilogy, *Foam*, is a description of the globalised space of contemporary society. The metaphor of foam describes a series of multi-chamber spaces that are separated by a thin layer or membrane, where each space exerts pressure on its surrounding spaces. Just like the foam produced by soap, the smaller bubbles conjoin to form larger bubbles that tend toward a stabilised space where the pressure from the outside and the inside is in equilibrium. The microspheres of the foam are worlds or places that are isolated and fragile. Each sphere can only ignore its neighbours to a certain extent, their immune nature also being dependent on the spheres around them. Whilst there are overlaps here with Manuel Castells's 'network society' and Deleuze and Guattari's 'rhizome', neither is as spatial and neither conceptualisation quite captures the limited perspective of each bubble.[28] A kind of treatise for a posthuman, non-modern world, *Foam* is an account of a world of spatial multiplicities. In Sloterdijk's posthuman stance, it is impossible to describe a human without describing what it takes to *live* as a human, what environment, atmosphere, or sphere is required – what support systems. Being-in-the-world here becomes an engagement with materiality and matter as the condition of our being human. Sloterdijk uses the metaphor of space stations to describe our relation to the world in which we live. Since the destruction of Mother Earth both physically and symbolically, the figure of the space station provides a way of thinking ecology in the sorts of relations that Donna Haraway's cyborg anticipated.[29] In the artificially generated atmosphere of the space station nothing is taken for granted, extreme care is required due to the fragility of the system. Sloterdijk speaks of the space station as 'a model for being in a world condemned to artificiality'.[30]

Thinking 'spheres' in this way as connected to our planetary relations rather than an abstract realm of communication proves useful for imagining 'diasporic spheres' (territories) as not only related to another national space, its cultures and politics, but enriches it with other concerns such as those related to ecology and the environment. We are enveloped in fragile skins that overlap environmental and bodily concerns, with a cultural 'double vision'.[31] Sloterdijk's *dyad*, the figuration of a coupling that is at the heart of his philosophy and replaces the absolute figure of the individual, is not a coupling made of two but several, and it is this important detail that allows diasporic thinking to extend beyond an 'us and them' or a 'here and there' dialectic. It offers a way of thinking across a multiplicity of relations and concerns. Alongside his insistence on the *'insurmountable spatiality'* of our existence, 'microspherology' provides a way of interrogating both the political and the biological dimensions of diasporic territories, whilst also interrogating these issues on both a globalised planetary scale as well as at the level of the body and personal relations.[32]

### *'Umwelt'* as Bio-Territory

Both Sloterdijk and Latour foreground the way in which the modern narrative has created an artificial divide between nature and culture, but for many in the global South and its diaspora this divide in not always so easily accepted or obvious. Here the role of science and technology also changes, and it becomes clear that for example the rural farming idylls of England so highly cherished by many, are also artificial landscapes engineered through hundreds of years of manipulating the earth. After our move from Pakistan and various trips around the UK, my father brought up in a farming family in rural Punjab on both sides of the border, would often point out to us the regimented nature of the English countryside, with a mixture of mischievousness and admiration (at how the British could not even leave nature alone to do what it wanted), being caught as we all were in the promises and false dreams of modernity's progress. I only found out later that others perceived what we took to be our slightly superior position in our closer connection to nature, as our complete lack of understanding of that very same 'nature'; apparently, 'the Asians don't understand the bucolic English countryside' – I guess we don't.[33]

Accepting the artificial divide between nature and culture also means that in conceptualising and representing diasporic territories relations other than those between humans need to be accounted for. I have already interrogated this in relation to 'quasi-objects' in the chapter, *Multiplying Borders*, and here I explore this non-anthropocentric line of thinking by discussing what the subjective worlds of trees, ticks and pigeons could contribute to a theorising of diasporic territories. They hint at the opportunity to conceive diasporic territories in relation to an ecological understanding of territory as the product of particular forms of expression. At the same time, such an engagement foregrounds the need to conceptualise diasporic territories through an appropriation of space and as a way of establishing a certain distinction from the environment. Finally, a non-anthropocentric engagement provides a radical instance of how we can encapsulate differences in the way space is perceived and mediated through our particular subjective understandings.

The first example of the *OneTrees* project by Natalie Jeremijenko foregrounds the relationships between the construction of territories and ecological concerns in relation to questions of representation.[34] Cloned trees were propagated in the laboratory and later planted at various sites across the Bay Area in California. These artificially grown, genetically identical trees became living tools for mapping. Their ongoing progress over the years not only indicates the environmental quality of their habitat but they also become social indicators; each tree was assigned a steward who would look after its welfare. Combined with a paper leaflet that gave the locations of the trees, information on wildlife in the area, flight paths of birds, toxicity and other data, the trees became part of a large-scale map that involves the local community in their environment, and as Jeremijenko comments the map itself becomes, 'an instrument that collects information as much as it disseminates it'.[35] These mappings could be seen as a way of representing the overlapping spatial envelopes of the trees, while also creating an affinity network around the trees and their welfare. Jeremijenko's trees are treated as quasi-subjects, they mediate just as the Bengali girls did in the previous chapter, and her practice stands out for taking plants and animals seriously as actors in our world. She does not anthropomorphise them but instead tries to understand reality according to them; the trees are in fact mapping their own bio-territory. How could I map the bio-territory of diasporic quasi-subjects whose spatio-temporalities also have a global scale? Whilst it is easy to conceptualise trees as being affected by various global conditions, such as air pollution, acid rain etc., it is harder to think of ourselves and our actions in a similarly interdependent way, proven by the wilful non-understanding of how our actions affect the lives of those living in other parts of the globe.

The concept of territory based on the subjective worlds of non-humans who have their own spheres is also influenced by the work of the theoretical biologist, Jakob von Uexküll.[36] He proposed his biological theory of sphere, *umwelt*, in the 1920s as a description of the world of living organisms, whose experience was seen not only as being very different from that of humans (as subjective beings) but as constituting a different world. His way of conceptualising different worlds or realities in fact foresaw many of the advances in quantum physics as well as in contemporary cultural and social theory. Uexküll used the term *umwelt* to describe a world beyond the merely scientific description of it as *welt*. His most famous example comes from his description of the *umwelt* of the tick – this simplest of insects whose world in comparison to that of the human seems so poor. Described as blind and deaf, the female tick's life is dominated by the reproductive urge and she has only three sense signals: a particular smell, a sensitivity to a precise temperature and a sense of touch. She requires warm blood for her eggs to mature and so needs to find a warm-blooded mammal to act as a host. Since she cannot see her sense of smell guides her: as a mammal approaches giving off the scent of butyric acid, which our sweat contains, the tick senses her chance and drops from her elevated position. If she has indeed managed to land on a mammal, she will know this through her sensitivity to the exact 37 degrees temperature of mammalian blood, and her sense of touch will guide her to a suitable place in which to burrow into the skin. Uexküll prefaces this account of the tick's world with a description of the same place as humans would perceive it, an idyllic meadow full of colour and smell and sound. In comparison the tick's world seems so meagre. But as Giorgio Agamben has pointed out, in ways that we humans could not come close to understanding, the tick's world is full of richness: 'Yet the tick is immediately united to these three elements in an intense and passionate relationship the likes of it we might never find in the relations that bind man to his apparently much richer world. The tick is this relationship; she lives only in it and for it.'[37]

What would a map of this world of the tick look like? Would it have three colours only, one for each of its three senses? Is it possible to map the subjective world of an animal? Or perhaps a better question would be: why map the subjective worlds of animals? The posthuman perspective of theorists such as Haraway, Braidotti and others is not only a radicalisation of the critique of the universal subject of western philosophy, and so entirely relevant to describing diasporic territories, but it is also a non-anthropocentric stance that is essential for the new challenges we face today related to the environment and the planetary scale on which we are now obliged to think.[38] To be able to create affinity networks that include not only animals, but rivers, ecosystems and people from varied cultures is crucial. And what the tick in particular could teach us is that an intensity of relations may sometimes be more important than an abundance of them. In our digitally connected world of constant media streams, intense corporeal relations also have a crucial place.

A pair of architects from New York, Terraswarm, have attempted to map the subjective world of an animal, through making a map of the visual world of a pigeon.[39] The harnessing of pigeon flight for the use of humans has a long history, but Terraswarm were attempting something different. They tried to apprehend the city from the pigeon's point of view as part of a flock in flight, technologically an ambitious undertaking that they have not yet perfected. A tiny camera was strapped to the pigeon's chest and they were set free. The photographs taken by the camera were then used to map their movements. This was carried out in the context of the Brooklyn Pigeon Wars, where homing pigeons are trained to fly high above the rooftops in which the aim of the pigeon coop owners is to increase their flock. The encounter of the birds in the sky merges the flocks in an intricate performance that results in 'disoriented' birds joining opposing flocks. The pigeon owners have an understanding of flock behaviour, planning strategies to win birds from different flocks. Terraswarm were seeking to understand flock behaviour through computer models developed by the games designer Craig Reynolds, but it seems that these models do not draw on the observational knowledge of the pigeon coop owners gained through years of experience.[40] The desire to use computational methods fails to valorise other ways of knowing, and in some ways Terraswarm do not manage to explore the pigeon's relationship to their context. This context did of course consist of all the environmental mappings that Terraswarm made, such as wind direction, local flight paths, the Earth's magnetic field, but it also included the humans that must have formed some sort of relationship with the birds. And what of the relations the birds may make in the sky? Does flock behaviour only ever consist of the kinetics of 'separation, alignment and cohesion'?[41] What of the reasons for these movements? Homing pigeons are also highly territorial birds, ready to defend their patch, but this urge to territory is not constant, it waxes and wanes according to the pigeon's life cycle, affected by age, seasons etc. All these factors form part of the subjective world, the *umwelt* of the pigeons and this endeavour to see the world from another point of view, whether of the pigeons, tick or trees, is a way of imagining how to live with the radically other, of establishing a common territory with them.

## DIASPORIC TERRITORIES

For Deleuze and Guattari territory is conceptualised as an act consisting of deterritorialisations and reterritorialisations and the agents of these processes could be humans or animals, but also the earth, planets, minerals etc. They use various examples to describe this process, including how the sun territorialises the earth through its gravitational pull, or how capital deterritorialises products into commodities.[42] They write: 'To begin with, the territory itself is inseparable from vectors of deterritorialisation working it from within: either because the territoriality is supple and 'marginal', in other words itinerant, or because the territorial assemblage itself opens onto and is carried off by other types of assemblages.'[43] This description of what they also call 'lines of flight' means that even the most entrenched of regimes (or territories) has the potential of resistance inscribed within it; from the perspective of diasporas it is the adapting and adopting of various cultural and bodily practices, the rhythms of these social and political processes that are capable of deterritorialising dominant practices and of their consequent reterritorialisation.

Diasporic territories can thus be thought of as a series of overlapping spatial envelopes made of many subjective spheres that continually deterritorialise and reterritorialise, producing a multiplicity of spheres. These spheres could be related to the stratifications of class, gender, ethnicity, but also ecology and the environment; sometimes fragile envelopes, other times entrenched positions, they can be challenged in the becomings of the diasporic subject that deterritorialises essentialised notions of the self and the dominant ways of conceiving nature and culture. In this sense diasporic territories are directly related to questions of how life takes place, urgent questions related to our survival on the planet.

The starting point of this chapter was a desire to understand the ways in which politics and the concerns of elsewhere are an essential part of the diasporic experience. The conceptualisation of diasporic territories starts with an understanding of migrant spatiality as inherently territorial, bringing with it the conflicts, nostalgias and attachments of another place. At the same time,

I wanted to counter the tendency of writing about diasporas and migrants through a single lens, whether that is of religion, politics or through an economic argument. Knowing that this was not the sum of my own experience, I was interested in conceptualising diasporic spatiality as a multiplicity of overlapping subjective spheres of sometimes highly conflicting positionings, related to politics, culture, religion, gender … for this, the concept of territories proved useful. Whilst territories are imagined differently across cultures and species, one aspect remains consistent, they are made up of appropriated space; sometimes bounded, static and militarised, at other times, temporal, inderterminate and contested. The nature of territories as appropriated also means that they are necessarily about bodily exchange, about the movement of bodies, deterritorialising and reterritorialising – bodies have always been at stake where territories are concerned.

In order to conceptualise territories as both political *and* biological, Sloterdijk's concept of 'spheres' allowed for an immediately spatial conception, imagining them as spatial envelopes that surround us all, overlapping and interacting with each other. This way of thinking also foregrounds the question of our relationship to the environment and to other species and I have explored this aspect through the experiential worlds of trees, ticks and pigeons. This non-anthropocentric perspective is not only a radicalisation of the non-unitary subject that has been so useful for post-colonial theory, but it also fits well with non-Western imaginaries that do not always subscribe to the modern division between nature and culture. The subjective world of the tick especially, shows the importance of an intensity of relations over their quantity. In human terms this intensity is seen to be the product of sharing time and sharing space, the establishing of common territories across cultures and sometimes species.

Political territories of migration and conflict add a further perspective that shows how the formation of territories is always related to questions of power and appropriation, and foregrounds the very different ways of conceptualising territories across cultures. The conceptualisation of 'diasporic territories' thus takes from this non-anthropocentric line of thinking the importance of the subjective nature of reality and counter to traditional architectural knowledge practices, moves away from looking for and always describing causal relations. Instead more open representations are sought that can accommodate the intricate interdependencies of the world in which we live, which is not really separated as nature and culture, subject and object. These insights are applied in the chapter *Diasporic Diagrams*, where I use walking as an embodied practice for mapping the spheres and spatial envelopes that diasporic territories consist of, and look for new types of representational practices for these multiple and fluctuating realities. Different types of territories are encountered and played out within the space of the high street, from social, political, religious and gendered territories to those of everyday life. Woven within this fabric is the possibility of deterritorialisation, the 'lines of flight' that are possible precisely because of the interactions between this multiplicity of spheres.

## NOTES

1.  For '*umwelt*' see, von Uexküll, *Theoretical Biology*; for 'the refrain' see, Deleuze and Guattari, '1837: Of the Refrain'.

2.  Delaney, *Territory: A Short Introduction*, 9.

3.  *territory (n.)* late 14c., 'land under the jurisdiction of a town, state, etc.', probably from Latin *territorium* 'land around a town, domain, district', from *terra* 'earth, land' (see *terrain*) + *-orium*, suffix denoting place … An alternative theory, somewhat supported by the vowels of the original Latin word, suggests derivation from *terrere* 'to frighten' (see *terrible*); thus *territorium* would mean 'a place from which people are warned off'. Harper, 'Online Etymology Dictionary'.

4.  Sack, *Human Territoriality: Its Theory and History*, 216.

5.  For more on the concept of 'counter-spatialisation' see, Altay and Altay, 'Counter – Spatialization [of Power] [in Istanbul]'.

6.  Weizman and Ramoneda, 'Archipelago of Exception: Sovereignties of Extraterritoriality'.

7.  For more details on the maps see, Segal, Weizman, and Tartakover, *A Civilian Occupation: The Politics of Israeli Architecture*.

8.  Weizman, 'The Politics of Verticality: The West Bank as an Architectural Construction', 65.

9.  Weizman, 'Introduction to The Politics of Verticality'.

10. Gordon, *Power/Knowledge: Selected Interviews and Other Writings 1972–1977 by Michel Foucault*.

11. Foucault, *The Birth of the Clinic: An Archaeology of Medical Perception*.

12. For a discussion on affinity networks in the diaspora see the chapter, *Trans-Local Practices*.

13. For an overview see, Biemann and Lundström, *Mission Reports, Artistic Practice in the Field: Ursula Biemann Video Works 1998–2008*.

14. From a discussion at, Biemann, 'The Mahgreb Connection'.

15. Castells, *The Rise of the Network Society*.

16. 'The term Schengen Agreement is used for two international treaties concluded among certain European states in 1985 and 1990 dealing with cross-border legal arrangements and the abolition of systematic border controls among the participating countries'. 'Schengen Agreement'.

17. For more on the *kahve*, see the chapter, *Trans-Local Practices*.

18. The Halkevi Kurdish and Turkish Community Centre was originally established in 1984 in Stoke Newington in the London Borough of Hackney. It became known as a place of political and cultural solidarity between Kurds and left-wing Turks. It was founded by Yashar Ismailoglu, an interview with whom is related in the chapter, *Diasporic Diagrams*. Some Turkish nationalists view the centre as a place from which the PKK (Kurdistan Worker's Party) is organised and supported through the Kurdish diaspora.

19. For a detailed discussion of the Peace of Westphalia see, 'Peace of Westphalia'. The concept of 'sovereignty' is described in the *Stanford Encyclopaedia of Philosophy* as: 'Sovereignty, though its meanings have varied across history, also has a core meaning, supreme authority within a territory. It is a modern notion of political authority.

Historical variants can be understood along three dimensions – the holder of sovereignty, the absoluteness of sovereignty, and the internal and external dimensions of sovereignty. The state is the political institution in which sovereignty is embodied. An assemblage of states forms a sovereign states system.' Philpott, 'Sovereignty'.

20.    Spivak, 'More Thoughts on Cultural Translation'.

21.    Habermas, *The Structural Transformation of the Public Sphere: An Inquiry into a Category of Bourgeois Society*.

22.    Fraser, 'Transnationalising the Public Sphere'.

23.    These topics have been discussed at length in, Gaonkar, Lee, and Editors, 'Special Issue: New Imaginaries'.

24.    Appadurai, 'Disjuncture and Difference in the Global Cultural Economy'.

25.    Sloterdijk and Hoban, *Bubbles*; Sloterdijk, *Sphären: Globen*; Sloterdijk, *Sphären: Schäume*.

26.    Sloterdijk and Hoban, *Bubbles*.

27.    Sloterdijk, 'Geometry in the Colossal', 30.

28.    Castells, *The Rise of the Network Society*; Deleuze and Guattari, *A Thousand Plateaus: Capitalism and Schizophrenia*.

29.    Haraway, *Simians, Cyborgs and Women: The Reinvention of Nature*.

30.    Sloterdijk, 'Cosmograms', 236.

31.    The phrase 'double vision' is borrowed from, Bhabha, *The Location of Culture*.

32.    Sloterdijk, 'Cosmograms', 229.

33.    A comment from a conversation about an art project with primary school children in Derby, a city in the Midlands with a large Asian population. The artist when speaking of her initial thoughts on the project was articulating her desire to engage the children with the surrounding countryside. I have heard the sentiment repeated several times in other situations, where the lack of Asian people living in the countryside is given as proof of the validity of this view. Whilst the assumption in itself is problematic, it shows an ignorance of the myriad social and economic reasons that would be more useful as explanation.

34.    Jeremijenko, 'OneTrees: An Information Environment'.

35.    Jeremijenko quoted in, Twemlow, 'Bark to Bytes', 256.

36.    von Uexküll, *Theoretical Biology*.

37.    Agamben, *The Open: Man and Animal*, 46–7.

38.    Haraway, *The Companion Species Manifesto: Dogs, People and Significant Others*; Braidotti, *The Posthuman*.

39.    Hall, Peter. 'Flight Paths'.

40.    Reynolds, 'Flocks, Herds, and Schools: A Distributed Behavioral Model'.

41.    These are the three behavioural properties given to each 'boid' or flock member, Ibid.

42.    Deleuze and Guattari, '1837: Of the Refrain'.

43.    Deleuze and Guattari, *A Thousand Plateaus: Capitalism and Schizophrenia*, 560.

## REFERENCES

Agamben, Giorgio. *The Open: Man and Animal*. Stanford, CA: Stanford University, 2004.

Altay, Can, and Deniz Altay. 'Counter – Spatialization [of Power] [in Istanbul]'. In *Urban Makers: Parallel Narratives of Grassroots Practices and Tensions*, edited by Emanuele Guidi, 76–101. Berlin: b_books, 2008.

Appadurai, Arjun. 'Disjuncture and Difference in the Global Cultural Economy'. *Public Culture* 2, no. 2 (1990): 1–23.

Bhabha, Homi. *The Location of Culture*. London: Routledge, 1994.

Biemann, Ursula. 'The Mahgreb Connection'. Presented at Zones of Conflict: Rethinking Contemporary Art During Global Crisis, Tate Modern, London, 29 November 2008. http://www.ucl.ac.uk/zones_of_conflict/bare_life.

Biemann, Ursula, and Jan-Erik Lundström, eds. *Mission Reports, Artistic Practice in the Field: Ursula Biemann Video Works 1998–2008*. Bristol: Arnolfini, 2008.

Braidotti, Rosi. *The Posthuman*. Oxford: Polity Press, 2011.

Castells, Manuel. *The Rise of the Network Society*. Vol. 1. Cambridge, MA: Blackwell, 1996.

Delaney, David. *Territory: A Short Introduction*. Oxford: Blackwell Publishing, 2005.

Deleuze, Gilles, and Félix Guattari. '1837: Of the Refrain'. In *A Thousand Plateaus: Capitalism and Schizophrenia*, 342–86. New York: Continuum, 2004.

_____. *A Thousand Plateaus: Capitalism and Schizophrenia*. New York: Continuum, 2004.

Foucault, Michel. *The Birth of the Clinic: An Archaeology of Medical Perception*. London: Tavistock Publications, 1973.

Fraser, Nancy. 'Transnationalising the Public Sphere'. *Republicart*, 2005. http://www.republicart.net/disc/publicum/fraser01_en.htm.

Gaonkar, Dilip Parameshwar, Benjamin Lee, and Guest Editors. 'Special Issue: New Imaginaries'. *Public Culture* 14, no. 1 (Winter 2002).

Gordon, Colin, ed. *Power/Knowledge: Selected Interviews and Other Writings 1972–1977 by Michel Foucault*. London: Harvester Wheatsheaf, 1980.

Habermas, Jürgen. *The Structural Transformation of the Public Sphere: An Inquiry into a Category of Bourgeois Society*. Cambridge: Polity, 1989.

Hall, Peter. 'Flight Paths'. In *Else/Where: Mapping New Cartographies of Networks and Territories*, edited by Janet Abrams and Peter Hall, 280–89. Minneapolis: University of Minnesota Design Institute, 2006.

Haraway, Donna. *Simians, Cyborgs and Women: The Reinvention of Nature*. New York: Routledge, 1991.

Haraway, Donna. *The Companion Species Manifesto: Dogs, People and Significant Others*. Chicago: Prickly Paradigm Press, 2003.

Harper, Douglas. 'Online Etymology Dictionary', 2001. http://www.etymonline.com/.

Jeremijenko, Natalie. 'OneTrees: An Information Environment', n.d. http://www.nyu.edu/projects/xdesign/onetrees/.

'Peace of Westphalia'. *Wikipedia, the Free Encyclopedia*, 2015. http://en.wikipedia.org/w/index.php?title=Peace_of_Westphalia&oldid=641520880.

Philpott, Dan. 'Sovereignty'. Edited by Edward N. Zalta. *The Stanford Encyclopedia of Philosophy*, 2014. http://plato.stanford.edu/archives/sum2014/entries/sovereignty/.

Reynolds, Craig. 'Flocks, Herds, and Schools: A Distributed Behavioral Model'. *Computer Graphics* 21, no. 4 SIGGRAPH '87 Conference Proceedings (1987): 25–34.

Sack, Robert David. *Human Territoriality: Its Theory and History*. Cambridge: Cambridge University Press, 1986.

'Schengen Agreement'. *Wikipedia, the Free Encyclopedia*, 2015. http://en.wikipedia.org/wiki/Schengen_Agreement.

Segal, Rafi, Eyal Weizman, and David Tartakover, eds. *A Civilian Occupation: The Politics of Israeli Architecture*. Tel Aviv/London: Babel/Verso, 2003.

Sloterdijk, Peter. 'Cosmograms'. In *Foreword to a Theory of Spheres*, Cosmograms New York: 233–40. Lukas and Sternberg, 2005.

_____. 'Geometry in the Colossal: The Project of Metaphysical Globalization'. *Environment and Planning D: Society and Space* 27, no. 1 (2009): 29–40. doi:10.1068/dst2.

_____. *Sphären: Globen*. Vol. II. Frankfurt am Main: Suhrkamp, 1999.

_____. *Sphären: Schäume*. Vol. III. Frankfurt am Main: Suhrkamp, 2004.

Sloterdijk, Peter, and Wieland Hoban. *Bubbles: Spheres I – Microspherology*. Vol. 1. 3 vols. Spheres. Semiotext(e). MIT Press, 2011.

Spivak, Gayatri Chakravorty. 'More Thoughts on Cultural Translation'. *Transversal. European Institute for Progresive Cultural Poliicies*. Accessed January 9, 2015. http://eipcp.net/transversal/0608/spivak/en.

Twemlow, Alice. 'Bark to Bytes'. In *Else/Where: Mapping New Cartographies of Networks and Territories*, edited by Janet Abrams and Peter Hall, 280-89. Minneapolis: University of Minnesota Design Institute, 2006.

von Uexküll, Jakob. *Theoretical Biology*. London: Kegan Paul, 1926.

Weizman, Eyal. 'Introduction to The Politics of Verticality'. *Open Democracy*, April 2002. http://www.opendemocracy.net/conflict-politicsverticality/article_801.jsp.

_____. 'The Politics of Verticality: The West Bank as an Architectural Construction'. In *Territories: Islands, Camps and Other States of Utopia*, edited by Klaus Biesenbach and Anselm Franke. Berlin: KW Berlin, Buchhandlung, 2003.

Weizman, Eyal, and Josep Ramoneda. 'Archipelago of Exception: Sovereignties of Extraterritoriality'. Centre for Contemporary Culture, Barcelona, Spain, November 10, 2005.

# PART II
# Mapping Otherwise

# A Diasporic Spatial Imaginary

Much has been written in geography about the world-making qualities of maps and on how they have been instrumental to the colonial endeavour. The power of representation and its entwined relationship to the claiming of territories and the creation of uneven global geographies is encapsulated, for example, in the ways in which we choose to project a spherical planet onto a two-dimensional plane. This mathematisation of the globe has been described by Peter Sloterdijk as the real beginning of the story of globalisation, which for him started with a spatial imaginary of the globe. 'Mathematical globalization' he states, 'proceeds terrestrial globalization by more than two thousand years'.[1] Whilst this mathematical globalisation relied on a Cartesian geometry, in this chapter I explore the consequences for architecture of an imaginary of the globe based on a topological understanding of space – one of the fundamental qualities of diasporic spatio-temporalities. As described in the previous section, linking diasporic agency to spatial inhabitations somehow exceeds the constraints of Cartesian space. What consequences will such a way of thinking about space, as topological rather than topographic, have on its representation? If the urge to map is linked to representation, is it possible to make a non–representational map?

---

[1] Peter Sloterdijk, 'Geometry in the Colossal: The Project of Metaphysical Globalization', *Environment and Planning D: Society and Space* 27, no. 1 (2009): 30, doi:10.1068/dst2.

# 6

## Maps and Agency

In the previous section I described how a topological understanding might transform three fundamental qualities that inform the way in which we think about the production of diasporic agencies. Firstly, the question of scale is exploded so that it transcends notions of distance to make connections based on affinities. This was explored through analysing for example the space of the *kahve* as being produced through specific forms of diasporic inhabitations that create trans-localities. Secondly, I explored how notions of value are rendered dynamic through an understanding of what Helen Verran refers to as the inventive qualities of numbers.[1] This way of thinking proved useful for understanding the city as a domain that exceeds the Marxist analysis of space through its lacuna of the religious and the ways in which it intertwines with the political. Here a perspectival engagement with value is required where the point-of-view is performed and contingent. Finally, if scale and value are no longer static then the idea of measurement itself is transformed. Rather than referring to an external or fixed metric, measure becomes a relational activity that is inscribed in the ways in which environments and territories are produced through the spatial inhabitations of diasporic subjects, rather than as a pregiven external backdrop. In this chapter I move on to discuss what modes of representation would be suitable for the multiple temporalities and power geometries embedded within the types of spaces discussed in the previous section.

Perhaps what this amounts to is a desire for a more critical engagement with the empirical in architecture and urbanism, where we often either ignore it in favour of more subjective approaches, or we see the empirical as a straightforward indexation of the quantitative. As Albena Yaneva points out, this divide between the quantitative and the qualitative leads to a comparative urge that is rooted in an unacknowledged universalism: 'We often assume that there is a unique, non-situated urban nature, which makes all cities have common features – infrastructure, markets, transport networks, city authorities. Whereas culture is taken as variable, relative, situated.'[2] Instead she advocates a way of approaching cities through measuring and tracing together, using narrative as a technique to mediate between the specific and the general. Maps and map-making could hold a privileged position here in the unexpected ways in which they are able to bring together disparate knowledge and claims, juxtaposing ways of seeing the world. But this is a practice of mapping that is far removed from the abstracted nature of standard cartographic modes, and also from the ubiquity of contemporary mapping tools such as Google maps.

## WHAT IS A MAP?

Perhaps a key feature of all maps is their ability to visually depict different realities by distilling and privileging some information over others. In this sense, maps are always political and should be read as such, including paying close attention to the conditions of their production. They are also always partial and perspectival, regardless of their claims to authority. The relation of maps to representation is therefore fundamental; they frame, codify and distil. That this quality of maps is often hidden or left unacknowledged might be one important issue for a diasporic mapping practice. How to draw a situated map that is still readable and useable, but does not resort to the bird's eye view of conventional maps? Or does the point of view matter, as long as the content is oppositional? In the collection, *An Atlas of Radical Cartography*,[3] the editors state that in choosing the maps to include in the book, they realised that for them it was the content that held a radical potential, and not necessarily the way that the maps were drawn. In a similar argument, the recent explosion of mapping has been described as holding a democratic potential by allowing the ordinary citizen to produce her own maps. The fact that mapping has become almost commonplace through the tools of mapping being made available is seen as more important than *how* the maps are made. In these claims Google Maps has been described as a game-changer, allowing anyone with an Internet connection and suitable hardware to make their own maps by adding content on top of the base layer that Google provides. Yet most of these maps, usually accessed through smart phones (and so only available to a fraction of the world's population), tend to be what Dodge and Perkins call 'self-centred "me maps"'.[4] There is also the uneasy reality that all of this apparently emancipatory cartographic potential is controlled by a single private company.

Whilst there is much that is new in this proliferation of digital mapping, there has been very little critical reflection on how power and representation come together in these new types of maps. Historically, maps have been produced by those in power to shape a world according to their own views and these maps have a long history of oppression. Whether enacted through the deployment of geometry, or the colonial mapping practices that literally carve up the land, or the production of facts on the ground such as those in the Occupied Palestinian Territories, or the city planning maps that refuse to acknowledge the existence of whole communities, it is clear that both historically and in the present maps have been used to control and to wield power. Specifically in relation to the new digital realm of mapping a similar landscape is emerging. For example, the virtual geographies produced through Google's collaboration with UNITAR's UNOSAT programme are making it a central player in humanitarian relief and co-ordination following a disaster.[5] But as Dodge and Perkins point out, much of the critical work required in understanding the relations between such types of mapping practices and decisions related to *'access, resource allocation, and even meanings attached to places'* has yet to be carried out.[6]

Embedded in the question of how to map is a necessary discussion on the types of representations that are being used. In the History of map-making the dominant maps have been those produced in the West according to a logic that privileges topographic representations above all others. Whilst the grid as a device for measuring and representing space was being used by the Chinese since the first century AD, it is the European conventions of map-making, such as the adoption of longitude and latitude, that have had such a profound effect on what we consider to be a map. Since the topographic conventions of western map-making, including the adoption of longitude and latitude, are fundamental to what we now consider to be a map, without such conventions we may be in danger of losing a sense of what a map is and what it is for. Yet, the dominant tropes of such map-making leave out much: scale, colour coding, longitude and latitude, do not account for temporality, touch, memory, relations, stories and narratives – in fact it is experience that is altogether removed. It may be that in a practice of diasporic mapping the abstractions of maps would be used to mediate between the realm of representation and lived realities. This could, for example, mean moving away from a dominant mode of mapping where experience is elided through a mode of representation that privileges precision over the messy reality of life. Maps could instead describe social relations or connections that transcend spatial proximity. At the same time, maps could be used to mediate between different types of knowledge and constructions of space, from the professionalised world of architects or cartographers to more accessible forms of representation.

## MAPPING AS A WAY OF WORKING WITH DIASPORIC AGENCIES

James Corner describes the agency of mapping as a tool for design where the focus is on mapping as an activity rather than the map as artefact.[7] In this sense, mapping is considered propositional and could be a way of imagining different futures. As Corner writes, 'mappings do not represent geographies or ideas; rather they effect their actualization'.[8] Corner is here writing on how mapping can be used within the disciplines of planning and architecture, of its role in design as an act that works with projections of the future. Citing David Harvey, he writes about 'a utopia of process rather than form' that mapping as practice can contribute towards.[9] Corner's account of mapping's agency is illustrated through maps that are grappling with ways of showing time and space in its dynamism through practices of drifting, layering and through the use of game boards on which to map out potential futures as scenarios. Yet, what is always missing in these accounts of mapping is the body. Perhaps this has something to do with Corner's original definition of mapping as abstraction, which according to him is the fundamental quality of all maps.

Whilst it is true that one way in which mapping operates is through abstraction, in representing diasporic agencies it would be an abstraction that is always returning to the real – it would be a movement back and forth. The feminist philosopher Elizabeth Grosz describes the real as: 'The uncontained, the outside of matter, of things, of that which is not pragmatically available for use, is the object of different actions than that of intelligence and the technological.'[10] The real therefore is the world before we apprehend it – it is outside representation. What Grosz refers to as 'the thing' is the necessary process of making sense of this multiplicity, it is 'the real we both find and make.'[11] If maps are both abstractions that strive towards the real and things that point to a spatial and temporal specificity of the real, then they should also operate in ways that are able to access both these registers. On the one hand, maps should deal with a knowledge that is related to representations, measurements and symbols, and this is something that maps are very good at. But on the other they should also deal with a knowledge that is more intuitive and is accessed through bodily gestures and idioms. In describing mapping as a practice that performs this movement back and forth, another conception of time also emerges, one that is related to matter – both matter in the sense of the map itself as object but also matter in relation to the bodies of those involved in the process of mapping. As Karen Barad states, 'one of matter's most intimate doings' is 'its materialising of time. Matter doesn't move in time, matter doesn't evolve in time. Matter materialises and enfolds different temporalities.'[12] This enfolding of different temporalities and spatialities could be one way of describing a diasporic practice of mapping and its relation to imagining other futures.

If maps are a way of working across the real, it is also useful to think what place such a practice of mapping could hold within a wider process. As described earlier in the chapter, *Diasporic Inhabitations*, the notion of spatial agency is concerned with an underlying idea that the potential of agency, that is the power and freedom to act for oneself, is somehow inherently spatial – that it has a spatial dimension.[13] We were interested in exploring how agency might emerge through spatial practices, and it is interesting to note that many of those featured in the publication were using forms of mapping as part of their work. Our conception of agency was based on the classical duality, the ability to act independently on the one hand and the constraints of social structures on the other. Following Anthony Giddens we wrote that spatial agency could occur through acting on behalf of others or acting with others. Corner's undefined notion of the agency of maps is aligned to this definition, where the agency of maps is embedded in their use by architects, planners, the users of spaces etc.

What is missing from this account of spatial agency and also from Corner's account of the agency of maps, is the question of materiality, the body and of imagining agency as not only the privilege of humans; or at the very least not *only* emanating from human social structures and their relation to individuals. The alternative definition of agency, introduced in the chapter *Diasporic Inhabitations*, leads to a different notion of the use of maps in imagining possible futures linked to the discussion of the real above. In claiming such a notion of agency embedded within free acts, a diasporic practice of mapping could be imagined that facilitates a move from abstracted possibilities caught within the oppositional logic of struggles, towards the production of materially real potentialities that are more open and creative. For Grosz this is more a capacity of the body than that of the mind, 'linked to the body's capacity for movement, and thus its multiple possibilities of action'.[14] Scott Lash also foregrounds the body in his discussion of agency thought through non-European conceptualisations, specifically in relation to Chinese philosophy. He suggests that an emphasis on the individual in western thinking coupled with a stance that is goal-directed remains problematic. Instead, Lash suggests the notion of activity: 'Activity is much less goal-directed, it is much more situational. It's like situationism in a way: you put yourself down anywhere, and see where it takes you.'[15] For this concept of agency to fit within the practice of mapping, conversations and everyday encounters would be just as legitimate a form of representation as making diagrams or archiving knowledge. According to Lash, simply doing could sometimes be enough, an indirect mode that is at once spatial, temporal and relational, contrasting with what he describes as the dominant western mode of subject-verb-object that is normally used to describe the agency of the intentional subject. Thus the notion of activity could allow mapping to perform the crucial movement back and forth between an abstracted realm that necessarily deals with representations towards a knowing *through* the body.

## MAPPING OTHERWISE

The term 'mapping otherwise' tries to capture some of these aspects of what a map could do. Choosing to use the word 'mapping' over 'cartography' is important in making a break from the professionalised world of cartographers and to valorise instead the amateur knowledge of the non-professional specialist. This reveals a different ethics of mapping, one that neither takes the position of the powerful and the elite nor an explicitly oppositional stance, preferring instead a mode where the politics of representation allows others to be included in the mapping process, as well as acknowledging the map-maker's own positioning. Some of what I am referring to here is covered by other terms such as 'counter cartography' or 'radical cartography', but I prefer to use the term 'mapping otherwise' as it also encapsulates my interest in a different tradition of mapping than the dominant western mode. It is a way of mapping that might not always be oppositional but is still able to contain political possibilities.[16] This way of thinking and doing also sits well within a diasporic sensibility, which rather than attempting open confrontations, ones that have had a long history of failure, looks for subtle subversions based in practices of mimicry and marginality. The use of the word 'otherwise' also recalls the feminist groundings of my work, the side-step that feminists often take to extricate themselves from hegemonic norms.[17] Above all in the practice of mapping otherwise experience is reintroduced as a way of exploring different futures by giving voice to other narratives and uses of space. In thinking about maps not just as drawings or objects, but also as ways of producing and disseminating knowledge about the world they take on a certain agency.

In this new practice the way maps act in the world also changes, whilst traditional maps made certain truth claims the maps that I am referring to operate differently. By not claiming complete authority, these mapping practices implicate themselves in the world around them. Mapping thus becomes an embedded activity that encompasses questions of the relationships between power and knowledge and access to knowledge. It also asks who makes the maps and with whom, as well as how and where they are made available. These are all important questions in understanding the agential potential of maps and here I describe three ways in which maps can take on agency – through making propositions, acting as mediators and creating possibilities for change.

### Maps as Propositions

Traditionally maps are used to convey information where a knowledge of the world already understood and known by the map-maker is represented in a form that can be disseminated. Conversely, when maps are propositions, it is the *process* of map-making itself that generates new knowledge. In being explicit about how knowledge is produced, these are situated maps that rather than making truth claims about the world, propose versions of it. Embedded in a certain point of view, certain knowledges and part of a certain tradition can often mean that these are specialised maps, the knowledge they contain is certainly authoritative but not authoritarian. These maps tend to take material form perhaps because they retain the traditional impulse of mapping to disseminate. As diagrams or objects they acknowledge the positioning of the map user as someone who interacts with the map as object, as well as that of the map-maker who may be included in the map. These maps have a common purpose of making relations, to somehow connect things, places and people, in order to reveal organisational structures or the way in which a certain space or project is working. What differs is the mode in which these connections are made; some connect topologically across space whilst others make connections according to cultural or social criteria. Often they are ongoing productions where new relations and forms are added as they are learnt. This can involve a collecting and collating of information, or could employ the act of drawing and making. The agency of these maps is in their ability to propose a different way of apprehending the world.

### Maps as Mediators

Maps as mediators have a very different function to traditional maps – they do not try to disseminate anything – instead their role is to translate and to act as go-between. They do this tactically through becoming an excuse to bring people together who would not normally meet, by acting as prompts for conversations

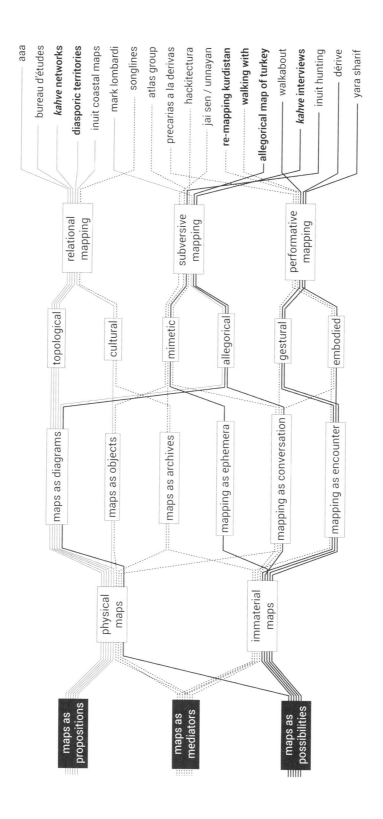

Agencies of mapping, 2010

or as catalysts for action. The mediation they enable could be between people or places or could equally be between fact and fiction. In all cases they create transformations through multiplying difference; sometimes they modulate space, through the bodily act of walking or through the deployment of technologies that create a mediatory space, a passageway or a channel worked through striated, surveilled spaces. From the migratory routes of transhumance to the elusive paths of asylum seekers, here maps are seen as tactics in the passing through to another place. These maps can be physical or immaterial, their assembling of collectivities meaning that they are subversive and performative. They can mediate in the realm of culture, at the level of the gesture, through mimetic and performed practices. Creating and collecting information, performing it through conversation or bodily acts, they tend to have the most diverse forms of representation.

## Maps as Possibilities

Maps as possibilities share many similarities with maps that are propositions. They also produce and disseminate knowledge, imagining other ways of being in the world. But they differ in one important aspect; they are almost never physical maps, remaining instead at the level of the immaterial. For this reason they are normally performative and embodied constructions. A definition of performativity in mapping cites examples from indigenous practices where mapping is said to be part of a *'a social tradition'*, where it is 'performed, by telling a story, recalling a dream, performing a dance, singing a song, or enacting a ritual'.[18] It could equally be part of an artistic practice that seeks to map affective registers perhaps as part of an urban installation. Performativity could also reside in everyday gestures, in mimetic practices and in the realm of the allegory. These are subtle, subversive and ephemeral practices where the map is a process rather than a product.

In the following chapter, I relate a series of diverse mapping practices that illustrate these categories as shown in the diagram 'Agencies of mapping' (see p. 121).

## NOTES

1.    Verran, 'Number as an Inventive Frontier in Knowing and Working Australia's Water Resources'.

2.    Yaneva, 'Traceable Cities'.

3.    Mogel and Bhagat, *An Atlas of Radical Cartography*.

4.    Dodge and Perkins, 'Reflecting on J.B. Harley's Influence and What He Missed in "Deconstructing the Map"', 39.

5.    UNITAR is the United Nations Institute for Training and Research, which runs UNOSAT (UNITAR's Operational Satellite Applications Programme). 'UNOSAT is a technology-intensive programme delivering imagery analysis and satellite solutions

to relief and development organisations within and outside the UN system to help make a difference in critical areas such as humanitarian relief, human security, strategic territorial and development planning.' 'UNOSAT.'

6.   Dodge and Perkins, 'Reflecting on J.B. Harley's Influence and What He Missed in "Deconstructing the Map"', 39.

7.   Corner, 'The Agency of Mapping'.

8.   Ibid., 225.

9.   Ibid., 228.

10.  Grosz, *Architecture From the Outside: Essays on Virtual and Real Space*, 179.

11.  Ibid., 168.

12.  Barad, 'Re-Membering the Future, Re(con)figuring the Past: Temporality, Materiality, and Justice-to-Come'.

13.  The publication, *Spatial Agency*, conceptualised a form of transformative spatial practice by drawing on a wide variety of historical and contemporary examples. Awan, Schneider, and Till, Spatial Agency: Other Ways of Doing Architecture.

14.  Grosz, 'Feminism, Materialism, and Freedom', 152.

15.  Lash et al., 'Agency and Architecture: How to Be Critical?', 8.

16.  See for example, 'Counter-Cartographies Collective'; Rankin, 'Radical Cartography'; Mogel and Bhagat, *An Atlas of Radical Cartography*.

17.  'Otherwise' invokes the 'otherhow', a term used by Blau DuPlessis to describe a multiplicity of possibilities over the binaries evoked by the word, 'otherness', while Katie Lloyd Thomas writes of 'drawing otherhow'. DuPlessis, *The Pink Guitar: Writing as Feminist Practice*, 154; Thomas, 'Building While Being in It: Notes on Drawing 'Otherhow''.

18.  Perkins, 'Performative and Embodied Mapping', 128.

## REFERENCES

Awan, Nishat, Tatjana Schneider, and Jeremy Till. *Spatial Agency: Other Ways of Doing Architecture*. London: Routledge, 2011.

Barad, Karen. 'Re-Membering the Future, Re(con)figuring the Past: Temporality, Materiality, and Justice-to-Come'. Presented at the Feminist Theory Workshop Keynote, Duke University, USA, 19 May 2014. https://www.youtube.com/watch?v=cS7szDFwXyg&feature=youtube_gdata_player.

Corner, James. 'The Agency of Mapping'. In *Mappings*, edited by Denis E. Cosgrove, 214–53. London: Reaktion Books, 1999.

'Counter-Cartographies Collective'. Accessed March 23, 2015. http://www.countercartographies.org/.

Dodge, Martin, and Chris Perkins. 'Reflecting on J.B. Harley's Influence and What He Missed in 'Deconstructing the Map'.' *Cartographica: The International Journal for Geographic Information and Geovisualization* 50, no. 1 (January 1, 2015): 37–40. doi:10.3138/carto.50.1.07.

DuPlessis, Rachel Blau. *The Pink Guitar: Writing as Feminist Practice*. Tuscaloosa: University of Alabama Press, 2006.

Grosz, Elizabeth. *Architecture From the Outside: Essays on Virtual and Real Space*. Cambridge, MA: MIT Press, 2001.

_____. 'Feminism, Materialism, and Freedom'. In *New Materialisms: Ontology, Agency, and Politics*, edited by Diana Cole and Samantha Frost, 139–57. Duke University Press, 2010.

Lash, Scott, Antoine Picon, Kenny Cupers, Isabelle Doucet, and Margaret Crawford. 'Agency and Architecture: How to Be Critical?' *Footprint* 4 (Spring 2009): 7–19.

Mogel, Lize, and Alexis Bhagat, eds. *An Atlas of Radical Cartography*. Los Angeles: Journal of Aesthetics and Protest Press, 2008.

Perkins, Chris. 'Performative and Embodied Mapping'. In *The International Encyclopedia of Human Geography*, 126–32. Oxford: Elsevier Inc, 2009.

Rankin, William. 'Radical Cartography'. *Radical Cartography*. Accessed March 23, 2015. http://www.radicalcartography.net/.

Thomas, Katie Lloyd. 'Building While Being in It: Notes on Drawing 'Otherhow''. In *Altering Practices: Feminist Politics and Poetics of Space*, edited by Doina Petrescu, 89–112. London: Routledge, 2007.

'UNOSAT'. *UNITAR*. Accessed March 23, 2015. http://www.unitar.org/unosat/.

Verran, Helen. 'Number as an Inventive Frontier in Knowing and Working Australia's Water Resources'. *Anthropological Theory* 10, no. 1–2 (March 2010): 171–78. doi:10.1177/1463499610365383.

Yaneva, Albena. 'Traceable Cities'. *City, Culture and Society* 3, no. 2 (June 2012): 87–9. doi:10.1016/j.ccs.2012.06.016.

# 7

# Representing the Non-Representational

## WAYS OF 'MAPPING OTHERWISE'

In this chapter I address, through discussing a series of different mapping practices, how maps can be used to represent a diasporic knowledge of space and how they can help in its navigation. Through an analysis of both contemporary and historical practices my aim is to build an assemblage of mapping techniques useful for representing diasporic agencies. Whilst these are diverse examples a number of common threads make them suitable for this purpose. They all in some way try to chart the voids and spaces that power hides and so are useful to the marginal claims of diasporas. They also have a topological sensibility meaning that they choose to see what they are mapping as producing their own spatio-temporalities.

It is an alternative history of maps, made by artists, architects and amateurs, all sorts of minor episodes in the history of a practice that has captivated many and that now seems to be having a renaissance. These include instances from other cultures that apprehend the world beyond the norms of the rationalised western model, there is a counter project of critical cartography and there are older maps that were made before the normalisation of the practice of cartography. A commonality of these diverse practices is that they all try to map something other than the earth and its geography; some map events and organisations, others map emotions and narratives, and the results are often very different from what we would usually consider a map. It is this other tradition that can prove useful for representing diasporic agencies, which need to account for the city seen as an aggregate of people, buildings and infrastructure, but also for the immaterial assemblages that are an integral part of diasporic city-space: trans-localities, atmospheres, networks, territories, borders …

## (a) Naming and Narrative

The **Aboriginal songlines** in Australia are a form of mapping from a completely different tradition to our own, where the relationship to the environment, the way of apprehending the world and representing it are all different. The question of mediation is tied to that of responsibility and rights over territory in the Australian aboriginal's relationship to their environment. Known for the intensity of relation to their environment, they view the bush as home, making camp through the simple act of sitting down. What is referred to in English as the 'walkabout' and 'songlines' expresses aspects of the same and most fundamental concept of their way of apprehending the world: *djalkiri* (in one of their many dialects). The walkabout is a system of routes that criss-cross Australia through which the Aboriginal people have mapped the entire continent. Yet it is much more than a simple map, it is a song, a story, a narrative of a journey and the making of worlds. The songlines tell the history of the Dream Time, of the origins of the world when the Ancestral Beings made journeys that named every thing and place, literally making the world through naming it; each shrub, stone, hill and ditch were named. The traces of these journeys have been left in the landscape and they circumscribe routes that tell stories: the songlines *are* the world as well as a way of being *in* the world.[1] Taken as such, *djalkiri* can be seen to embody a topological sensibility where the representation or naming of something is also its production, being at the core of the Aboriginal way of seeing their world. First the ancestors socialised the world, making places through their journeys, literally sculpting the landscape, and now humans are maintaining these same places through their own negotiation, intervention and actions.

This way of describing the world changes everything, including the status of knowledge, territory and space. Here the songlines take on another extremely important quality, they are valuable in the sense of a commodity and they can be traded as such. Since the walkabout is a series of routes that cross and overlap, they do not define space as a bounded entity but as an open, overlapping system; having a knowledge of the song gives rights over territory, very similar in this sense to the way in which birds use song to mark their territory. The points at which songs meet are the places of negotiation, where songs are exchanged, territory could be extended and questions of responsibility raised; in this sense the songs as techniques of mapping are *mediators of territory*. In what seems an aporia to the western mind, the songlines *are* the landscape, the territory, and maps of it; one of their many functions being that of a navigational device, used to cross vast stretches of land that to us would seem completely featureless. The question of detail is present here too, giving importance to the smallest of things, the way a stone lies on the ground, the relationship of a shrub to a mound in the land. This privileging of indiscernible features, of the infra-small, makes use of two qualities that are missing from the dominant practices of mapping: the representation of time and an explicit practice of naming. In some ways these two aspects are intertwined, when the world is laid out flat for us to view in its entirety, the time it

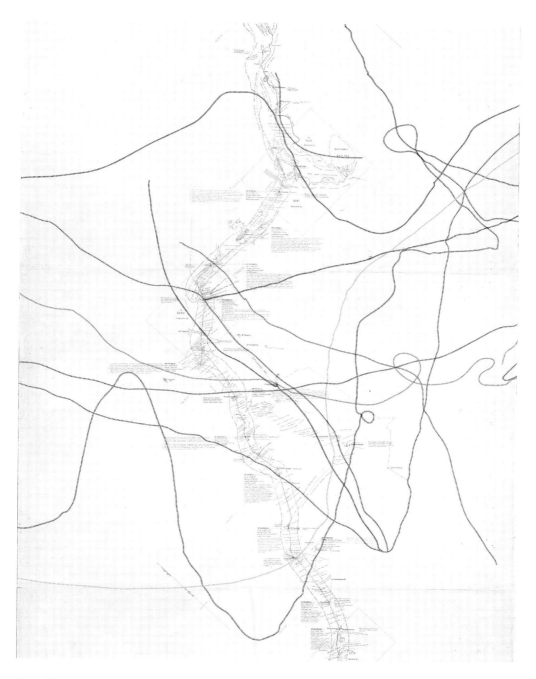

Map of Dreaming tracks crossing the northern end of the Canning Stock Route – surveyed in the early
1900s, the route was a source of conflict between indigenous groups and colonisers
*Source:* National Museum Australia, 2006.

takes to understand and represent it in parts, partially and subjectively, from our own perspective, is not accounted for. Narrative and naming are both elided.

The Aboriginal songlines hint at the type of mapping practice required for migrant lives, it is also a question considered by Doina Petrescu in her article on Romanian migrants who move back and forth across old and new Europe in pursuit of material wealth.[2] Living in the interstices of the French capital with semi-legal status, they return home to build large villas with the fruits of their travels. In her discussion of their active seeking out of marginality for economic profit, Petrescu notes that new spaces are created in the city that sit within an invisible network of economic value that the migrants are able to exploit. This and other networks made through mobility create another map of Europe that is, 'crossed over by *meandering lines* that go around and around, making detours and deviations from country to country, looking for that "something that attracts"'.[3] The movement of the Aborigines thus has its echoes in the detours of migrants across Europe, the tactical and subversive moves of those without power gaining advantage through the wily use of time and space.

## (b) Walking and Wandering

Walking as a form of everyday practice has a history of being used as a way of understanding the city through experience, ranging from the purposeless nature of the stroll to the walk as march that becomes a deliberate means of protest. Rebecca Solnit, in her extensive history of walking writes: 'Paris is the great city of walkers. And it is the great city of revolution. Those two facts are often written about as though they are unrelated, but they are vitally linked.'[4] The western history of walking as revolutionary act is Parisian, from Baudelaire's nineteenth-century *flâneurs* to Benjamin's appropriation of the act within the arcades of Paris to the Surrealist's stroll and the Situationist's *dérive*. In contrast in many contemporary cities walking is hindered by the morphology of the city as sprawl making it difficult to travel by foot alone. With the ubiquity of motorised forms of travel the economy of walking works in a different register, taking too much time, slowing time.

The figure of the flâneur where this story of walking starts is perhaps outdated for the twenty-first century, the bourgeois male experience of the city sits uneasily with feminist critiques of the aloofness with which he surveyed the city, being in it but not always a part of it. Yet Benjamin's writings on the newness of the crowd, the contrast between walking in the city and his childhood walks in the Alps reveal a contrasting attitude to walking in the city as opposed to the countryside.[5] In the nineteenth century, the strangeness of the crowd bestowed radicality on the *flâneur* who walked in an unknown city, discovering its pleasures; in the twenty-first century these are no longer new worlds. Although a getting lost in the city has been theorised by many, perhaps what is interesting for the practice of walking is to no longer marvel at its strangeness (which only ever translates itself in the exoticisation of places and cultures) but to find again the familiar through a shared and collaborative practice – walking alone is no longer the radical gesture it once was, but 'walking with' or a collective practice of walking could hold this potential.

Starting with the visit-excursions of the Dada walking became a collective activity that was usually carried out in groups and was part of a series of actions, from the handing out of gifts to passers-by to the reading of passages from books, but finally it was the conceptualisation of the act of inhabiting space as an aesthetic practice that mattered.[6] The Surrealists took this further from a single visit to an unconscious journey, exploring the countryside and also those areas of the bourgeois city that escaped the dominant modes of planning and control. The Situationist's **dérive** is an explicit extension of these earlier explorations, using a specific way of walking, the drift, to explore the city.[7] In the *dérive* there is an explicit rejection of utilitarian time for free time and playing – a time that is inherently creative. Getting lost in the city has its own rules and sometimes the *dérive* seems bizarrely prescriptive: 'the objective passional terrain of the dérive must be defined' or 'the average duration of a dérive is one day' etc.[8]

Yet, the Situationist *derive* as walking practice has its shortcomings. As Mary McLeod has pointed out, 'their visions of pleasure are permeated with sexism, a sexism inextricably entwined with their revulsion against bourgeois family life. They categorically ignore issues such as domesticity, childcare, reproduction – indeed, all aspects of women's situation in society …'.[9] The artist Helen Scalway salvages a walking practice for women from the debris of this gendered critique; in her essay 'Contemporary Flaneuse', she writes of a walking practice that is specifically borne of the situation of a woman in the city, afraid at times, wanting to explore, yet having to protect herself whilst doing so. Referring to Steve Pile's definition of walking as a lack of place, she writes '… because I cannot easily stand in the city street – so walking is what enables me to look round, while precisely, not occupying any space'.[10]

A collective walk could also be a useful tactic, transforming this simple act into a negotiation or collaboration. A group of women from Madrid, **Precarias a la Deriva**, have used walking in this way; walking with other women who like them were employed in a range of precarious employment, from working in universities as technicians or research assistants, to working in cafés or doing domestic work – they all had jobs that were not guaranteed, being either temporary, part-time or consisting of shift work. The group acknowledged that this situation did bring certain advantages but also many disadvantages, for example the unions that called the general strike of June 2002 in Spain, did not take this type of informal work into consideration. The project started on the day of the strike with the women carrying out interviews with workers at the picket line, asking questions about their work conditions, reasons for striking etc. From these initial conversations, the project of the walks came into being, as a way of 'mapping the metropolis from within'.[11]

Precarias carried out walks with workers through the city of Madrid and beyond, having conversations and recording interviews. They took the Situationist *derive* and made it more purposeful, attempting to record the everyday lives of the people that they were walking with, their routes from home to work and back again. Walking together meant that they acknowledged their own positioning and the drift itself started to create solidarities between disparate women. In

A *dérive* with students from Sheffield School of Architecture, UK in Nowa Huta, Kraków, Poland *Source:* Author, 2007.

this sense, the walks were an excuse, a *mediation* that allowed the women to spend time together, knowing that the duration between destinations was often the only time available for such conversations in lives that were already busy. The mapping process was therefore both embodied and performative and in describing its public nature Precarias write; 'if we want to break social atomisation, we have to intervene with strength in the public sphere, circulate other utterances'.[12] Here mapping is an encounter between women that empowers those who inhabit other geographies through a material and embodied engagement. It is a way of addressing the issues raised by the women's lives not just as employment issues but as the result of the intersection of many different social realities: gender, class, ethnicity, education. It is also a way of analysing these realities as social *and* spatial. Although Precarias also produced standard maps showing the routes that they took, it was at the level of the walks themselves that their mapping practice actually occurred, these *immaterial maps* being the basis for those produced later.

The artist Anne-Lise Dehée also uses the mode of 'walking with' as part of her artistic practice but here it is enunciated differently as a therapeutic practice.[13] Her walks were carried out with women who live on the streets, homeless women, drug addicts and sex workers. On the pretext of her research and art practice, Dehée took the women out of their usual neighbourhood, the exploitative *milieu* of pimps, drug dealers, and others. The change of scene, along with their conversation and the unconscious activity of walking, combined to give a little psychological space to the women; a space for them *to imagine other possibilities*, other ways of living. An embodied practice, walking here becomes both subversive and nurturing. To view unconscious, embodied gestures as therapeutic is to place an emphasis on their mechanical and shared qualities, for example the lover's stroll shares time and space, often saying nothing and doing nothing, its pleasure in time spent together. Fernand Deligny's drawings of the movements of autistic children also use this particular quality of spending time as therapy. Following the children in their daily routines, tracing their movements, he produced maps that were a layering of the children's walks, their movements and gestures. Commenting on this mapping practice, Petrescu writes; 'There where nothing is common, instead of language, what is shared is the "place" and its occupation – and this place together with its different activities, gestures, incidents and presences is drawn on the map with different lines and signs'.[14] These sensitive maps of those who are vulnerable and yet whose experiences need to be engaged with, open up important questions about the politics of representation. Giving away information about where the women could be found was dangerous as they operated through their ability to remain hidden, whilst the children's maps also needed to be protected. For Dehée, it is crucial to find a subtle balance between what is shown and what is not. Whilst the women's privacy must be respected, their experiences also need to be related, they may operate through remaining in the background but for many people those living on the streets are invisible, easily ignored and walked past.

The urban collective Stalker use walking in an explicitly Situationist tradition as a way of rediscovering people and places forgotten by others. They started out using the method of collective walking to explore territories within the indeterminate or void spaces of the city, which they felt had for too long been disregarded or considered a problem in traditional urban planning. Stalker refer to their walking practice as 'transurbance', a collective mode of expression and a tool for mapping the city and its transformations.[15] Since the mid-1990s they have explored the indeterminate zones of various cities starting with the edges of the Tiber River on the outskirts of Rome, and later in Milan, Paris, Berlin and Turin amongst others. In describing the purpose of their walking they write: 'The idea is to rediscover, in the metropolitan territory, a sense that springs from the experience of the present state of things with all its contradictions, from an unopinionated perspective, free of reassuring and at the same time frustrating historical or functional justifications'.[16] It is a way of engaging freely with whatever they find in these places; in Rome they met individuals and communities living along the riverbanks forgotten by the general public and ignored by the city authorities. In response to that particular situation they decided to produce an atlas of the riverbanks, describing the excluded places as a 'fractal archipelago', made up of a fractured space that inhabits the cracks of the ordered consumerist city.[17] Through their transurbance Stalker discovered the voids to not be empty after all but filled with the city's forgotten inhabitants – migrants, the homeless, the Roma population and others.

Since then Stalker's emphasis has shifted and they set up projects that address those they have encountered on their walks. For this they have changed their way of operating, setting up a trans-local network of practitioners, researchers, artists, and architects; Osservatorio Nomade is a platform that allows Stalker to engage in long-term projects in collaboration with others. Via Egnatia is the first and longest running of such projects, following the route of the ancient Roman road between

Rome and Istanbul along which migrants and displaced people have travelled between East and West for centuries. It is also a highly contested territory with the nationalistic claims of Macedonian Greeks, Turks, Kurds and Albanians overlapping and across which the Ottoman Empire's long shadow still falls. Osservatorio Nomade's project carried out in collaboration with Oxymoron from Athens and Atelier d'Architecture Autogérée (AAA) from Paris, gathered stories along this route of past and present displacements and migrations. Their practice is one of mediation, making the conditions necessary for informal meetings and encounters between disparate people. Stalker's Lorenzo Romito defines their practice and themselves: 'Stalker is a desiring community where no one belongs and where individuals encounter each other. It is an unstable entity, a temporary community, which is founded on possibilities, on desire, on intention, on promise and waiting.'[18] Taken as such, the whole of Stalker's practice whether carried out through walking or as part of a larger curatorial project that arranges encounters and meetings, is working towards establishing a community through the *mediatory practice* of mapping.

The various practices of walking described here allow space to be experienced as it is lived, and they bring a degree of chance into what is encountered. It is a way of mapping that is able to discover the marginal and interstitial spaces of the city, which are also often occupied by diasporas.

### (c) Tracing and Drawing

The group **Atelier d'Architecture Autogérée (AAA)** have developed a highly specialised practice of mapping to gain a relational understanding of the spatial politics at play in their project, Ecobox. In it gardening acts as a catalyst for urban change in La Chapelle, an area of Paris with high unemployment and a large proportion of migrants. Ecobox consists of a series of temporary, self-managed spaces that take advantage of underused and leftover pockets of land with the aim of encouraging residents to take greater control of their city. Here AAA have used mapping as both a representational device and as a way of understanding the different agencies and relationalities that operate within their project. Used at each stage mapping and diagramming are a fundamental part of their methodology, used to identify potential sites, to map local resident's groups, to record the progress of the project, and finally deployed as a means of understanding their own and other people's actions and involvement. In AAA's practice, mapping is *propositional* for its usefulness in understanding the relationships between everyday practices, the formation of desire in the social field and how these are affected by spatial configurations that encourage or discourage certain ways of inhabiting space. Mapping thus becomes a powerful tool in their architectural and urban practice.[19]

In one map loops are drawn between people, places and objects that represent the different networks operating within Ecobox. They show how certain people gradually become embedded within the project as they make new relationships and involve themselves in more activities. Doina Petrescu, one of the founding members of AAA, writes: 'The role of this mapping was not only to 'represent' or 'conceive' but to enhance experience.'[20] This is an important distinction as the enhancing of experience means that the mapping is not carried out as an afterthought at the end of the project but is considered a part of it. The map also shows the role of what they call tactical devices; mobile units for cooking, a library and a DJ station become infrastructural nodes in the network, their position in space as well as the social *milieu* of the project providing insights into the workings of Ecobox.

Petrescu also refers to their maps as tactical devices that the collective use to represent social and subjective processes, such as how people's involvement in the project changed over time according to which groups and activities they were a part of. One example that AAA often cite is the change in a number of families who came to garden each week but did not take part in any of the other related cultural or social activities. But when the garden was threatened with eviction these passive users who had never before involved themselves in politics became urban activists, petitioning the town hall for a new space. In AAA's intricate and highly detailed maps this process of subjectivation is visible as coloured lines whose trajectory changes gradually or suddenly, either in the day-to-day exchanges of the project or in a moment of crisis. AAA have not forgotten their own important role, their activities are also included charting the transition from a project initiated and run by themselves to one that is taken over and managed by others. Petrescu characterises their mapping of these processes or *'agencements'* as drawing 'the evolving portrait of the fluid and elusive socio-cultural and spatial entity made by informal and temporary relationships'.[21] In AAA's practice, as part of an activist project, mapping becomes a way of creating agencies.

The tactical drawings of AAA trace the different spatial and temporal possibilities within their project envisaged as a growing trans-local network. **Yara Sharif**, whose work is situated in Palestine, has also used this method of mapping that traces the social and spatial possibilities in a given situation. Here she uses mapping as a tool to imagine the 'spaces of possibility' within the Palestinian/Israeli conflict.[22] In a context where architecture and urbanism stand accused of being used as 'a continuation of war by other means', her work re-imagines these practices as tools that can bridge the gaps between fragmented communities.[23] Walking is used performatively as a way of creating subjective maps, mixing narrative, sketches and photos; a journey is related from the Dead Sea to the Mediterranean Sea. Sharif traces the trajectories of people living and working in the West Bank, her encounters with different people allowing her to relate the tactics that allow them to pass through borders. In this unique context space itself reconfigures continuously as checkpoints are relocated daily. For Sharif this fluctuating landscape creates restrictions and blockages, but also moments of opportunity where everyday practices are able to transgress the regimes of surveillance and control. Even the minutes and hours spent waiting to go through checkpoints or for crossings to open become opportunities where everyday life re-forms and continues; a whole host of small-scale, informal economies emerge, such as vendors selling food and drink.[24] Sharif names these mobile practices that are able to adapt

Walk from
Dead Sea to
Mediterranean Sea
*Source:* Yara
Sharif, 2009.

and negotiate the changing daily reality as 'social calligraphy' and through her mapping she creates an architecture that can imagine counter-strategies of resistance.

There is a sensitivity to her drawings that map the empty spaces of Ramallah and overlay them with the movement of people. The voids and empty blocks are overlaid with the routes of people characterised as 'floating social clusters' of migrants, refugees, the unemployed and street vendors. Thin fragile lines demarcate the routes whilst fuzzy patches of colour indicate the places that are empty, the overlaying of this information produces a beautiful map entitled 'Absence and the Will to Survive', that reveals the places of possibility for another narrative within the harsh and changing urban environment. These ambiguous maps reveal some things but not all; their ability to be read in a number of different ways protects the sensitive information contained within them. In this sense, these maps are allegorical, revealing a hidden meaning to those that know what to look for, subversively relating the will to survive. It is interesting to compare them to those maps produced by Esther Polak and the Waag Society in the project RealTime. Here people with GPS trackers are linked to a screen that creates a map of their movements as they go about their daily lives in Amsterdam. Their movements in real time create lines in light on a black background that overlay each other and fade with time. The maps are beautiful and aesthetically similar to those produced by Sharif but they raise questions of security and surveillance, where individual movements are traced, recorded and exposed for all to see. The problematic use of military technology not only exposes but the lack of proximity and time spent together means that GPS maps can never create the spaces of possibility, full of potential, that Sharif's maps are able to. Her time spent on the ground with those going about their daily lives, her own presence in the maps means that they are able to answer the challenge articulated by Petrescu towards architectural practice: 'how to operate with a space which is traced at the same time as it is lived and how to use this tracing to understand and eventually create more relationships between those who inhabit it.'[25]

## (d) Collecting and Curating

**Bureau d'études** are a group of artists and graphic designers whose maps address the growing role of networks in our everyday lives, from the vast corporate, consumerist and military networks that are an integral part of the workings of capital, to the diffuse cultural and social networks that resist their power and offer alternative possibilities. The maps and accompanying texts are available freely on their website, *Université Tangente* (Tangential University) which is an integral part of their project for autonomous knowledge production.[26] In what they call the archives of capitalism their maps display meticulous compositions that chart the links between think tanks, governmental organisations, financial firms, regulatory bodies, intelligence agencies, media groups, weapons makers, satellite companies … in effect they chart the complex workings of the neo-liberal economy. Over the past 15 years, Bureau d'études have developed an extensive iconographic language to represent this highly detailed and complex information. Set alongside their collaborations with the critic Brian Holmes, it has produced an ongoing discourse on the possibilities of using cartography to promote social movements. Holmes describes their maps as 'subjective shocks', remarking: 'There's a wager here: paint a totalitarian picture, crystal clear, and people will look for the cracks into some other dimension.'[27] In this sense, described by Holmes the dense maps of Bureau d'études have a *propositional potential*. The information they hold is extremely useful and has the potential to empower citizens. For example, their map European Norms of World Production, shows the organisational and power structures behind the European Commission (EC), revealing the dominant sources of power to be the Court of Justice, the European Roundtable of Industrialists and the rather obscure, Burston Marsteller. The existence and power of this private company, which promises to navigate you through the maze of bureaucracy that is the EC – at a price – demonstrates the use-value of the map. It has the potential to act as a navigational device, as all good maps do, allowing the ordinary European citizen to grasp the relations between the hundreds of lobby groups associated with the EC and whatever issue they are interested in. These, and other maps like it, are produced in large print runs to be handed out for free at activist events, such as the European Social Forum or the No Border Camp, or to be found at various autonomous social centres.

The other side of Bureau d'étude's work explores anarchist positions, from dissident knowledge producers to those living in squats – a diffuse network that embodies various forms of non-capitalist exchange. Here again the question of access to knowledge is paramount; they have collaborated with the unemployed, squatter communities and the *sans papiers* through the self-organised space in Strasbourg, the *Syndicat Potentiel*. The space was set up in frustration with the art world in order to produce and disseminate work collectively, outside the institutionalised space of the art gallery. Bureau d'études write of the importance of these other types of groups, practices and spaces: 'These manifestations of autonomous knowledge/power provoke a crisis in the monopoly of access to possibilities held by the productive organisations of consumer society.'[28] Bureau d'études describe the actual production of their maps as artisanal and have written recently on the insufficiency of such an approach, which is extremely time consuming. Instead they hint at a new collaborative project that will produce a map generator, an online tool to which bits of information can be uploaded by the general public. The accumulated knowledge of a potentially large number of people could produce quickly maps that would take the collective months to research. This new approach of a map produced collaboratively, also allows for a mechanism of exchange, solving the problem of a lack of dialogue within the original maps; the relational connections that could be made by the new maps would not only be those described by the map itself but also those created through its production.

Whilst Bureau d'études produce their maps through a meticulous collecting and collating of facts, *The Atlas Group* does the same but with *potential* facts. The group is a fictitious foundation set up by the artist, Walid Raad, to record the contemporary history of Lebanon, in particular the period of civil war from 1975–1991. The project consists of documents allegedly produced by them and presented in exhibitions as images, videos and artefacts, or in lecture performances by the artist. Although Raad explicitly highlights the imaginary nature of his project, it is telling that at many of his lectures people forget this detail, assuming that the work is claiming complete authenticity. In one part of the archive entitled, Let's be Honest, the Weather Helped, Raad puts together a series of photographs of buildings peppered with bullet holes. The photos are gathered in a notebook with coloured dots indicating each hole, the colour apparently corresponding to the coloured tips of the bullets, a categorisation system for the country of manufacture. Part of the description accompanying these files, which are attributed to the artist, reads: 'It took me 25 years to realise that my notebooks had all along catalogued the 23 countries that armed or sold ammunitions to the various militias and armies fighting the Lebanese wars, including the US, UK, Saudi Arabia, Israel, France, Switzerland, and China.'[29] Whilst the salient facts here are true, that is these countries did arm the Lebanese militia, the story of the collection of the bullets with coloured tips is a fiction.

Another part of the archive is a collection of notebooks, photographs and videos allegedly donated to **The Atlas Group** by Dr Fadl Fakhouri, who is identified as a famous Lebanese historian of the Civil War. It includes notebooks that contain a photograph of a racehorse near the finish line with an accompanying text relating the story of how the historians of the Lebanese civil war had a penchant for gambling. They had persuaded the race official to take only one photo of the winning horse, and they would bet on the distance between the finish line and the horse in the photograph. The notebooks include the photographed image cut out from the following day's newspaper annotated with descriptions of the winning historian and details of the bets placed. The work hinges on the fact that the photo finish, a supposedly authoritative record of the winning horse, could never be completely accurate. Being well aware of this detail the historians chose instead to bet on the margin of inevitable error.

Walid Raad's retelling of the work of The Atlas Group questions the thin line between fact and fiction. Here mapping is an archival project that collects and collates the versions of history that circulate, inflected through the subjectivity of the narrator and the continual work of constructing collective memory. Through a subversive, mimetic practice these mappings play with the politics of representation, questioning notions of authenticity and authorship. The fabricated history they relate is nonetheless grounded in serious research using archival material such as news clippings, press photographs etc. It is also based in actual events that were broadcast around the world on television sets and radios. Raad's practice thus serves to highlight the subjectivity inherent in individual accounts of history and the workings of collective memory.

## (e) Telling and Transmitting

**Mark Lombardi's** drawings can be seen as a precursor to the maps produced by Bureau d'études. Using information publicly available on news wires or the early Internet he produced intricate drawings, most often in pencil or pen. Thin lines make connections between different types of actors – people, organisations, groups – relating a narrative of corporate fraud or the secret deals of governments. Lombardi worked alone, initially making diagrams to aid his writing and later realising the value of his compositions that managed to distil and relate complex events. Whilst his work has been critiqued for not sufficiently representing the strength of relations or distinguishing between the different types of relations, his drawings follow another logic. In what are static images made without the use of computers, Lombardi succeeds in relating an impression of the speed and rhythm of connections and their intensities. The artist called his drawings, Narrative Structures, and as is the case with narrations these are situated representations of events based on facts, but arranged according to the account that Lombardi wanted to relate. Displayed in galleries, Lombardi's maps are able to tell their sometimes explosive stories in a quiet way, the gallery setting allowing certain connections and leaps to be made which in the context of a news story would be immediately questioned as conjecture. The neo-liberal machine that is often exposed in his drawings would be set in motion to discredit any rumours before they could become claims. It is perhaps of no surprise that Lombardi, whose drawings were having an increasing impact, committed suicide in circumstances that have aroused suspicion.

Hackitectura is a group of architects, artists, computer specialists and activists based in Seville, whose practice uses new technologies to create temporary spaces that can escape the formal structures of control and surveillance in contemporary society. Inspired by hacker culture they use free software and communication technologies to subvert established power structures through bottom-up organisation and by creating alternative connections between disparate spaces. The group often works collaboratively carrying out research into the effects of communication and technology on physical spaces, the formation of social networks and how these can be put to work for an activist agenda. They have

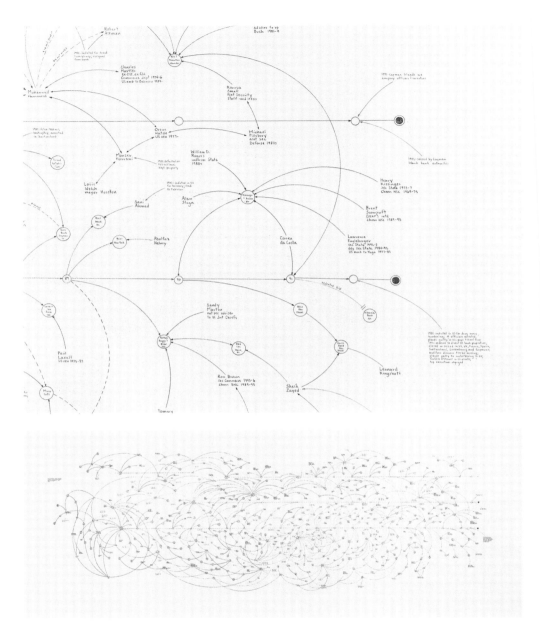

*BCCI, ICIC, FAB c. 1972–91* (4th version), 1996–2000, Graphite on paper, 52 × 138 inches. Collection of The Whitney Museum of American Art, New York, NY
*Source:* Courtesy Donald Lombardi and Pierogi Gallery.

collaborated with Indymedia Estrecho in creating links across the Straits of Gibraltar or *Madiaq*, the militarised ocean that is the shortest distance between Africa and Europe.[30] As part of a series of projects they established a network link that became a free public interface between the two continents. They also produced maps that chart a geography of the Straits and describing the role of these representational spaces within their work they write: 'Making a cartography of an 'Other-territory' – a border zone of high strategic importance co-inhabited by social processes of great intensity and violence – became a necessary tool to orient ourselves and our practices/praxis.'[31]

One side of the map charts the security and surveillance regimes of the border that surrounds Fortress Europe, whilst the other side charts the resistances to it, groups of activists and NGOs that work against and across the border, constructing networks of collaboration. The maps are a way of getting to know the territory but also a way of reinventing it; here the border is not a militarised line but an inhabited space filled with other desires and counter-spaces. The project also included a series of regular events that took place on either side of the Straits. Called *Fada'iat* or 'through spaces' the events included workshops, actions, and seminars bringing together migration, labour rights, gender and communication activists, political theorists, hackers, union organisers, architects and artists in a temporary media lab that could become a permanent public interface between Tarifa in Spain and Tangiers in Morocco. Combined with direct actions against the detention of migrants, for a time the event created a network of communication, action and solidarity between the two continents. Hackitectura's mapping practice thus consists not only of the maps they produced but also the transmitting of signals across the Straits, creating a mediatory space, a channel through the striated, surveilled space of international borders.

### (f) Mimicry and Being Present

In the context of what they choose to represent, the coastal maps of the **Greenland Inuit** are fairly standard, recording aspects of the landscape for seafarers, much the same as that other more famous map that Mercator produced. But the Inuit maps vary in the *way* they map the landscape, whilst sight and scale may take precedence in the maps that we are used to, they use different senses. Pieces of driftwood are carved in the shape of a coastline with separate pieces that could represent off-shore islands. Kept in the pockets of seafarers, they can be used without looking and without exposing your hands to the cold. It is a radically different way of conceiving the map, making no use of vision – these are touch maps. Being *objects* rather than lines drawn on paper they demand a different relationship to us. They are everyday objects that can be thrown in a kayak, left on the side, or kept in a pocket, whilst fragile paper maps containing their expensive and professionalised knowledge need to be stored straightened and smooth for next time. But to understand just how these and other maps produced by the Inuits function, it is important to place them within their wider culture. The anthropologist, Robert Rundstrom, writes that map-making is not a specialist exercise but something that everyone participates in; the nomadic lifestyle and the long journeys necessary for hunting in a landscape that would look completely homogenous to us, means that mapping is a necessity and men, women and children all take part in it regardless of social status. Thus maps are not precious objects, in fact some are ephemeral maps made in the snow, air or sand, they last only a while – what is cherished is the detailed knowledge behind the maps rather than the map itself.[32] The rugged coastal maps work in conjunction with these other temporary maps and show an attitude to knowledge that is very different from that encapsulated in western maps; an everyday knowledge that is generated through continual *exchange* as people move across the terrain. In this important sense, the Inuit maps are propositions for a collective cross-generational map of the landscape.

Early European explorers to the Arctic were indebted to this detailed knowledge and the Inuit's ability to transmit the information to them in a way that they could comprehend. Rundstrom points out that what makes the Inuits good map-makers was not that they necessarily used similar conventions to the Europeans, as some early anthropologists suggest, but that they deliberately tried to present information in a way the Europeans could understand, using their ability to mimic in order to communicate.[33] Rundstrom explains the role that mimicry plays in Inuit culture in general and how this informs their approach to mapping. Whilst hunting caribou in a landscape that lacks cover or camouflage, the Inuit stalk their prey through gestural mimicry, bending down, moving their arms and legs together, they imitate the gait of the caribou allowing them to get close enough to their prey. The hunting of seals uses a similar technique, this time lying on the ground and rolling as the seals do. The Inuit's believe that humans and animals had a much closer relationship in the past, being able to speak to each other; good hunters recall

Gestural mimicry – 'An Eskimaux Watching a Seal'. In Parry, William Edward, 'Journal of a second voyage for the discovery of a North-West Passage …', London: J. Murray, 1824
*Source:* Library and Archives Canada, reproduction copy number C-127963.

this lost ability and converse with their prey, imitating their sounds. But this is not just a way of fooling the animal it is also an 'appeasement of the soul of the highly respected animal'.[34] Through a practice of mimicry, the Inuit can be said to remake these connections topologically across time and space, a cultural inscription onto the bodies of animals and humans alike. It is an integral part of everyday life that was used not only in hunting but as an art form and to relate stories of journeys, it also gave the Inuit a special relationship to their environment. They imitated it, enveloped themselves in it, wearing animal skins, living in igloos, but most of all they *knew* it, completely immersing themselves in their environment.

Another example where mimicry proved to be a powerful tool is in the mapping practice of the organisation, **Unnayan**, which worked with the urban poor on housing and dwelling rights Kolkata, India, in the 1980s. Set up by Jai Sen and a number of other professionals, their work was based around Sen's 1974 essay, 'The Unintended City', which critiqued the use of western planning ideals in India and other developing nations.[35] The essay argued that whilst in industrialised western cities most people could be said to live an urban existence, in India this was not the case; the vast majority of the population led a rural existence, unnoticed within the interstices of the legitimate urban city. Unnayan was concerned with the dwelling rights of such people, helping them to gain legitimacy within the planning system through community organisation and advocacy work. As Sen himself stated, although mapping started out as a peripheral activity within the organisation, its impact grew through its use in their overall campaign.

The informal settlements that Unnayan worked with were not marked in any official map, meaning that bypasses, flyovers, infrastructure of all sorts could be drawn by city planners in ostensibly empty space passing through these invisible settlements. Conversely and for the same reasons, the sort of infrastructure that these communities desperately needed – drainage, electricity, water – was not provided. The maps produced by Unnayan may look unexciting, as they use the same representational techniques as official maps, but they also work for this reason. Through mimicking official representations Unnayan's maps legitimised the squatter settlements with the status of the maps as official objects mediating this shift. Here again it is *what* is mapped and *how* this mapping is deployed that creates agency. Sen writes of the large-scale map that they produced through visiting the settlements and painstakingly measuring them, creating an image that was slowly filled through their collective effort. 'The collage that loomed over the Action Room in our office always reminded us of the realities of the city.'[36]

Almost all of the maps and documentation produced by Unnayan were destroyed in floods and a fire at their office, leaving behind very little trace of 18 years of work and effectively ending the organisation. Despite this, Unnayan's mappings helped a number of communities who were either saved from being evicted or compensated for it. In a later essay, Sen has commented on what else these maps could have achieved had the mappings been carried out more collaboratively and performatively with the communities concerned, and whether a bigger legacy in the form of memories and learnt skill would have survived the destruction of paper.[37]

**A DIASPORIC MAPPING PRACTICE**

The practices described in this chapter provide a vocabulary and a toolkit for 'mapping otherwise', the titles of each subsection relating particular techniques developed over a wide range of contexts. In the following chapter, I have used many of these techniques to map diasporic agencies, and in doing so they become more specific and the vocabulary transforms somewhat.

In mapping diasporic agencies, narrative and naming could also be described as the relating of stories, the representation of snatched conversations and snippets of gossip. Touch and relations form an affective world of gestures, ways of inhabiting and movements that are a reminder of another place. In the diaspora the workings of memory become so important and the ability to recall without nostalgia, or to at least compensate for it, is a necessity but almost always a failure. The practice of naming becomes crucial to this negotiating of memory in the city for those who can read the signs. Here the role of performativity and the practice of mimicry become important, in particular the ways in which they are able to transform mapping into a practice that can connect and relate disparate groups and places. It is an approach to mapping that is embedded within its context, a site-specific activity that happens whilst walking with others, speaking to them, through observing and being present, it reveals the workings of power and with it the making of agencies.

Collecting, collating and informing, whether carried out in an empirical manner or as an interpretative practice that plays with ideas of fact and fiction, are useful for representing diasporic agencies that are embedded in marginal ways of inhabiting space and in making visible hidden histories. The mediatory spaces created through practices of transmission hold an important place in diasporic culture, whether this is through satellite television, popular music or the Internet that is now perhaps the most important medium. Tracing and drawing as mapping techniques are especially useful in representing such trans-local connections and experiences spatially. Whilst these processes have often been described verbally in other disciplines such as sociology and geography, for architecture and urbanism making the connection to spatial inhabitation is crucial. Finally, the ethics of working with marginalised groups means that often being present and observing are just as important ways of representing than the other more interpretative techniques described here. To be present and to witness those events, conversations and acts that mainstream practice chooses to ignore or thinks unimportant is crucial to representing diasporic agencies.

**NOTES**

1.    For a detailed discussion of the songlines see, Chatwin, *The Songlines*.

2.    Petrescu, 'Pl(a)ys of Marginality: Transmigrants in Paris'.

3.    Ibid., 262.

4.    Solnit, *Wanderlust: A History of Walking*, 218.

5.    Benjamin, *The Arcades Project*.

6.    For a detailed discussion and history of walking see, Careri, *Walkscapes: Walking as an Aestheic Practice*.

7.    See, Debord, 'Theory of the Dérive'.

8.    Ibid.

9.    McLeod, 'Architecture and Feminism', 16.

10.   Scalway, 'Contemporary Flaneuse', 252.

11.   Precarias a la deriva, 'A Drift Through the Circuits of Feminised Precarious Work', 161.

12.   Ibid., 160.

13.   Dehée, 'Anne-Lise Dehée'.

14.   Petrescu, 'The Indeterminate Mapping of the Common', 90–91.

15.   See, Stalker, 'Stalker: Laboratorio d'Arte Urbana'.

16.   Careri, *Walkscapes: Walking as an Aestheic Practice*, 178.

17.   This conceptualisation is very similar to Jai Sen's concept of the 'unintended city' that inhabits the cracks and voids of the 'legitimate' city in India and other countries of the global South. See Sen, 'The Unintended City'.

18.   Romito quoted in Papastergiadis, 'Glimpses of Cosmopolitanism in the Hospitality of Art', 149.

19.   For a detailed discussion of AAA's use of mapping see, Petrescu, 'Relationscapes'.

20.   Ibid., 137.

21.   Ibid.

22.   For a detailed discussion see, Sharif, 'Searching for Spaces of Possibility within the Palestinian/Israeli Conflict'. Unless otherwise stated all quotes are from, Sharif, 'Spaces of Possibility'.

23.   Weizman, *Hollow Land: Israel's Architecture of Occupation*, 85.

24.   These are exactly the sorts of processes related by Nabeel Hamdi in his book *Small Change* that describes the role that informality plays in urban life. It sets out a way of approaching cities that gives precedence to small-scale, incremental change over large-scale projects. He shows how the trickle-down effect advocated by conservatives everywhere does not produce the sort of large-scale changes that are predicted. It is instead the trickle-up effect of self-organised systems that produce the biggest changes. Hamdi, *Small Change: About the Art of Practice and the Limits of Planning in Cities*.

25.   Petrescu, 'The Indeterminate Mapping of the Common', 96.

26.   For an account of Université Tangente see, Bureau d'études, 'Autonomous Knowledge and Power in a Society without Affects' .

27.   Holmes, 'Cartographies of Excess (Bureau D'études, Multiplicity)'.

28.   Bureau d'études, 'Autonomous Knowledge and Power in a Society without Affects'.

29.   Nakas and Schmitz, *The Atlas Group (1989–2004): A Project by Walid Raad*, 126.

30. *Madiaq* is the Arabic name for the Straits of Gibraltar.

31. Hackitectura and Indymedia Estrecho, *Fadaiat*.

32. Rundstrom, 'A Cultural Interpretation of Inuit Map Accuracy'.

33. On the alleged use of hachuring to show topographic features in maps produced by the Eskimo see, Spink and Moodie, *Eskimo Maps from the Canadian Eastern Arctic*.

34. Rundstrom, 'A Cultural Interpretation of Inuit Map Accuracy', 163.

35. Sen, 'The Unintended City'.

36. Sen, 'Other Worlds, Other Maps: Mapping the Unintended City', 20.

37. Sen, 'Other Worlds, Other Maps: Mapping the Unintended City'.

## REFERENCES

Benjamin, Walter. *The Arcades Project*. London: Belknap Press, 1999.

Bureau d'études. 'Autonomous Knowledge and Power in a Society without Affects'. *Université Tangente/Tangential University*, 2002. http://utangente.free.fr/anewpages/holmes.html.

Careri, Francesco. *Walkscapes: Walking as an Aesthetic Practice*. Barcelona: Gustavo Gili, 2003.

Chatwin, Bruce. *The Songlines*. New edition. London: Vintage Classics, 1998.

Debord, Guy-Ernest. 'Theory of the Dérive'. *Internationale Situationniste* 2 (1958). http://library.nothingness.org/articles/all/all/display/314.

Dehée, Anne-Lise. 'Anne-Lise Dehée'. Accessed January 12, 2015. http://annelise.dehee.free.fr/.

Hackitectura, and Indymedia Estrecho. *Fadaiat*. Observatorio Tecnologico del Estrecho, 2006.

Hamdi, Nabeel. *Small Change: About the Art of Practice and the Limits of Planning in Cities*. London: Earthscan, 2004.

Holmes, Brian. 'Cartographies of Excess (Bureau D'études, Multiplicity)'. *Mute: Culture and Politics After the Net*, 2003. http://www.metamute.org/en/node/6243.

McLeod, Mary. 'Everyday and "Other" Spaces'. In *Architecture and Feminism*, edited by Debra Coleman, Elizabeth Danze, and Carol Henderson, 1–37. New York: Princeton Architectural Press, 1996.

Nakas, Kassandra, and Britta Schmitz, eds. *The Atlas Group (1989–2004): A Project by Walid Raad*. Cologne: Walther König, 2006.

Papastergiadis, Nikos. 'Glimpses of Cosmopolitanism in the Hospitality of Art'. *European Journal of Social Theory* 10, no. 1 (2007): 139–52.

Petrescu, Doina. 'Pl(a)ys of Marginality: Transmigrants in Paris'. In *The Hieroglyphics of Space: Reading and Experiencing the Modern Metropolis*, edited by Neil Leach, 260–70. London: Routledge, 2001.

_____. 'Relationscapes: Mapping Agencies of Relational Practice in Architecture'. *City, Culture and Society*, Traceable Cities, 3, no. 2 (June 2012): 135–40. doi:10.1016/j.ccs.2012.06.011.

_____. 'The Indeterminate Mapping of the Common'. *Field:* 1, no. 1 (2007): 88–96.

Precarias a la deriva. 'A Drift Through the Circuits of Feminised Precarious Work'. *Feminist Review* 77, no. 1 (2004): 157–61.

Rundstrom, R.A. 'A Cultural Interpretation of Inuit Map Accuracy'. *Geographical Review* 80 (1990): 155–68.

Scalway, Helen. 'Contemporary Flaneuse'. In *Radio Temporaire*, edited by Sylvie Desroches Zeigam Azizov, 251–62. Grenoble: National Centre for Contemporary Arts, 1998.

Sen, Jai. 'Other Worlds, Other Maps: Mapping the Unintended City'. In *An Atlas of Radical Cartography*, edited by Lize Mogel and Alexis Bhagat. Los Angeles: Journal of Aesthetics and Protest Press, 2008.

_____. 'The Unintended City' Life and Living Seminar 200 (April 1976). http://www.india-seminar.com/2001/500/500%20jai%20sen.htm.

Sharif, Yara. 'Searching for Spaces of Possibility within the Palestinian/Israeli Conflict'. University of Westminster, 2012.

_____. 'Spaces of Possibility'. *Lines of Flight Research Group*, 11. http://linesofflight.wordpress.com/2009/01/19/seminar-10-spaces-of-possibility/.

Solnit, Rebecca. *Wanderlust: A History of Walking*. London: Verso, 2002.

Spink, John, and D.W. Moodie. *Eskimo Maps from the Canadian Eastern Arctic*. Vol. 5. Toronto: York University Press, 1972.

Stalker. 'Stalker: Laboratorio d'Arte Urbana', n.d. http://digilander.libero.it/stalkerlab/tarkowsky/tarko.html.

Weizman, Eyal. *Hollow Land: Israel's Architecture of Occupation*. London: Verso, 2007.

# 8

# Diasporic Diagrams

The new agency of maps discussed earlier in this section as the practice of 'mapping otherwise', is here developed as a tool for the representation of diasporic agencies. This way of mapping borrows techniques from these other practices but also adds to them with theoretical insights of the potentialities of diasporic space. The mappings are carried out in a variety of spaces and address questions related to spatial inhabitation and its relation to subjectivity, temporalities and difference. These occur at different scales from the public to the semi-private to mental spaces. The topics identified earlier, 'trans-localities', 'borders', 'territories', 'quasi-subjects' and 'topological spaces' are mapped in an embodied spatial practice that valorises the everyday, the bodily and the material in an attempt to represent diasporic agencies. Such a practice of mapping creates 'diasporic diagrams' that are a way of uncovering narratives, making relations and actuating potentialities. This unique ability of maps to create relational ecologies that work across the real and enfold different spatio-temporalities means that they became an integral part of my methodology of spatial research. This section relates how and why the maps were created, including the specific methods used.

## TYPES OF MAPS

### Digital Mappings of Topological Connections

One of the central questions for mapping diasporic spatio-temporalities is how to engage the multiplicity inherent within it.[1] As described in the chapter, *Difference and Belonging*, it requires a change in the way space is understood in order to move beyond Euclidean notions to a move that Deleuze and Guattari have described as the transition from 'the multiple to multiplicity'.[2] Here the two properties conflated in Euclidean mathematics, order and value, are brought together in relation to each other as described by sociologist, Celia Lury:

> *In the topological thinking of multiplicity, however, ordering and value are brought together without reference to an external measure, but rather by – or in – relations in which the performative capacities of number to order and value are locally combined in different ways to produce spaces more general than those described by Euclid.*[3]

It is this move to more general spaces that is of importance in the attempt to map space topologically and to understand the consequences of thinking and representing multiplicity in architectural and urban practice. Here space is n-dimensional and inherently performative; it is the co-production of space-time that privileges difference and is the socialised space of the Aborigines or the lived space of Lefebvre. Topological relations are represented in all the maps related in this chapter but two sets use digital techniques to make these connections explicit; they have been produced in close collaboration with computational designer, Phillip Langley.[4]

Firstly, the mapping of diasporic territories as spheres and spatial envelopes uses a series of walks as input in order to represent the fluctuating territories of different people as manifold, lived and performed, whilst attempting to foreground the relational nature of this type of space. Here we were concerned with how to represent the complexity of such a space without losing the inherent subjective, social and political qualities of the original walks – put simply, how to map using the powerful capabilities of the computer without the limitations in representation that often come with this tool? In the second example, a similar approach was applied to the mapping of the *kahve*, this time our aim was to map each of these individual spaces in relation to each other, to try to represent what was essential in constituting them as important nodes within the construction of a diasporic home. Of all the networks in which the *kahve* operated and which constituted it as place, which were the most important and what relationships did they have with each other? Again the notion of space as being produced through rituals, habits and gestures, was the basis from which we carried out our mappings.

## Interpretative Mappings of Relations, Symbols and Spaces

A second set of maps is concerned with representing trans-local practices, where certain spaces or situations (in this case the *kahve*) are represented through an interpretation of the relations and symbolic meanings they hold. The aim is to reveal how city-space is transformed through diasporic inhabitations. The first map is based around the naming of the *kahve* and describes the reterritorialisations of the street by its displaced diasporic users. These spatial practices produce another geography that remains hidden from those who do not know how to read the signs – the objects, colours and words that relate to allegiances elsewhere in the guise of decorations and graphics.

The second type is the network (loop) maps of individual *kahve* that highlight the ways in which each space functions through representing the various networks that it is a part of. Here space is at first deterritorialised, the shop fronts of Victorian terraces now inhabited very differently from how they were first imagined, and then reterritorialised in an attempt to mimic practices from various regions of Turkey. Both types of maps attempt to represent diasporic agency by interpreting how place in taken through the deployment of symbols and through bodily postures, rituals and gestures.

## Performative Mappings of Gestures and Embodiments

Nearly all the mappings described here were produced using data collected through interviews and walks with various people. These occurred in a performative mode, either through being situated in public, or through consciously using techniques such as drawing as part of the interview process. Particularly in the walks, the body itself acted as a transducer and was used as a means of mapping. Whilst some drawings mapped gestures, others were maps made of gestures. The aim of the mappings in this section was to represent the multiplying borders that are the result of a diasporic inhabitation of space.

The first set of maps was produced in interviews where I asked various people to draw Kurdistan, the act of drawing itself creating a space for the recalling of journeys and the imagining of other possibilities. In these examples the map consists not only of the drawing that was made but also the person's words, their hand that drew, as well as facial or linguistic expressions. These were also ephemeral maps, difficult to represent but they foregrounded the importance of the body in diasporic agency, communicating in its own language the affective dimensions of diasporic subjectivity. The second map relates to the chameleon like Shaheed Minar, changing according to location and enunciated in the mimetic mode – it is an object that stands in for the passions of nation-states, for the failures of them and for the segue into language. Here language is made of words, but also of practices and gestures that are all modes of performative mapping.

## MAPPING DIASPORIC TERRITORIES

I have previously described the production of diasporic space using the concept of dispersed and overlapping territories that cause topological deformations to the actual lived space. This deformation refers to the way in which space, subjectivity and politics influence each other and are co-produced, foregrounding issues of difference and belonging. Each person's inhabitation of space opens up moments of agency and affect in city-space. Here I experiment with ways to represent these deformations through focusing on the micro-scale and the everyday. The mappings foreground an understanding of the production of diasporic space as a process of reterritorialisation and deterritorialisation that occurs through our bodily practices in the local space of a city. In this section I discuss how these can be mapped in a dynamic manner that foregrounds the importance of the body in producing territories and actuating potentialities. Thus, the mapping starts at the level of bodily detail using various techniques, including photographing, conversations, walking, and then finally using computational methods to map the topological relations of and between the territories that emerge in these practices. In doing this, the aim is to keep the poetic and political dimensions of the original walks and conversations – to try not to lose their subjective qualities. In the desire to think territories as both political *and* biological I used the everyday practice of 'walking with' as a method because reality is never the same for two people and the street on which I walk is very different from the one others may walk and experience. Both the act of walking itself, and its later mapping and analysis, were a way of trying to discover how the reality of a space that I was highly familiar with differed from person-to-person.

The walks occurred along a single stretch of road, Stoke Newington High Street/Kingsland Road, in the London Borough of Hackney, which is situated in the north-east of inner London. At the time, the street was the site of regular protests by Kurdish groups in the area, thus walking on this particular street was already a highly charged activity, being used regularly to mark out and traverse territories. The southern tip of the borough sits adjacent to the City of London with private development encroaching northwards. The street in question runs north-south and extends from Stoke Newington to Dalston, areas where recent gated developments sit next to large social housing estates. The project ran from summer 2007 to the end of 2008, a particularly intense moment in the transition of the area where significant development was underway, including the demolition of prominent existing buildings and the construction of new residential towers, as well as new transport infrastructure related to the London Olympics of 2012.

Such private/public regeneration is accompanied with the production of many maps, such as development plans indicating opportunities, constraints, zones and phases. These maps represent a bureaucratic exercise intended to create a formal record of a process rather than encouraging a situation in which dialogue and participation are possible. They do not describe an urban condition at that particular moment nor an idealised situation in the future that could be realised, instead they are merely a pre-determined stage in the process of regeneration. These maps are linked to the requirement for participation and user consultation in the planning process. Although opinions are sought and questions asked, in the end the limited nature of the choices and what is highlighted and enframed, leaves no room for any real discussion or conflict – the outcome is predetermined and the maps record a process in order to meet the obligation to participate. It is within this context that the mappings described here proposed as an alternative tool that would be more situated in the local context, rather than generically applied to it.

Mapping can also be a continual, cyclical practice that does not occur simply to legitimise development but instead is a critical practice that questions easily held assumptions regarding the use and value of city-space. At that moment, hard-won communal spaces, whether in the form of the semi-private *kahve* or the community centres set-up in disused buildings, were being pushed out as the area became more desirable. For example, Halkevi, an important Kurdish and Turkish community centre, occupying part of the ground floor of a building on Stoke Newington High Street, was forced out of its premises through large-scale

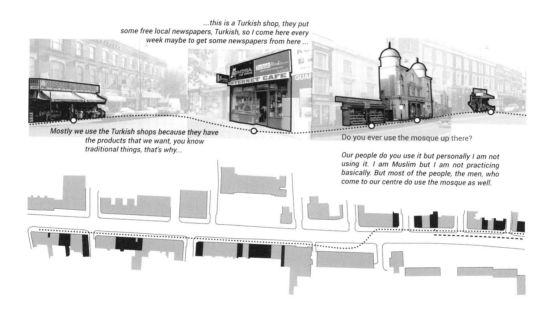

A walk with a Kurdish woman involved in organising the frequent protests on the high street, 2007

So the posters you have seem to be all in Turkish?

*Some of them are in English. For the important day, for example for May Day, we do it in English as well.*

I am also interested in the protest that happens on this street ... Is that something that you are involved in?

*Yes, some of them, for example there was a hunger strike in Turkey, in Turkish prisons, political prisoners were doing it because of the condition of the prisons. It was very bad, still very bad, so they do hunger strike for about seven years, one hundred and twenty-two people have lost their lives. So to protest this massacre and to make people aware what's happening in Turkey, you know and to take attention from the government, so we were doing peace demonstrations here, just from the centre to the graveyard - there is a cemetery.*

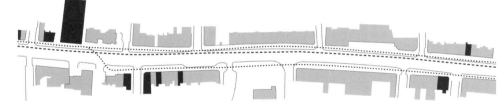

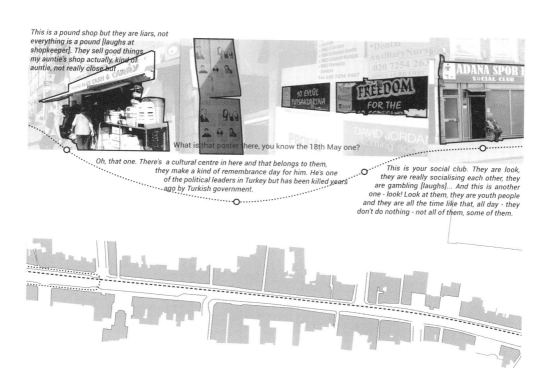

This is a pound shop but they are liars, not everything is a pound [laughs at shopkeeper]. They sell good things my auntie's shop actually, kind of auntie, not really close but...

What is that poster there, you know the 18th May one?

Oh, that one. There's a cultural centre in here and that belongs to them, they make a kind of remembrance day for him. He's one of the political leaders in Turkey but has been killed years ago by Turkish government.

This is your social club. They are look, they are really socialising each other, they are gambling [laughs]... And this is another one - look! Look at them, they are youth people and they are all the time like that, all day - they don't do nothing - not all of them, some of them.

rent increases and the building itself converted to expensive loft-style apartments, while the ground floor was let to a fashion retailer. The type of walking and mapping practice that is described here is therefore a political act that seeks to valorise the neglected and overlooked narratives of the city and is conceived in opposition to the developmental maps described above. These maps could become tools to be used within an alternative and participatory planning process.

## New Tools for Mapping Diasporic Space

The diasporic subject is by condition political, both due to past events and present realities, and any mapping of diasporic territory therefore needs to engage with the ways in which the geopolitical realities of other places are inscribed on to the bodily practices of those in the diaspora. Using 'walking-with' as a technique allowed a privileging of the personal *and* the political, conceptualising this inhabitation of the space of a street as a way of mapping micro-territories that form, dissolve and overlap around us all, influenced by our specific circumstances and spatial politics. They can be considered as a kind of field or sphere of influence, overlapping, constricting and merging as we encounter different people and places. These fluctuating diasporic territories were mapped by carrying out walks with people who had differing, sometimes highly opposing political views. The juxtaposition and overlaying of these walks produced a representation of diasporic territory that was also a way of taking what were highly individual points-of-view (the mapping of personal territories) and representing them collectively through mapping affiliative or political territories. Whilst walking I carried out informal interviews along the individualised trajectories of those I walked with and we spoke together about the neighbourhood, in particular about the street, exchanging experiences about the different places we frequented and the people we knew (see pp. 151–3). The walks were therefore performative, acted out within the public space of the street, and any representation of them needed to convey their spatial, durational and experiential logic. Such a mapping technique also gave importance to small-scale details and events, mixing this close looking with specific architectural strategies, including computational methods. The question of technology is also of interest here – how is it possible to use new technologies without fetishising the technique and without losing the poetic and personalised quality of a method of working that privileges the subjective and the narrational. The use of computational methods was also an attempt to transform walking, which is viewed within a certain tradition as an artistic practice, into a specific architectural tool that could be reused in another setting.[5] Such techniques allow for a level of generality and repetition to be inserted into what is a highly subjective process. Here the mappings can also be thought of as new ways of imagining the city and its spaces through foregrounding the conflictual nature of city–space.

Proposed as both a methodology and a resource, the maps are intended to contribute to an open, web-based archive where simple bits of information can be added and readily translated into territorial maps. Made in collaboration with a computational designer the software for the maps was scripted in the open source platform *Processing*.[6] Currently, it is at the level of an interface for exploring the territories as visualisations and as a means of reconnecting these abstracted representations back into the context of the street. The photographic elevations at the top and bottom of the screen act as a navigational device allowing the user to explore the territorial maps in section (see p. 156 and p. 164).[7] We were interested in creating a mapping tool where the architect or designer was no longer essential to the process of mapping. This acceding of the responsibility for mapping to others has the potential to allow for a long-term and participatory mapping process to occur.

## Neural Territories

A practice that consisted of the collective mapping of diasporic space through emphasising the relations between different people's territories, and the way in which they affected each other, required a shift in our thinking: from the Euclidean space of normative architectural practice to a different kind of space, one that is heterogeneous, multiple and communicative.[8] Starting in Euclidean space, a representation of the street as a standard map, our walking practice provided spatial inputs: 'what shop do you use, which cafe do you go to?' In addition, this simple information was enriched with time – 'when do you use that shop, when do you go for coffee?' This small step of adding temporal information to spatial location already moved us beyond the Euclidean. However, the question here is not simply about how to map four-dimensional information, instead the dimension of time implies an overlapping and intersecting of spatial occupancy and appropriation. In order to map the fluctuations of someone's territory, we needed to move away from ideas around three-dimensional or even four-dimensional systems, and into a relational or topological space. This can be understood as the removal of Euclidean metrics so that instances are no longer defined through orders of magnitude (1, 2, 3 …) but are replaced by relations (convergence, continuity, connectedness …). The map no longer simply indicates which shop someone went to and when, instead it starts to show a field of influence, including how certain events or the presence and absence of certain people and places changes the mapped territory. In this sense, the mappings move into a topological space of possibilities and the mapping tool becomes propositional. The need to map in this way is demonstrated by how certain places on the street are important and have their own field of influence that affect some people but not others. For example in one of the walks, a young Turkish man commented that he did not like to walk past a particular community centre as he thought that the Turkish secret police were operating there. In another walk with a Kurdish woman, the mosque was a place to go into only on certain specified days. It was therefore clear that both these places and various others had an influence on people's behaviour and they not only acted independently but also influenced each other.

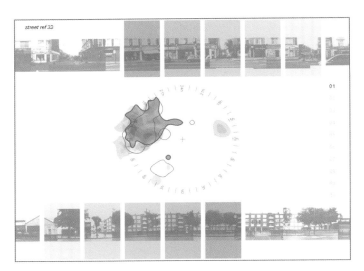

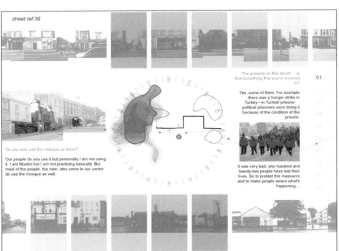
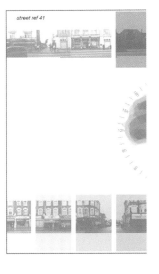

Screenshots of a walk viewed in the web interface designed to explore each walk in section.
The elevations at the top and bottom are used for navigation
*Source:* Nishat Awan and Phil Langley, 2009. To view the interactive version see: www.openkhana.net.

01

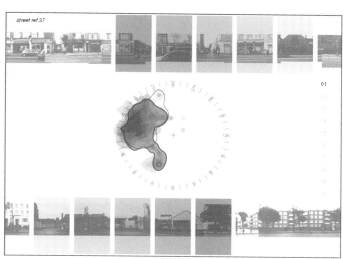

*street ref 37*

01

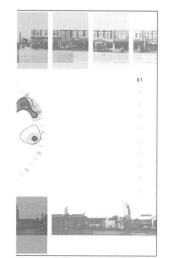

01

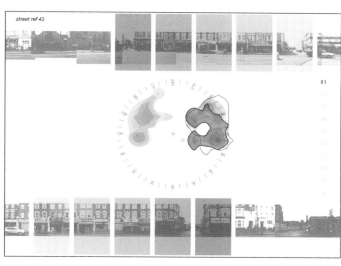

*street ref 43*

01

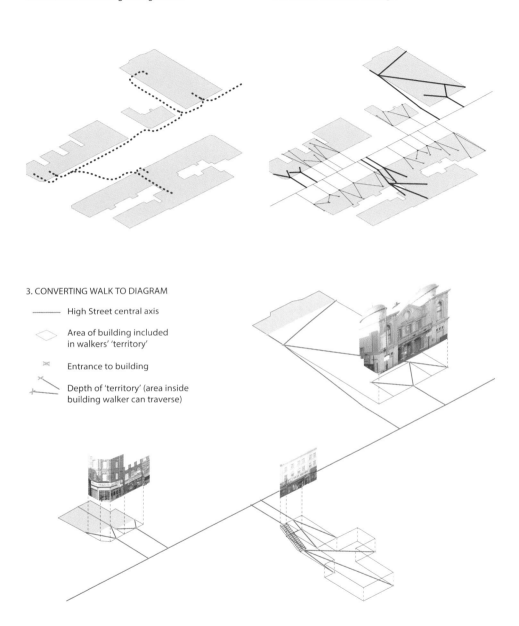

1. PHYSICAL TRAJECTORY OF WALK
I asked people from different cultural backgrounds to take me for a walk along the high street

2. ENCODING OF PHYSICAL SPACE
Calcualted according to the entrance of each building and how far inside we could go

3. CONVERTING WALK TO DIAGRAM

———— High Street central axis

◇ Area of building included in walkers' 'territory'

✕ Entrance to building

✕ Depth of 'territory' (area inside building walker can traverse)

Mapping the walks as territory, 2007

## 4. SPATIAL AND TEMPORAL REPRESENTATION OF THE TERRITORY

A volume is created through an approximation of the points generated through the walk, creating a three dimensional representation of the territory

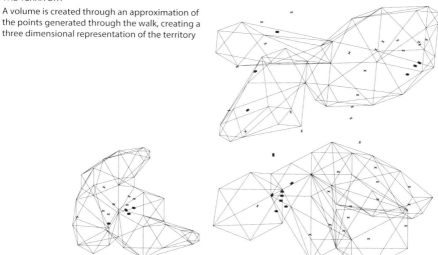

## 4. ENCODING OF TIME

Each arm is rotated according to the time the walker goes there. A semi-circular rotation represents 24 hours, therefore each semi-circle represents one side of the high street

..... Original position according to plan

—— Position following rotation

▓ Area indicating time spent

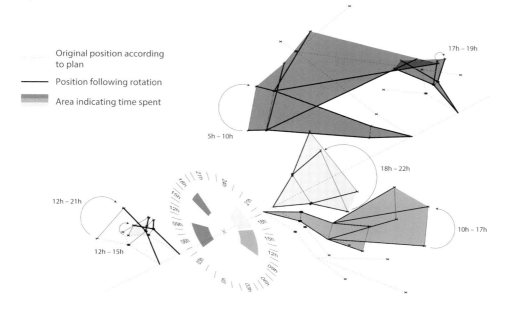

In order to create a map that is able to respond in such ways to people, places and events, we used the technique of Artificial Neural Networks [ANN]. ANNs are mathematical models inspired by the structure and functional aspects of biological neural networks, where the transmission of information through synapses and neurons in the brain is represented by nodes and connections within a computational system that is able to process inputs and create outputs. Usually such programmes are used to model complex relationships and patterns in datasets, typically being used for classification, for example in face recognition software. There are a range of different types of neural networks that vary in topological organisation, and consequently in the transmission of data. For this project, a specific ANN was developed derived from the Self Organising Map (SOM), a type of ANN that is typically a two-dimensional map of $n$- dimensional inputs.[9] In cognitive and computational science the SOM is used as a tool for categorisation; a simple example of its use would be for determining a colour range as RGB values. The basic algorithmic principle consists of two stages, training and calibration. The first stage involves the training of the network with a limited range of inputs (in this case sample RGB values). The second, calibration, is carried out through the classification of further, discrete input data into the trained map, for example by using further RGB input values and identifying the colour zone into which these are mapped.

Before describing this mapping further, it is important to relate why we chose to use such a highly complex technique, which also relates to a cautionary point about the use of algorithmic techniques in understanding social phenomenon. There is a certain fallacy of exactness surrounding the use of computational methods that the ANN addresses, which is borne out of a conflation of precision and accuracy. Whilst standard computational processes are very precise, they are not necessarily accurate since this quality depends on the original input. The ANN is also computationally very precise but the output it produces is quite imprecise or fuzzy – it is, in fact, attempting to map complex but incomplete inputs. In the example above, the SOM was presented with a set of input data, consisting of eight colours described as RGB values. These were interpolated and then re-presented as a generalised output, in order to fill the missing gaps between the original inputs. Therefore, the network created the range of colours in between the discrete set of initial data. Thus, the nature of ANNs is to take precise but incomplete data and to create from it an imprecise but complete output map. It is this quality of ANNs that is crucial to our mapping, and which we sought to develop.

Whilst the network used for the RGB inputs was very simple – a two-dimensional array – the walks required a more sophisticated approach. In the RGB example described above, the SOM has a fixed topology (structure of connection) and a fixed size (number of nodes). For mapping the walks we used a type of growing ANN that could adapt both its size (i.e. it could both grow and shrink) and topology according to the initial inputs.[10] Rather than adopting the typical classification mode of SOMs, we took a different approach, based in the observation that just as in real life the relations between people, objects and spaces are altered as soon as something extra is added or someone else arrives, so the same is also true for a neural network, which is in essence a map of relations. It is solely a representation of the original inputs – there is no field upon which inputs are distributed and therefore there can be no categories, *only* relations. Therefore the advantage of using an ANN did not lie in its ability to produce classifications of data but in its approximations of the missing data through inference. This means that the ANN was able to create a map of topological relationships rather than topographic descriptions.

The ANN was thus developed to create a relational map of each person's walk, the input data being a quasi-spatial-temporal point cloud that was generated from the initial walks and conversations (see p. 159). Through comparing different walks in a relational map, it became possible to analyse the *significance* of difference or similarity, rather than its mere existence. This was due to the sensitivity of the network to even very small changes in the input data meaning that we were able to address the proximate scales of everyday life. Using the walks as input also gave a level of lived accuracy to the original information, which can be contrasted to the technical accuracy of some other mapping systems. Unlike the recent use of technologies such as Global Positioning System (GPS) tracking, this way of gathering information is grounded in actual experience. Most GPS systems map to a 1.5m–2m accuracy and in the space of a street, for example in London where Victorian pavements are generally two meters wide, it is the difference between being inside or outside. The politics and poetics of those two meters is what the walks have attempted to map. At the same time, to walk with someone is to spend time with them, which could also be considered an ethical choice. Whereas the use of GPS, a military technology, keeps a distance and brings back the detached perspective of the traditional cartographer. But this is not a rejection of the technological merely a desire for a more critical use of it. The mapping of diasporic territories used technological means as a way of layering and over-coding narrative, data and interviews for a representational style that allowed a topic or an issue to be addressed from multiple perspectives. The aim was to represent the walks in a way that did not flatten them, but that instead opened up points of access and possibility as different maps were overlaid to allow a tracing of trajectories from one person's territory to another. The tracing, understanding and multiplication of these diasporic agencies described as spatial deformations was central to the purpose of the maps, which attempted to transcend simple descriptions of physical space in order to describe the complex processes that produce diasporic agencies.

## Mapping Diasporic Territories as Topological Deformations of Space

In this attempt at mapping diasporic space I have privileged the method of 'walking with', using it as a tool for the corporeal mapping of a diasporic inhabitation of space. The maps describe topological deformations to the actual lived space of the street through how we affect and are affected by our surroundings, our politics, our subjectivity. These deformations were mapped spatially and temporally using computational methods that allowed a move beyond the conventions of traditional architectural representation that is restricted to the Euclidean space described by the x-, y- and z-axes. The use of ANNs allowed a switch to a type of representation that rather than mapping instances, mapped relations, overlaps and intensities, by allowing the territories of different people at different times to communicate and to connect topologically according to their particular spatial politics.

In addition, the developmental context in which these maps were produced, and in opposition to which I have tried to create an alternative planning tool, demanded a form of representation that could somehow mediate between the representational space of local government plans and the lived, actual space of the walks. They needed to bring these everyday and often marginal experiences to the planning table as equally legitimate and as having their own authority. The eventual aim of relinquishing control over the mapping process through a web-based application in development, allows a shifting of agency from the professionalised space of architects and developers to that of the engaged user.

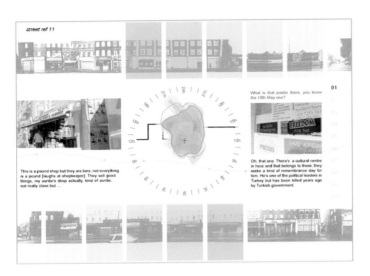

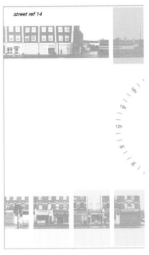

Screenshots of a walk viewed in the web interface designed to explore each walk in section.
The elevations at the top and bottom are used for navigation
*Source:* Nishat Awan and Phil Langley, 2009. To view the interactive version see: www.openkhana.net.

01

*street ref 17*

01

01

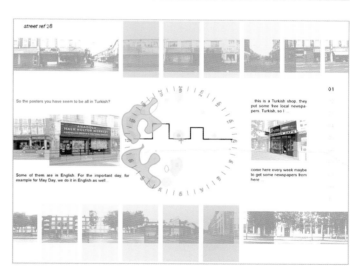

*street ref 28*

So the posters you have seem to be all in Turkish?

Some of them are in English. For the important day, for example for May Day, we do it in English as well.

this is a Turkish shop, they put some free local newspapers. Turkish, so I

come here every week maybe to get some newspapers from here

01

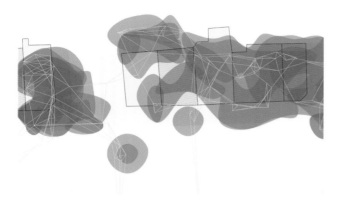

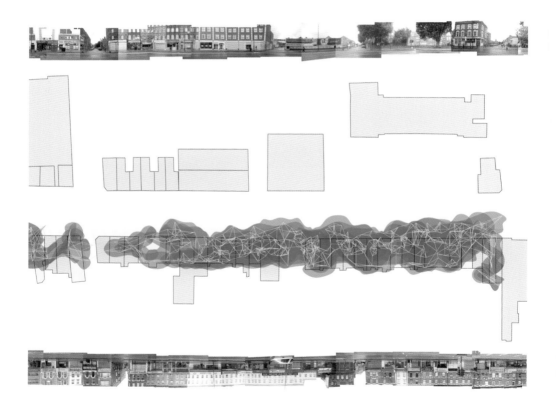

*Bottom*: The walk represented using an ANN that traces the use and occupation of the street as intensities and rhythms, 2009; *Top Left*: Detail
*Source:* Nishat Awan and Phil Langley, 2009.

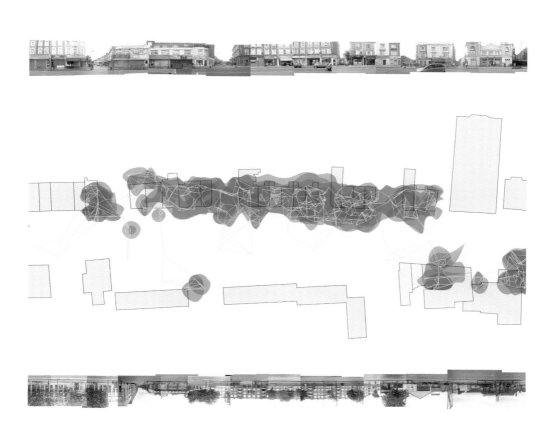

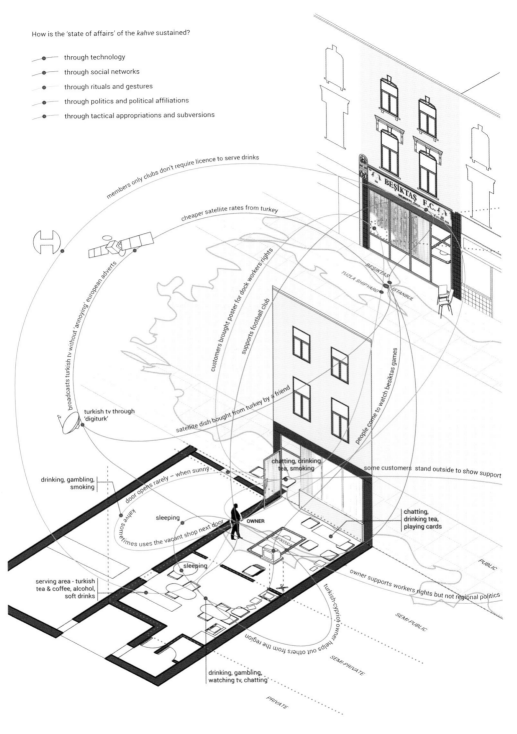

How is the 'state of affairs' of the *kahve* sustained?

- through technology
- through social networks
- through rituals and gestures
- through politics and political affiliations
- through tactical appropriations and subversions

members only clubs don't require licence to serve drinks

cheaper satellite rates from turkey

broadcasts turkish tv without 'annoying' european adverts

customers brought poster for dock workers rights

supports football club

BEŞİKTAŞ

TUZLA SHIPYARD

BEŞİKTAŞ ISTANBUL

people come to watch beşiktaş games

turkish tv through 'digiturk'

satellite dish bought from turkey by a friend

chatting, drinking tea, smoking

some customers stand outside to show support

drinking, gambling, smoking

door opens rarely – when sunny

kahve sometimes uses the vacant shop next door

sleeping

OWNER

chatting, drinking tea, playing cards

PUBLIC

sleeping

serving area - turkish tea & coffee, alcohol, soft drinks

owner supports workers rights but not regional politics

turkish-cypriot owner helps out others from the region

SEMI-PUBLIC

SEMI-PRIVATE

drinking, gambling, watching tv, chatting

PRIVATE

*Kahve* network map of Beşiktas, 2008

BEŞİKTAŞ F.C.

protests by kurdish groups against
events in turkey

**Beşiktas** is named after an Istanbul football team that the owner supports but the customers are mostly Turkish-Cypriots and are older first generation migrants. It carries out the normal functions associated with *kahve* but there was a sense that it was an overtly political place where the '*kahve* talk' revolved more around politics than sports.

**atmospheric**
scale of interaction [y-axis]
**semi-transparent screening**
visibility [x-axis]
**continuous**
temporality [size of sphere]

**technology**

**Yusuf's Place (or Upstairs of Pub)** is located adjacent to a popular pub on the high street. It is a spacious family oriented *kahve* with a welcoming feel. Due to its location over the pub, it is one of the few place where 'foreigners' also come but only to watch popular football matches when the pub is too full or is not showing a particular game.

**territorial**
scale of interaction [y-axis]
**solid screen**
visibility [x-axis]
**regular**
temporality [size of sphere]

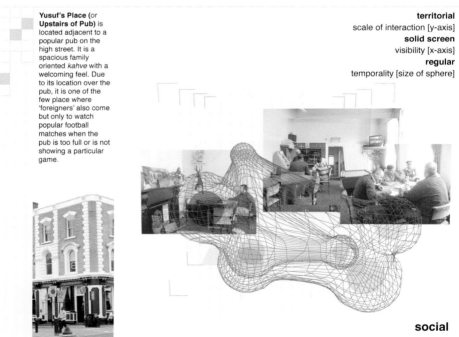

**social**

Web interface for navigating the networks operating within the *kahve*
*Source:* Nishat Awan and Phil Langley, 2009. To view the interactive version see: www.openkhana.net.

The *kahve* in
**Gülensu** is located in
a gecekondu
neighbourhood of
Istanbul that has a
strong tradition of
local activism since
the 1970s and at the
time was mobilising
against attempts to
evict residents for
development
purposes. The *kahve*
is an important node
in the neighbourhood
for discussing the
fractious local politics.

**local**
scale of interaction [y-axis]
**fully visible**
visibility [x-axis]
**continuous**
temporality [size of sphere]

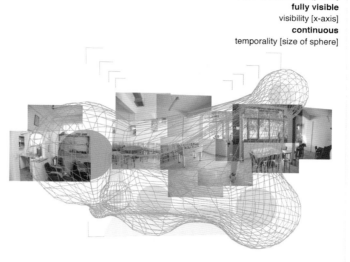

**political affiliation**

**Guben** is located on
a side street just off
the high street and is
a *kahve* with a young
clientele. It takes its
name from the
internet café that
occupied the
premises before it
and although
established for a
number of years it
has not been
renamed.

**territorial**
scale of interaction [y-axis]
**semi-transparent screening**
visibility [x-axis]
**regular**
temporality [size of sphere]

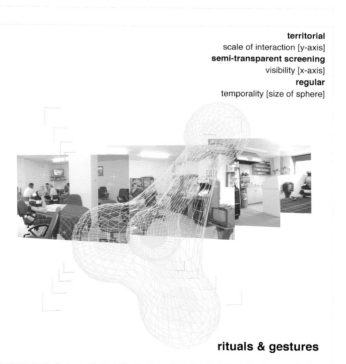

**rituals & gestures**

## MAPPING TRANS-LOCAL PRACTICES

From a mapping of walks on the high street, I now turn to mapping the *kahve* on and around the same street. These mappings are two-fold, first I mapped the actual physical locations of the *kahve* on the street and then I mapped the interiors of these spaces. The map of the various *kahve* on the high street is certainly not definitive and is out-of-date already. It attempts to represent an other geography overlaid onto the physical space of the street (see pp. 68–9). This map uses the most conventionally architectural mapping techniques: a visual survey of the buildings and the marking out of them onto a standard ordinance survey. What is unusual about the map is its content, where the standard information is layered with an analysis of the names of the *kahve* that describe their affinities to regions in Turkey. This was then overlaid with maps of Turkey that are deformed according to the affinities of each *kahve*. It is a mapping of how the street could be read by someone who knows the geo-political situation of the area and for whom the politics of that region are a lived and felt reality. It is another way of representing the reterritorialisation of the street through diasporic inhabitations, and specifically the effect of multiplying borders that is produced in the everyday comings and goings of diasporic subjects.

### Mapping *Kahve* Space as the Servicing of Networks

The mapping of the *kahve* interiors was based on a number of interviews I carried out with the owners and their customers. I wanted to discover how these places functioned as diasporic space through trying to understand what purpose they served in the lives of their users. This type of space has been identified as taking part in a 'fictional urbanism' that Diego Barajas describes as being based, 'on mental but tangible constructions – that [are] manifested in the city as fragments, micro-environments of global circuits, each of which establishes its own identity, time, rules, and aesthetics – its own atmospheres'.[11] What was the atmosphere that the *kahve* strove for and how was it maintained? I had been observing them for a while and I was aware that many of the businesses were short-lived, easily opened and closed, and one of the first casualties of the slowly encroaching gentrification that was moving northwards along the high street from the City of London. I had already attempted to trace a pattern of dispersal of the *kahve*, a mapping of location and regional allegiance signalled through a naming practice, I now wanted to go inside and discover what type of space these unassuming façades hid – a space that was undoubtedly traditional but one that held the promise of another more contemporary space.

It was difficult for me to gain access to the *kahve* as they are places for Turkish or Kurdish men only. Not only was gender a barrier but also language, because most *kahve* are opened by people who cannot speak English and therefore have difficulty finding jobs. I visited the *kahve* with a Turkish man who was a regular visitor to many of them and was happy to act as my guide. We went to a number of places together and I realised that even after what I thought was a thorough and intensive mapping of *kahve* locations I had missed many. Occupying first floors of buildings, hidden behind façades that claimed a different function, they were easy to miss. I had prepared a number of questions for the interviews that were practical in nature such as: 'when did the *kahve* open; who were their customers; which products and objects were essential to have or to serve; whether it was a good business to be involved in; how were the decorations and furniture chosen; and whether the *kahve* were modelled after those in Turkey etc..' The idea was to gain an understanding of how these places functioned and to find out what was essential in transforming what was usually a drab and nondescript interior into a *kahve*.

Alongside the interviews I took photos but this was not always possible. The images are therefore sparse but are added to with my own observations and notes. Using this information, I later drew maps that tried to show both the spatial configuration of the *kahve* and also their organisational structure. I paid particular attention to the networks within which theses spaces operated, the ways in which they maintained connections to Turkey and how they involved themselves (if at all) in regional politics. The maps reveal that while the networks cross long distances and have an air of ephemerality about them, they are actually embedded in very particular physical locations, in certain objects, and in certain practices. The combination of these highly material and located practices with the deterritorialised condition of migration constituted the *kahve* as place.

The networks were grouped in order to answer the question: How is the 'state of affairs' of the *kahve* sustained?[12] There were a number of different types of networks and in the maps these were colour-coded according to their function. The first type of network, *technology*, was perhaps the most obvious. In the diaspora technology is used to maintain connections and relations across large distances and in the specific case of the *kahve* this technology took the form of satellite dishes and mobile phones that were able to transmit images, messages and voices from another place. The majority of the *kahve* had satellite television, especially through the provider 'DigiTurk', which was popular with younger audiences as it screened football matches and music videos. But this technology was also made immediately material for me through the observation that most of the satellite dishes were not bought in the UK but in Turkey. This meant cheaper rental as they were charged at the Turkish tariff, and crucially for many I spoke to, they received advertisements from Turkey rather than from Germany. 'It is much better and makes you feel as if you are still at home and the Turkish accent is right too.'[13] This alerted me to another type of network that dealt with *tactics of appropriation and subversion*. The purchase of the satellite dish subverted certain laws while the status of the *kahve* as member's only clubs meant that they could operate under different regulations to a standard café. Appropriation of space also seemed common with a slow encroachment onto the pavement or into adjoining shops, where clandestine activity such as illegal gambling or the provision of a hostel of sorts could take place. There were also other more subtle networks at work, such as *social networks* that were the main source of custom for the *kahve*, and others that were maintained primarily through *rituals and gestures*. These could be seen in the use of the samovar for tea, a certain way of pouring it, the playing of particular card games, the relation of the games to the drinking of tea etc. The enactment of these gestures connects the *kahve* to another place, and their mapping needed to keep some of their performative quality that actively created these links. Through observation and encounters I came to know well these bodily movements and they informed the maps that I have produced. Finally, there were *political networks* of solidarity and conflict that played a great part in determining who could be a customer and who could not. Some *kahve* were more overtly political than others but they all seemed to be involved in the politics of the region in one way or another. Some places were exclusively Kurdish others were for Turks only, whilst one was self-consciously apolitical, its owner having banned such talk from his premises.

In the chapter, *Trans-Local Practices*, I write of the *kahve* as a place where the bodily production of locality occurs through its positioning within a trans-local network that is serviced through regular and material work. How could this production of locality within the *kahve* space be mapped? My mappings have been influenced by those produced by Atelier d'Architecture Autogérée, where they represent networks that can at times feel intangible and ephemeral by paying close attention to the very precise physical locations in which they operate.[14] This mapping technique reveals the importance of the way space is organised and its influence on the workings of trans-local networks. Certain spatial interfaces were important in the functioning of the *kahve*, for example the threshold and the manipulation of the layers of screening on the shop, as well as the small strip of pavement in front of the *kahve*, which often acted as a place to meet, chat and observe. In the case of one *kahve*, the shop-front was used to display posters for a discussion they were hosting regarding the worker's struggle at the Tuzla shipyard in Istanbul, making it one node in a network that stretched from the Victorian pavement of London to the industrial edges of Turkey. Through mapping the *kahve* as networks the multiplicity of its space is revealed, as well as the specific ways in which diasporic inhabitations transform a nondescript physical space into a kind of surrogate home through processes of reterritorialisation. These spaces, hidden from the view of the other users of the high street are hubs of diasporic agency and the representations try to show this.

### *Kahve* Talk

The phrase '*kahve* talk' refers to the prominent activity that takes place there; sometimes used derisorily, other times with affection, for some it is the essence of the place. Here I describe some of the *kahve* I visited (including one on the outskirts of Istanbul) and describe the talks we had there.

*Beşiktaş* was one of the 'sports club' type *kahve* I visited (see p. 168). It was a small place on the high street in a typical shop unit that was fairly run-down but serviceable. The owner, a Turkish-Cypriot, told me that it used to be a branch of the Wimpys franchise in the 1970s, then an independent burger bar and finally he decided to open a *kahve* on the same premises. His reason for choosing to open the *kahve* was that it had the advantage of being easy to manage. Although it was

named after an Istanbul football team that the owner supported, the customers were mostly older Turkish-Cypriots who were first-generation migrants.

Different levels of privacy operated within the *kahve* space, from the public nature of the chairs that were placed on the pavement to the area behind the bar and the outdoor space at the back that were completely private. The adjacent shop unit was owned by the same person and since he had not been able to let it for a while, the *kahve* was allowed to spill into this space from time-to-time. I was not allowed inside this part and the roller shutter of that shop unit is rarely opened except on a few warm, sunny days.

Beşiktas carries out the normal social functions associated with *kahve* but there was a sense that it was an overtly political place where the *kahve* talk revolved more around politics than sports. This may well have been due to the owner's own support of worker's rights, which he promoted through advertising and sometimes helping to arrange meetings and talks related to labour movements.

*Kahve* network
map of Yusuf's
Place (or Upstairs
of Pub), 2008

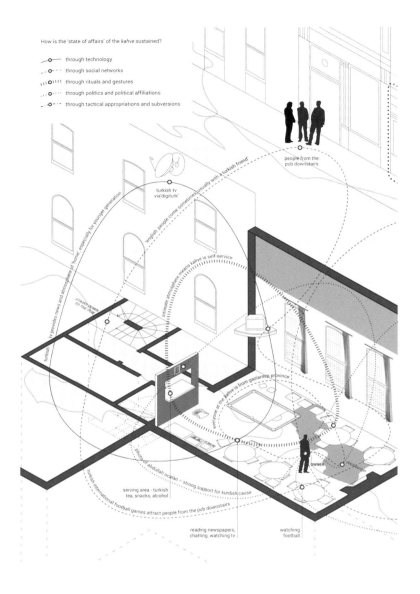

*Yusuf's Place* (or *Upstairs of Pub*) was located next to and above a popular pub
on the high street. It was a spacious family-oriented *kahve* with a welcoming feel.
The current owner had taken over the business from a friend eight years ago.
Everyone seemed to know each other and the owner confirmed that customers
were relatives of relatives, meaning that it was associated with one particular
region of Turkey, Gaziantep in the south-east. Due to its location over the pub,
it was one of the few places where 'foreigners' (that is, people who were not of
Turkish origin) sometimes came, but only to watch popular football matches
when the pub was too full or if it was not showing a particular game.

There was a photograph of Abdullah Ocalan over the serving hatch and there was strong support for the Kurdish cause.[15] Many people from the *kahve* took part in the protest marches or would at least go out on the street to show their support when it passed by. The *kahve* talk revolved as much around regional politics as it did around family politics. The presence of the Turkish samovar, the drinking of tea whilst playing the 101 card game and the reading of newspapers and chatting were all ways of initiating the younger generation into their cultural ways. Most of the people who attended this *kahve* were settled in London with their families and although they were deeply embroiled in the politics of Turkey they generally did not anticipate moving back.

*Kahve* network
map of
Guben, 2008

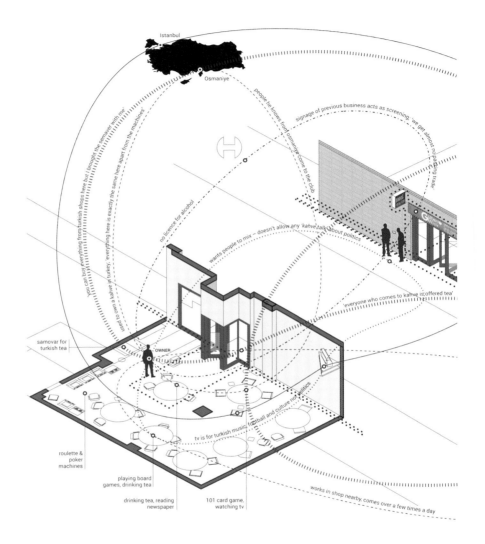

Guben was a *kahve* with a younger clientele, which was located on a side street just off the high street. It took its name from the Internet café that used to occupy the premises before it and although established for a number of years it had not changed its signage. The owner told me that he used to run a *kahve* in Turkey and so decided to set up the same business when he moved to London.

It provided all the usual services and had a relaxed atmosphere, allowing customers to make their own tea and serve themselves snacks. The owner stated

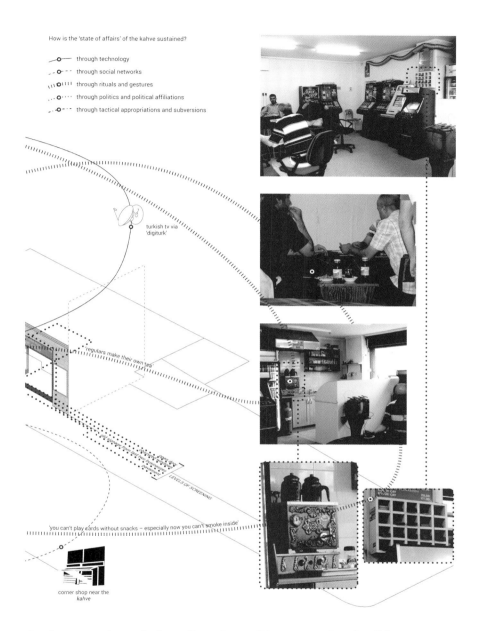

How is the 'state of affairs' of the kahve sustained?

—o— through technology

- o - - through social networks

ıııoıııı through rituals and gestures

...o···· through politics and political affiliations

.-o--- through tactical appropriations and subversions

turkish tv via 'digiturk'

'regulars make their own tea'

LEVELS OF SCREENING

'you can't play cards without snacks – especially now you can't smoke inside'

corner shop near the *kahve*

that he stopped people from discussing politics too much as he did not want to spoil the atmosphere. He was derisory of '*kahve* talk', which he claimed was idle chit-chat that only started arguments. Although most of the people who come to the *kahve* were from his home province of Osmaniye, he said that he tried to encourage people from all over Turkey to come to his place. His hope was that Guben would become a more cosmopolitan *kahve,* much like those found in parts of Istanbul.

*Kahve* in Gülensu
neighbourhood of
Istanbul, 2009

The *kahve* in *Gülensu* was located in a *gecekondu* neighbourhood of Istanbul, which had a strong tradition of local activism since the 1970s, and at the time I visited was mobilising against attempts by the authorities to evict residents.[16] The *kahve* was one amongst many places in the neighbourhood that acted as hubs for discussing and organising the fractious local politics. Having arrived there after completing my interviews in the *kahve* in London, I was struck by how similar the place looked and felt. But there was one major difference – this *kahve* was not a marginal space, it was deeply embedded in its immediate locality and in fact held a position of considerable power. The men who met there were able to affect local lives and although they were connected to other city-wide or national networks through political mobilisation these were not trans-local networks. There was also one conspicuous absence: the television set whether large or small, in a remote corner or taking pride of place in the London *kahve,* was missing here. There was no need for the constant humming presence that was so important for those other spaces that needed the connection back to Turkey.

## Representing *Kahve* Relationally

Whilst the drawings described above showed the operation of the individual *kahve*, I was also interested in representing them in relation to each other, in a similar way to the mapping of diasporic territories. The navigational tool for exploring the *kahve* space was also developed in collaboration and the idea behind this was to create a way of exploring the different networks of the *kahve* through multiple entry points. Unlike the interface developed for the walks, where there was a pre-determined way of navigating the information, in this instance the navigation was left up to the user.

The *kahve* networks (the loops of the earlier diagrams) are displayed as spheres in a virtual environment that is described according to set criteria (see p. 170). The size of the spheres represents the *temporality of the network* being described. This can range from a spontaneous act or a chance meeting, to intermittent events such as the meeting organised at Beşiktas to discuss the worker's situation at Tuzla shipyard, to regular encounters or actions such as the weekly card-game organised by a group of friends at the Guben *kahve*, to finally those functions of the *kahve* that happen on a regular basis, such as the serving of tea. The y-axis describes the *scale of interaction* of the network, from the intimate scale of face-to-face encounters between people, to local interactions at the neighbourhood level, to territorial connections that could be regional or national in scale and finally, atmospheric interactions that refer to those that are usually mediated through technology or are somehow more global in scale. The x-axis describes the most physical aspect of the networks, their *location and visibility*, from being fully visible in the space of the street or on the *kahve* threshold, to being situated just inside the *kahve* space but visible from the street as views through, to being located behind semi-transparent screening, to finally being completely invisible in a back room or behind some kind of solid screening device. The z-axis describes each of the *individual kahve* so that the networks for each are located in a single plane and can be viewed individually, if desired. Finally, the colours of each of the spheres indicate the network type and correspond to those used in the network drawings described earlier.

The *kahve* diagram can be navigated in a number of different ways, the navigational panel at the side contains three strips of buttons, the first cycles through all the different networks, the second strip corresponds to each of the four *kahve*, and the third to the network types. This last view adds a mesh around networks of the same type, which map a topological space arranged according to the type of network being described. Whilst the mapping of the diasporic territories kept a topographic quality through always being viewed in relation to the street, here the maps are not placed on a physical ground. Since the physical space being described is an interior that is overlaid with other connections, interactions and atmospheres, it seemed more appropriate to create a navigational tool that foregrounded these relations. Panoramic photographs are displayed behind the map to give an idea of the interior space but act as backdrops only.

Finally, the maps are designed to be easy to use and are extendable. Coding the network data according to fairly simple criteria of scales of interaction,

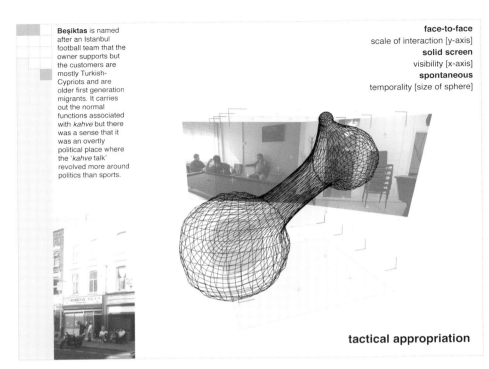

**Beşiktas** is named after an Istanbul football team that the owner supports but the customers are mostly Turkish-Cypriots and are older first generation migrants. It carries out the normal functions associated with *kahve* but there was a sense that it was an overtly political place where the '*kahve* talk' revolved more around politics than sports.

**face-to-face**
scale of interaction [y-axis]
**solid screen**
visibility [x-axis]
**spontaneous**
temporality [size of sphere]

**tactical appropriation**

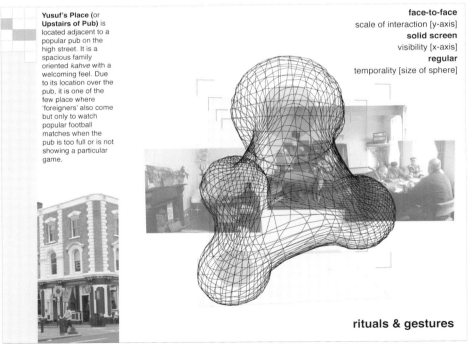

**Yusuf's Place (or Upstairs of Pub)** is located adjacent to a popular pub on the high street. It is a spacious family oriented *kahve* with a welcoming feel. Due to its location over the pub, it is one of the few place where 'foreigners' also come but only to watch popular football matches when the pub is too full or is not showing a particular game.

**face-to-face**
scale of interaction [y-axis]
**solid screen**
visibility [x-axis]
**regular**
temporality [size of sphere]

**rituals & gestures**

Web interface for navigating the networks operating within the *kahve*
*Source:* Nishat Awan and Phil Langley, 2009. To view the interactive version see: www.openkhana.net.

visibility, temporality and type, allows information from casual conversations and interviews to be translated into a representation of the *kahve* space (in this instance, although it could be any number of other spaces) as networked and relational. In comparison to the drawn representations these diagrams were quick to produce and therefore can be added to and amended easily. They could be used to show how the networks operating in the *kahve* may change over time and crucially, they can be used to analyse dynamically rather than in the static fashion of a standard drawing.

## MAPPING MULTIPLYING BORDERS

As I have argued previously, the diasporic space of a city like London is made up of multiplying borders. How to map these dispersed and invisible borders is the central concern of this section. Through interviews, observations and narrative modes I have attempted to create a figuration of Kurdistan in London through its contested borders. A second mapping represents the effects of the replicating Shaheed Minar and its attendant networks on a public park. Whereas in the mapping of the *kahve* space there was an attempt to map gestures, in these examples often it is the gesture itself that is the map.

### Re-Mapping Kurdistan

In the following I attempt to map borders through emphasising the role of diasporic bodies in both producing borders and of being inscribed by them. These mappings and observations attempted to explore how Kurdistan as a figuration emerges in the reterritorialisation of space by the diasporic Turkish and Kurdish community within their local neighbourhood. In order to create a heterogeneous account, I started by conducting a series of interviews with people who had very different social and political backgrounds. I wanted to understand how Kurdistan as an imagined home was constructed in the psyche of the Kurdish people strewn across national borders, but also in the psyche of those who were opposing their desire for an independent Kurdish state. These mappings ask the question of how to map such border struggles without resorting to the dominant narratives of those in power? Where contested borders are not even allowed the ambiguity of dotted lines on official pieces of paper, where the 'line of control' or the 'line of ceasefire' never came to be named as such – how do you map the experience of those whose lives are touched by a phantom line that is always a thick line, a zone, a borderland?[17]

During the interviews I asked people to draw a map of Kurdistan as they saw it in their mind. The conversations together whilst drawing the maps revealed how their experience of urban space in London was also inflected through the way in which they conceptualised Kurdistan, whether as a geographic location, a concept, a hope, a person (for example, Abdullah Ocalan, the PKK leader) or an ideology. Drawing and speaking thus became a tactic for mapping these highly

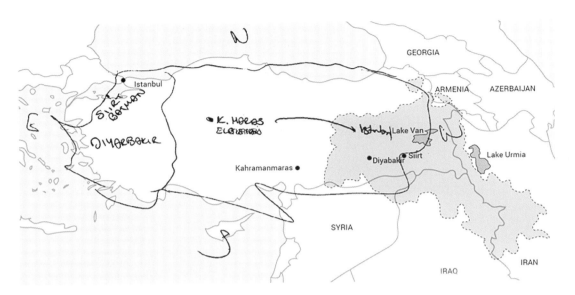

Kurdish woman's map drawn as a personal journey across Turkey, 2007

contentious borders that are inscribed onto the subjectivity of those I spoke to. The maps produced during these sessions varied enormously, both in what they chose to represent and in the way they were drawn. It was a way of creating narratives that are usually hidden by the accounts of those in power, for example until recently the Turkish state refused to recognise a separate Kurdish ethnicity, instead referring to them as 'mountain Turks'. Mapping therefore functioned as a mediatory practice, a ruse for speaking about difficult journeys and personal stories. The gesture of hand-to-paper, which began as a self-conscious, deliberate stroke, slowly became a non-articulated movement, sometimes almost an auto-drawing, tracing maps made of gestures. They explored ways of representing affects, of a person embodying and diffusing the border, of somehow internalising it. They were also a way of exploring broader questions around how feelings of nostalgia, exile and the relationships with the host community affect the construction of a subjective space that could be considered a diasporic home.

For some the drawings were a description of home, for others a journey or a narrative, as the act of drawing provoked stories that augmented the maps. For some the map was drawn following their own journey so that the compass directions changed to follow their path. Where someone chose to start the map was also important. Diana, an Iranian Kurd who worked for a women's rights organisation, was the only person to start her map in the area designated Kurdistan. She had lived in the Kurdish areas of Iran, Iraq and Turkey and said that she felt at home in all of them. For her the continuity of this space was a reality and her map reflected this attitude, the national borders of the surrounding states being just sketched out in the barest of lines, as a quick gesture. Another map tells the story of the invasion of Iraq as described by Derin, a young Turkish waiter who worked in a local café. Here the map is a narrative of politics and promises. For him drawing Kurdistan was almost impossible. The story of the US invasion of Iraq, and what he saw as their complicity in establishing a Kurdish state, was the main topic of concern.

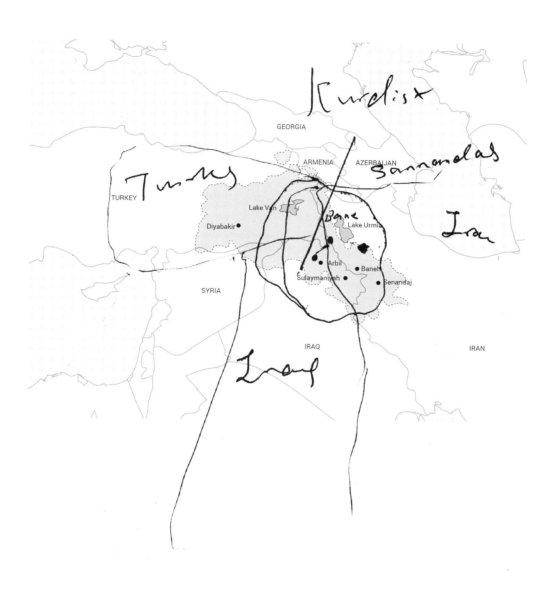

Diana's map was the only one that escaped the dominance of Turkey and showed a contiguous Kurdish territory, 2007

In each of these maps the words are just as important as the drawings. It is the *process* of mapping rather than the final product that is of importance, including the movement of hands and the words spoken. If I had permission, these sessions were recorded on film and some of the mappings include stills from these videos. Whilst the drawings produced could be described as mental mapping they were also a material mapping.[18] The places where we spoke, the props that were used, such as a map of the area brought over by one of the interviewees are all part of the map. In a similar way, the artist Helen Scalway has produced mental maps of the London Underground, asking passengers to draw their own network. Scalway writes that she was interested in 'the personal geographies of Tube travellers whose private copings with city's space might mingle strangely with the authoritative suggestions of official maps'.[19] The maps in these sessions were drawn similarly to those that Scalway describes, but unlike hers which established a dialogue with official maps, in the case of the Kurdistan maps it was exactly the absence of official maps that was being represented. Drawing and speaking together, these maps were mental constructions of what always fails to be represented in the hegemonic accounts of those in power, and so the maps also asked the question: 'does where you are affect what you draw?' In this case it certainly did. Deleuze writes on mapping: 'The trajectory merges not only with the subjectivity of those who travel through a milieu, but also with the subjectivity of the milieu itself, insofar as it is reflected in those who travel through it. The map expresses the identity of the journey and what one journeys through.'[20] In this sense, the maps that were drawn during the interviews superimposed reality with an imagined space so that the mappings were both trajectories of journeys made as well as the varied figurations of Kurdistan that they produced.

Yashar's map – an almost 'perfect' map from someone with a long-term involvement in the Kurdish cause, 2007

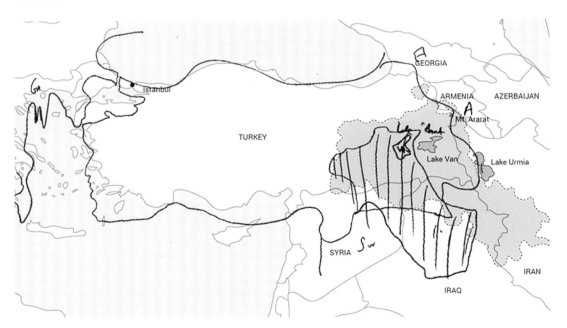

Derin's map – he could only draw Kurdistan as a narrative of the Iraq war, 2007

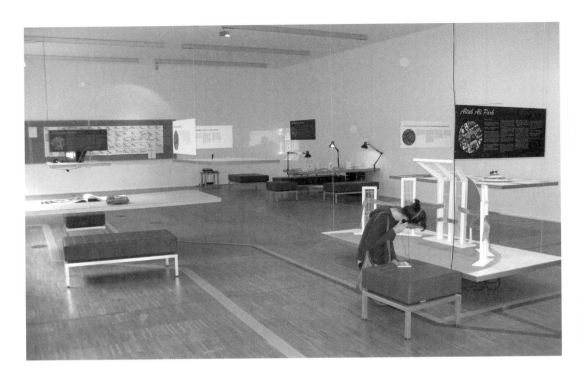

A replica of the Shaheed Minar with extracts from interviews with the Bangladeshi girls on display at the Architektur Forum, Linz, Austria, 2008

## The Shaheed Minar as Map

In some ways the mapping of the Shaheed Minar is the least like a traditional map. For the exhibition that prompted my discussion of the park and the minar, I created a model of the minar, which stood in for a place (the park), while the interviews with the teenage girls around questions of language, subjectivity and borders could also be listened to on headphones.[21] The model of the minar was decorated with ribbons as the original minar in Dhaka, Bangladesh often is on days of celebration. On the ribbons extracts from the girl's conversations were inscribed, written in the script of the language in which they spoke – sometimes in English and sometimes in Sylheti. Together the ensemble could be said to constitute a map, but the map is also formed by the monuments dotted around the globe, wherever there is a Bangladeshi population. Here the Shaheed Minar itself is an allegorical map of the amorphous borders of Bangladesh and in each new location it is different: shiny and bright in Tokyo, made of concrete in a schoolyard in the small town of Ijjatpur in Bangladesh itself. Whereas in London the Minar became a more general symbol of political struggle, in Dhaka on the site of the original monument it is proto-nationalistic. In contrast a minar in the area of Chittagong in Bangladesh has become a place to commemorate the atrocities of a State that turns a blind eye to violence against its ethnic minorities and indigenous groups. Here the laying of flowers is forbidden whilst in Dhaka the monument is continually decorated. The adaptability of the Shaheed Minar, its mimicry of the original monument, adapted and readapted to local conditions makes a powerful diasporic diagram.

## DIASPORIC DIAGRAMS

The maps described in this chapter are 'diasporic diagrams' of the agencies inherent in the particularities of our spatial inhabitations. They are attempts to represent beyond the physical in order to understand how diasporic agency is produced and enacted within urban space. The maps, therefore, attempt to foreground questions of difference and belonging in the city through focusing on ways in which the specificities of a diasporic inhabitation of space can be represented. Their aim is to foreground questions of subjectivity and politics within spatial relations. In this sense, the diagrams represented qualities often left out of traditional maps through operating in the different registers identified in the chapter, *Maps and Agency*. They attempted to be propositional, to create possibilities and to mediate situations. Through representing the relationship between the production of space and subjectivity the diagrams were able to relate the processes through which diasporic agencies are constituted in an urban metropolis like London.

In these diagrams I mapped space at different scales and in different guises. This ranged from the exterior public spaces of a street and a park to the interior trans-local space of the *kahve*. Overlaid on top of these representations were the mental or psychic spaces produced and inhabited by diasporic subjects. I used different ways to map these, from the walks that were represented as spheres and spatial envelopes, to the *kahve* mapped as networks and as topological spaces that were then mapped on top of physical space. Finally, Kurdistan and the Shaheed Minar were mapped as imagined mental spaces and as reterriorialisations of lived space. A common characteristic of all these mappings was their dynamic nature, which not only reflects the unsettled nature of diasporic subjectivity itself, but also highlights the importance of this quality in constituting diasporic agencies.

Different audiences were addressed by these varying representations. Some diagrams were highly specialised and were attempting to intervene in a professional and academic discourse, whilst others were more immediately engaging for the lay viewer. The digital maps in particular were imagined as tools for architects and urbanists to expand their understanding of how space is affected and produced by diasporic subjects. They also attempted to describe the urgent need to represent space beyond the traditional methods of orthographic drawing, which is caught in the restrictions of Euclidean space. As has been described earlier, there is a complexity to the spaces produced through diasporic inhabitation, not least because of the way in which they collapse notions of scale and therefore require novel methods of representation. Whilst the specificities of the diasporic condition prompted these mappings, they are also more general and could be applied in other situations where there is a need to acknowledge the heterogeneity of space, or where there is a desire to represent it through experience.

Digital techniques were chosen over other means of representation due to the complexity of the information. The walks, for example, not only indicated the places that were visited but the times at which they were frequented; in addition what we discussed, that is the conversations we had, also needed to be represented alongside images of the street itself. In the *kahve* the overlapping networks and the way they interacted with each other demanded a mode of representation that would not flatten the information. For both these maps the digital method was also generative, creating new relations between data or highlighting those relations that would not be visible otherwise. A second quality of the digital maps was that they required a collaborative approach in order to engage other expert skills and knowledge, for example those of computational design. My collaboration with architect and computational designer, Phil Langley, was therefore crucial to the digital mappings described in this chapter, and our decision to make all the underlying code for the software freely available online was a way of allowing others to make future iterations and adaptations to suit their own purpose.[22]

The interpretative maps are geared towards a more general audience and are designed to give an overview of each spatial situation. They can be reproduced easily for other spaces and have the ability to be used in participative processes with users and inhabitants. Discussing such maps together transforms a static image into a mediatory tool, facilitating a conversation through bringing up issues and highlighting certain narratives. These maps are useful for describing the important role of symbolic spaces in diasporic lives, spaces that are too often not recognised as such and are therefore not accounted for. The performative maps also function in this way using diverse methods to produce other representations. These maps that started as encounters, conversations and walks needed to be processed in such a way that they could foreground the relationships between subjectivities, politics and spaces. These mappings took standard ethnographic methods and added to them an explicitly spatial dimension.

In producing these diasporic diagrams, I have viewed my mapping practice as inseparable from the understanding of diasporic agencies and their embodied spatial practices. The techniques of representation, or the discovering of diasporic diagrams has been an integral part of the research carried out for this book, being not only the method of research but also the subject of it. Above all, the maps and stories recalled here have been experiments in ways of working that could in the future become constituent part of a 'diasporic urbanism'.

## NOTES

1. This is also the concern of what has been termed the 'topological turn' in social theory. For more on this see, Lury, Parisi, and Terranova, 'Introduction'.

2. Deleuze and Guattari, *A Thousand Plateaus: Capitalism and Schizophrenia*, 3–28.

3. Lury, 'From One to Multiplicity', 80.

4. For more on Langley's work see, Openkhana; www.openkhana.net.

5. For example Careri provides a detailed history of walking and discusses it as a specifically aesthetic practice. See, *Walkscapes: Walking as an Aesthetic Practice*.

6. Processing is an open source programming language and environment initiated by Ben Fry and Casey Reas whilst at MIT Media Lab, see 'Processing.org'. The maps were made in collaboration with Phillip Langley. For more on the computational aspects of these mappings see, Langley, 'Meta Cognitive Mappings: Growing Neural Networks for a Generative Urbanism'.

7. Future iterations of the software will incorporate the scripts that generate the maps themselves, allowing users to directly create and store their own maps.

8. A number of feminist critiques of architecture have also explored ways of 'multiplying' the restricted Euclidean space of normative architectural practice. See for example, Petrescu, *Altering Practices: Feminist Politics and Poetics of Space*; Rendell, *Gender, Space and Architecture*.

9. Kohonen, *Self-Organizing Maps*.

10. The specific type of ANN was a SOM based on the algorithms developed by Teuvo Kohonen. The most common use of ANNs is in algorithms for pattern recognition in images or language. ANNs have been used previously in an architectural context, usually in the mapping of 'real-world' spatial information. For example, the Centre for Evolutionary Computing and Architecture (CECA), based at University of East London, carried out a number of projects. For more information see, Ibid.; Derix, 'Building a Synthetic Cognizer'; Derix and Izaki, 'Empathic Space: The Computation of Human-Centric Architecture'.

11. Barajas, *Dispersion: A Study of Global Mobility and the Dynamics of a Fictional Urbanism*, 1.

12. Here I am referring to Actor-Network Theory. See, Law and Hassard, *Actor-Network Theory and After*; Latour, *Reassembling the Social: An Introduction to Actor-Network Theory*.

13. From an interview with one of the *kahve* owners.

14. Petrescu, 'Relationscapes'.

15. Abdullah Ocalan is the leader of The Kurdistan Worker's Party or *Partiya Karkerên Kurdistan* (PKK) who is currently incarcerated by Turkey. The group was established in 1978 and 'from 1984 to 2013 fought an armed struggle against the Turkish state for cultural and political rights and self-determination for the Kurds in Turkey'. 'Kurdistan Workers' Party'.

16. *Gecekondu* is a Turkish word that refers to informal housing that has been built quickly. In Turkish '*gece* means 'at night' and *kondu* means 'placed' (from the verb *konmak*, 'to settle' or 'to be placed'); thus the term *gecekondu* comes to mean 'placed (built) overnight'. 'Gecekondu.'

17. The term Line of Control (LOC) refers to the military control line between the Indian and Pakistani controlled parts of the former princely state of Jammu and Kashmir – a line which does not constitute a legally recognised international boundary but is the de facto border.

18. Mental maps have been used widely, for example in geography, architecture and in art practice. See for example, Lynch, *The Image of the City*; Harmon, *Personal Geographies and Other Maps of the Imagination*.

19. Scalway, 'Travelling Blind', xvi.

20. 'What Children Say' in, Gilles Deleuze, *Essays Critical and Clinical,* trans. by Michael A. Greco and Danile W. Smith (London: Verso, 1998), p. 61.

21. The exhibition, *Revisit: Urbanism Made in London*, was curated by Peter Arlt and shown at Architekturforum Oberosterreich, Linz (2 February–3 March 2007) and Haus der Architektur, Graz, (19 June–24 July 2008) Austria. See chapter, *Multiplying Borders* for more detail.

22. The scripts used in the mapping of diasporic territories and in the topological representations of the *kahve* space are available at www.openkhana.net.

## REFERENCES

Barajas, Diego. *Dispersion: A Study of Global Mobility and the Dynamics of a Fictional Urbanism*. Rotterdam: episode publishers, 2003.

Careri, Francesco. *Walkscapes: Walking as an Aestheic Practice*. Barcelona: Gustavo Gili, 2003.

Deleuze, Gilles, and Félix Guattari. *A Thousand Plateaus: Capitalism and Schizophrenia*. New York: Continuum, 2004.

Derix, Christian. 'Building a Synthetic Cognizer'. *MIT Design Computational Cognition Conference*, 2004.

Derix, Christian, and Åsmund Izaki. 'Empathic Space: The Computation of Human-Centric Architecture'. *Architectural Design* 84, no. 5 (October 2014).

'Gecekondu'. *Wikipedia, the Free Encyclopedia*, August 13, 2014. http://en.wikipedia.org/w/index.php?title=Gecekondu&oldid=621053555.

Harmon, Katherine. *Personal Geographies and Other Maps of the Imagination*. New York: Princeton Architectural Press, 2004.

Kohonen, Teuvo. *Self-Organizing Maps*. Berlin: Springer, 2001.

'Kurdistan Workers' Party'. *Wikipedia, the Free Encyclopedia*, January 21, 2015. http://en.wikipedia.org/w/index.php?title=Kurdistan_Workers%27_Party&oldid=643436925.

Langley, Phillip. 'Meta Cognitive Mappings: Growing Neural Networks for a Generative Urbanism'. Centre for Evolutionary Computing in Architecture, University of East London, 2007.

Latour, Bruno. *Reassembling the Social: An Introduction to Actor-Network Theory*. Oxford: Oxford University Press, 2005.

Law, John, and John Hassard. *Actor-Network Theory and After*. Oxford: Blackwell, 1999.

Lury, Celia. 'From One to Multiplicity'. In *Cultures of Change: Social Atoms and Electronic Lives*, edited by A. Ascione, C. Massip, and J. Perello, 80–81. Barcelona: Actar, 2009.

Lury, Celia, Luciana Parisi, and Tiziana Terranova. 'Introduction: The Becoming Topological of Culture'. *Theory, Culture & Society* 29, no. 4–5 (July 1, 2012): 3–35. doi:10.1177/0263276412454552.

Lynch, Kevin. *The Image of the City*. Massachusetts: The MIT Press, 1960.

Petrescu, Doina, ed. *Altering Practices: Feminist Politics and Poetics of Space*. London: Routledge, 2007.

_____. 'Relationscapes: Mapping Agencies of Relational Practice in Architecture'. *City, Culture and Society*, Traceable Cities, 3, no. 2 (June 2012): 135–40. doi:10.1016/j.ccs.2012.06.011.

'Processing.org'. Accessed January 15, 2015. https://processing.org/.

Rendell, Jane, ed. *Gender, Space and Architecture*. London: Routledge, 2000.

Scalway, Helen. 'Travelling Blind'. In *City A-Z: Urban Fragments*, edited by Steve Pile and Nigel Thrift. London: Routledge, 2000.

# A Diasporic Urbanism to Come

Nomadic subjects are not quantitative pluralities, but rather qualitative multiplicities. The former is merely a multiple of One – multiplied across an extended space. This is the political economy of global capitalism as a system that generates differences for the purpose of commodifying them. Qualitative multiplicities, however, pertain to an altogether different logic. They express changes not of scale, but of intensity, force, or *potentia* (positive power of expression), which trace patterns of becoming.

Braidotti, *Transpositions: On Nomadic Ethics*, 94.

The space of possibilities does not represent a fixed horizon within which the social location of knowers can be mapped, nor does it represent a homogeneous, fixed, uniform container of choices. Rather, the dynamics of the space-time manifold are iteratively reworked through the inexhaustible liveliness of the manifold's material configuration, that is, the ongoing dance of agency immanent in its material configuration.

Barad, *Meeting the Universe Halfway*, 246.

This book charts my exploration of the spatialities of the diasporic experience and in doing so it sets up the possibility of a 'diasporic urbanism to come'. Whilst much has been written in geography, sociology and anthropology on the subject of diasporas, architecture has remained mostly silent. I started this project with an understanding that a prerequisite for any architectural engagement with diasporas would be an approach that could switch scales – from the intimate to the institutional, from the local to the global, from systems to bodies. What has emerged over the course of writing this book is that this switching of scales is far too binary a way of thinking. It is in the multiplicity inherent within diasporic notions of space and time, what I have chosen to call diasporic spatio-temporalities, that the difficulty of representing and working with diasporas emerges. This is especially true within a discipline that is not only inherently spatial but is also incredibly deterministic. And yet, to engage multiplicity within the practices of architecture and urbanism is not a concern that is limited to diasporas because in many ways the diasporic subject is paradigmatic. The effects of what we have come to call globalisation mean that the other is always already here, and the multiple belongings and hybrid nature of diasporas can also be considered radicalised versions of contemporary subjectivities.

In some ways the two quotes above say all there is to say in this conclusion – that qualitative differences and material configurations are the key to an understanding of diasporic agencies.[1] Qualitative differences for us emerge out of the initial act of displacement that allows for a multiple, dislocated and sometimes disjunctive approach to the world and to time and space. In the chapter, *Difference and Belonging*, I asked how we might include temporal and spatial dislocations within our ways of conceptualising diasporic agencies. Some of what has been included in the Part II (Mapping Otherwise) attempts to do this, for example in the mappings of Kurdistan in London I describe a relation to the city that is inflected through an imagined nation-state that often manages to dislocate the here and the now. But through this dislocation it also creates a mode of diasporic agency that is both able to challenge the hegemony of the nation-state whilst at the same time demanding the state as such. This ambivalence and instability in the ways in which diasporas engage with hegemonic constructs is an important form of diasporic agency.

Material configurations emerge through processes of reterritorialisation that are the key to an inhabitation of space that produces differentiation. In the chapter *Diasporic Inhabitations* I explored how mimicry as inhabitation can allow for an imaginative relating to the radically other and works within an affirmative model of agency based in the notion of free acts. Whilst the critique of space as being much more than a static, timeless backdrop has been well rehearsed in architectural theory as social space, what is perhaps less developed is the relationship with time. This is especially true for the practice of architecture where we lack representational tools that can account for the passing of time. When the linear, clock time of history is replaced by the cyclical, lived time of everyday life, and the folding of time that occurs through diasporic inhabitations, traditional architectural representations become increasingly redundant. One of the most important aspects left unaccounted for is the relationship between these fluctuating spatio-temporalities and the production of subjectivity, a connection that is brought back to architecture through the forgotten place of matter, materiality and the body. The specific inhabitations of space by displaced and dislocated diasporic bodies are therefore crucial to diasporic urbanism.

Spatial figurations were a way of expressing diasporic agencies through lived examples of the diverse ways in which we inhabit the city. Whilst not being completely explicit, I hope that the concerns mapped out in the section *Potentialities of Diasporic Space* have found their echoes here. Whether it is in the trans-local practice of making a diasporic home within sprawling networks of kinship, or in the mediation of a shared present through the proliferation of replicas and imitations, or in the fragile envelopes that we all depend on to negotiate our place in the world. These have all been instances of diasporic agencies that have demanded a different mode of representation that exceeds the constraints of Euclidean space. It requires a different spatial imaginary one that places emphasis not on walls, objects and buildings but on materialised networks, dispersed territories and on multiplying borders. *Mapping Otherwise* was my way of *practicing* spatial (con)figurations. I hope that the images, drawings and code that I have worked with (often in collaboration with others, as is the key to any attempt at representing multiplicities) provide glimpses of what a diasporic urbanism could be. It would be an urbanism that no matter how difficult would insist upon a topological approach, that would deny fixed notions of measure and value, would stubbornly confuse ontology with epistemology and vice versa, and would also know that the movement back and forth across the real is the space of figuration that we as architects and designers inhabit.

I have learned how to do this through the wonderful practices of mapping otherwise that I relate in the chapter, *Representing the Non-Representational*. They gave me diverse ways of working with an abstracted realm that is necessarily about representations to moving towards a non-representational knowing *through* the body. This movement back and forth has emerged as a key modality of working with diasporic agencies. The mapping of diasporic territories perhaps did this in the most explicit way. By going for walks with others on a street that I knew so well and walked on almost everyday, I came to know it differently. Then through drawing that experience collaboratively with someone else in the computational language of code was a move back into the realm of abstraction. This was then re-presented in a mock-up of a web interface that played with the standard architectural representations of sections and elevations to give room to that which architecture never accommodates – inhabitations and the intensities of occupation and use. Finally, in the placing of the stories back into the maps, through adding extracts from our conversations and photos taken whilst we walked, was an attempt to bring back the material and the bodily. This movement is of course also a movement from the topological to the topographic and back again – back and forth, back and forth … It is the making of what I have called *Diasporic Diagrams*, an attempt to show how all of these instances of diasporic agency are embedded within spatialised relations.

So then where exactly does diasporic agency lie? It lies in the indeterminate nature of the mimetic effect. It is also in the disjuncture and dislocation of the diasporic experience. It is in the spaces of figuration that we create, as the teenage Bengali girls that I spoke with about the Shaheed Minar knew only too well. It is in the transposition of images and objects across borders, in the constitutive instability of such movements and the uncertainty in meaning that this brings. The doubled nature of all of these instances that I have described, their often openly ambivalent stance towards standardised notions of belonging should not be considered problematic – this is both the potential and the risk inherent within diasporic agencies. Perhaps I could be accused of only seeing the positive side in this ambivalence and I hope that I have not idealised the diasporic experience. I have attempted to describe the affirmative potential of living between times, spaces and cultures. It is a good place to be. But it is also a place from which, as we can see from countless news stories, all sorts of divisions and conflicts emerge. I have chosen to direct my gaze towards more positive engagements because as someone who is embedded within one of the more 'problematic' diasporas in Europe, I am also tired of forever discussing how we did not integrate, did not speak out, did not condemn, did not say that we are worthy of being here now. This book is for all those who insist on their right to be here now.

## NOTES

1.    Braidotti, *Transpositions: On Nomadic Ethics*, 94; Barad, *Meeting the Universe Halfway*, 246.

## REFERENCES

Barad, Karen. *Meeting the Universe Halfway: Quantum Physics and the Entanglement of Matter and Meaning*. Duke University Press, 2007.

Braidotti, Rosi. *Transpositions: On Nomadic Ethics*. Oxford: Polity Press, 2006.

# Index

Aboriginal space 126, 128, 148
Abrams, Janet 35
Actor-Network Theory; *see* ANT
Adkins, Lisa 22
affect 51, 122, 149, 184
affective
    body 7, 35
    world 142
affiliation 8, 50, 54, 97
affinity
    networks 54, 61, 96, 102–3
    politics of 39
affirmative agency 7, 9, 23, 30, 32–4, 196
Agamben, Giorgio 39, 103
Altab Ali Park 82–3, 87
ambivalence, in subjectivity 4–5, 30,
    196, 198
ANN 160–61, 191n6
ANT 60–61, 83
Appadurai, Arjun 9, 33, 58, 81, 99–100
architecture
    and diasporas 10n2, 195
    discipline of 2–3, 142,
    practice of 35, 95, 133, 191n8, 196
artificial neural network; *see* ANN
Atelier d'Architecture Autogérée (AAA)
    132, 133, 174
The Atlas Group 136–7
atmospheres 7, 11n24, 54–7, 58, 100,
    137, 172, 178–9, 181
Aydemir, Murat 58

Badiou, Alain 23
Bal, Meike 58
Bangladesh 36–7, 82, 84, 86n24, 188; *see*
    *also* Bengali
Barad, Karen 118, 195
Barajas, Diego 172

becoming 2, 4, 15, 18–19, 24–5, 31, 34,
    97, 104, 195
being present 15, 139, 142
belonging
    and inclusion, 7, 15, 23–5
    multiple, 3, 18, 84, 196–7
Bengali 37–8, 82–3, 84, 102, 197; *see*
    *also* Bangladesh
Benjamin, Walter 79, 128
Beşiktaş 55, 168, 174–5, 181
Bhabha, Homi 29–31
Biemann, Ursula 96–7
bio-territory 101–2
bodily practice 2, 39, 93, 97, 104, 149,
    154
body
    affective; *see* affective body
    and agency 7, 29, 31, 118–19, 149
    and difference 25
    knowing through 2, 15, 21, 101, 118,
        196–7
    performative 34–5, 39, 98
    and rhythm 7, 17–18
borders 76
    colonial 77–8, 86n3, 133
    contested 78–9, 183–4, 191n17
    diffused 75, 183–4
    European 96–7, 106n16, 139; *see also*
        Europe
    invisible 50, 57, 79–80, 183
    movement across 25, 63n17, 85, 197
Brah, Avtar 5
Braidotti, Rosi 18, 43, 87n26, 103, 195
Bremner, Lindsay 21
Brick Lane 8, 62, 82
Bureau d'études 135–6, 137

Caillois, Roger 30–31, 39
Cartesian space 17, 100, 113; *see also*
    Euclidean space
Castells, Manuel 63n20, 96, 100
de Certeau, Michel 31
Cho, Lily 29
citizen 1, 2, 32, 36, 78, 83, 98, 116, 135
city-space 29, 32, 43, 98, 125, 148–50
coloniser/colonised relation 29–30, 33,
    40n35
community 32, 82–3, 132
    cohesion 1, 23, 58
    and protest 79
complexity 148, 189
conflict 40n35
conversation
    informal 37, 84, 183
    in mapping 119, 120–22, 129–30, 142,
        150, 183, 188, 190, 197
Corner, James 117–18
counter
    cartography 35, 95, 116, 119, 125,
        135, 139
    narrative 35, 120, 147, 152
Cruz, Teddy 3

decolonisation 110
Dehée, Anne-Lise 130
Deleuze, Gilles 2, 6, 18–19, 21, 22, 100,
    104, 147, 186
Deligny, Fernand 60–61, 131
Demos, T.J. 81
*dérive* 128–9
Derix, Christian 191n10
Derrida, Jacques 61
design research 2–3, 147, 190
deterritorialisation 81, 97, 104–5, 148,
    149, 173
diasporic
    domesticity 53, 54–5, 61
    embodiment 9, 25, 38, 149
    home 1–2, 4–5, 7, 23, 37–8, 43, 49,
        52–3, 59, 61, 148, 184, 196
    urbanism 6, 8, 9, 190, 195, 197
diasporic experience
    of multiplicity and dislocation of 24,
        33, 197–8
    and politics 38, 104–5
    of space 6, 15, 17, 21, 43, 195
diasporic subjectivity 4–6, 196
    and agency 7, 31–2, 34, 37, 80, 149,
        189

and belonging 25, 154
and deterritorialisation 97, 98, 104,
    172
and mediation 2, 18, 20–21, 75–6,
    84–5, 98
representation of 61, 149, 154, 172,
    189
displacement 4, 5–6, 18, 24, 29, 39, 49,
    196
diversity 3, 5, 18
Dodge, Martin 116, 117
drawing
    borders 79, 134, 183–6
    relations 3, 120, 137, 181–3
    and speaking 35, 149, 183–6
    as tracing 9, 60–61, 132–3, 142
duration 15, 18, 24, 34

enunciated practice 31–2, 130
environment
    distinction from 8, 30–31, 93, 101,
        126, 141
    as envelope 100–101, 104
    as habitat 102, 115
ethnicity 18, 31, 36, 58, 81, 98, 104, 130,
    184, 188
Euclidean space 20, 147–8, 155, 163,
    189, 192n8, 197; *see also* Cartesian
    space
Europe
    and borders 76, 78, 85, 90, 96–7, 98,
        106n16, 128, 139
    and diasporic communities 1, 3, 23,
        38, 43, 75–6, 198
European norms 33, 43, 98, 117, 119,
    135, 140
everyday (the) 3, 97, 147, 149
    acts 31–2, 50, 58–9, 119, 122, 172
    experience 4, 5, 17–18, 25, 39, 52, 80,
        162
    knowledge 140
    practice 32, 128, 132–3, 150
exclusive space 8, 174
exotic space/culture 8, 39, 49, 58, 61,
    62n1, 128

fact and fiction 122, 136–7, 142
feminist politics 22, 29, 33, 51, 119, 128,
    191n8
football 34–5, 50, 55, 56, 173, 175, 176
Foucault, Michel 40n24, 95
Fraser, Nancy 98

free acts 34, 39, 119, 196
freedom 25, 33, 40n24, 118

geo-politics 8, 38, 78, 85, 94–5, 96, 172
gestures
    as bodily performance 2, 18, 31, 36,
        52, 58–61, 130–31
    and habit 8, 38, 148
    in mapping 9, 35, 118, 122, 142, 149,
        173–4, 183–4, 60
Giddens, Anthony 46, 118
global flows 5, 57, 63n17, 63n20, 76
globalisation 5, 17, 18, 36, 76, 85,
        99–100, 113, 196; see also global
        flows
gold 54, 61, 63n14
gossip 51, 53, 61, 142
Grosz, Elizabeth 7, 15, 18, 24, 33–4, 119
Guattari, Felix 6, 18, 100, 104, 147
guesthouse 52, 53–4, 62n9

Habermas, Jürgen 98
Hackitectura 137, 139
Hackney 36, 79, 106n18, 150
Hall, Peter 35
Hall, Stuart 5
Haraway, Donna 22, 100, 103
Hirsch, Michael 79
home 10n3, 61, 126, 128, 174, 183; see
        also diasporic home
homeland 4, 37, 40n35
hooks, bell 53, 59
hospitality 61

imitation 31, 75, 81–2, 85, 140–41, 197
imprecise, imprecision 78, 160
inclusive space 8, 99
indeterminate 24, 33, 78, 131, 197
intensity of relations 7, 19, 26n12, 103,
        105, 126, 137, 139, 162, 166, 195,
        197
introverted 5, 49, 61, 99
Inuit 139–41
Islam/Islamic 27n32, 37, 62n4

Jeremijienko, Natalie 102

kahve 37–8, 50–61, 62n11, 76, 97, 115,
        148, 150, 168–83, 189
kahve talk 53, 56, 174–9
knowledge
    access to 120, 122, 135

amateur 51, 103, 117, 119, 125, 140,
    situated 22, 120
Kracauer, Siegfried 20, 26n13
Kurdistan 38, 79–80, 85, 149, 183–6,
    191n15, 196
Kurds 37, 38, 40n35, 54, 79, 80, 97, 98,
    106n18, 132, 191n15

Lahore 20, 24, 43, 77–8
landscape 35, 101, 126, 133, 139–40
Langley, Phil 148, 156, 164, 166, 170,
    182, 190, 191n6
Lash, Scott 21, 119
Latour, Bruno 32, 83–5, 101
Lefebvre, Henri 18–19, 148
Leibniz, Gottfried Wilhelm 19–20, 99
Leung, Simon 60
locality 50, 57–60, 63n18, 84, 174, 180,
    189
Lombardi, Mark 137–8
London
    Brick Lane 8, 62n1, 82
    Hackney 36, 79, 150, 196n18
    Spitalfields 37; see also Brick Lane
Lury, Celia 20, 22, 147–8

Manto, Saadat Hasan 78
map
    allegorical 49–51, 68, 134, 188
    counter; see counter cartography
    digital 9, 116, 147–8, 189–90
    immaterial/ephemeral 122, 125, 130,
        140, 149
    interpretative 9, 60, 142, 148–9, 190
    mental 61, 147, 186, 189, 192n18
    as navigational device 125, 126, 135,
        155, 181
    network; see network maps
    official 94, 95, 141, 186
    performative 9, 60, 122, 130, 133, 141,
        148, 149, 190
    relational 132, 136, 161, 181–3
map-making 116, 117, 120, 139
Marcus, Julie 54
marginal
    claims 63n17, 119, 125, 162
    spaces 49, 53 132, 180
    subjects 6, 9, 25, 53, 128, 142
martyr 81, 82
Massey, Doreen 36, 57, 63n18
Massumi, Brian 34
materiality 58, 100, 118, 196

McLeod Mary 129
mediation 20, 34, 36, 38–9, 43, 122, 126,
    130, 132, 197
memory 18, 117, 137, 142
Miéville, China 49
migrant 1, 50, 55, 60, 94, 97
    economic 54, 128
    integration/inclusion 3, 23, 32, 37, 75
    projects concerning 131, 132, 134,
        139
migration 1, 4, 17, 25, 57, 75, 96, 99, 105,
    132, 139, 173
military 30, 81, 134, 135, 161, 191n17
mimicry 7, 29–31, 32, 39, 119, 139–41,
    142, 188, 196
Min-ha, Trinh T. 53
moments 18, 21, 25, 36, 63n18, 149
Mooshammer, Helge 50
Mörtenböck, Peter 50
Mouffe, Chantal 36, 84
Muhurram 24, 27n32
multiplicity 18, 19, 23–4, 53, 61, 101,
    104–5, 118, 147–8, 174, 195–6
Muslim 1, 23, 37, 50, 75; see also Islam

naming 9, 31, 32, 50–51, 58, 126–8, 142,
    148, 172
narrative
    and nations 5, 25, 29, 75
    as technique 9, 19, 79, 116, 117,
        126–8, 133, 134, 137, 142, 161, 183,
        184, 190
nation-state 5, 7, 29, 37, 79, 94, 98–9,
    149, 196
network
    actor; see ANT
    affinity 54, 61, 96, 102–3, 196–7
    maps 148, 173–4, 181–3, 189
    neural; see ANN
    performative 2, 60–61
    power 96–7, 128, 135, 137–9
    social 35–6, 50, 55–6, 84–5, 148, 172,
        180
    society 58, 63n17, 96, 100
non-anthropocentric 8, 101–3, 105
nostalgia 7, 15, 50, 83, 104, 142, 184

object 19, 21, 25, 31, 37, 43, 75, 79, 81,
    83, 85; see also quasi-object/subject
observe, observing 9, 37, 142, 174, 183

occupation of space 60, 76, 95, 131, 166,
    197
other, the 7, 8, 19, 31, 39, 60, 77, 104,
    196
    geography 50, 130, 148, 172

Pakistan 4, 20, 24, 26n16, 27n32, 43,
    77–8, 79, 82, 99, 101, 191n17
parallel worlds 5, 36, 49–50, 97
participation/participative 22, 32,
    40n15, 98, 150, 190
performative
    body 34, 58
    act/enacting 80, 95, 154
Perkins, Chris 116, 117
Petrescu, Doina 60, 128, 131, 132–3, 134
pigeons 8, 101, 103–4, 105
politics of representation 119, 131, 137
post-colonial geographies 5, 40n35, 77,
    96–7, 98, 99
posthuman 100, 103
power 40n24, 94–6
    colonial 30, 33, 97
    hegemonic 59, 186
Precarias a la Deriva 129–30
protest 26n16, 37, 51, 79–80, 84–5, 128,
    150, 177
proximity 21, 38, 50, 80, 117, 134, 161
public space 8, 32, 37, 38, 49, 76, 80, 81,
    82, 84, 154, 189

quasi-object/subject 83–4, 101, 102,
    147, 161

Raad, Walid 136–7
radical cartography; see counter cartog-
    raphy
refrain 94
Rendell, Jane 6
replica 81, 82, 83, 85, 188
representation
    of agency 6, 147, 154
    of space 94, 96
    politics of; see politics of representa-
        tion
resistance 30, 31, 59, 79, 81, 96, 104,
    134, 139
reterritorialisation of space 5–6, 29, 37,
    104, 148–9, 172, 174, 183, 196
Reynolds, Craig 103

rituals 8, 31, 38, 58, 59, 61, 122, 148–9, 173
Rogoff, Irit 51
Rundstrom, R.A. 140

scale 2, 7, 15, 20, 21–2, 32, 78, 115, 181, 195
Scalway, Helen 141, 186
scapes 21, 98, 99
secular 75, 99
seed-eating 58, 59
segregation 1, 3, 23, 58
Sen, Jai 141
Sennett, Richard 78
Shaheed Minar 81–5, 149, 183, 188, 197
Sharif, Yara 133–4
signage 51, 52
signs 33, 43, 49, 52, 81, 131, 148
Situationists 128, 129, 131
Sloterdijk, Peter 8, 99–101, 105, 113
social club; see kahve
songlines 126, 128
souvenir 7, 8, 11n24
sovereignty 78, 98, 106n19
space
    actual 51, 149, 162
    Cartesian; see Cartesian space
    mediatory 25, 122, 139, 142
    multiple 3, 15, 18, 36, 61, 105, 115, 147, 155, 196
    relational 3, 17, 19, 22, 25, 100, 147–8, 155, 183
    social 49, 126, 148, 196
space-time 3, 18, 81, 84, 148, 195; see also spatio-temporalities
spatial
    agency 34, 118, 123n13
    deformation 173
    figuration 21, 25, 36, 39, 43, 57, 80, 94, 183, 186, 196–7
    geometries 20, 100, 113, 116
    inhabitation 6, 29, 31–2, 35, 43, 50, 99, 113, 115, 142, 147, 149, 154, 161, 189
    politics 29, 51, 132, 154, 162
spatio-temporalities 2, 7, 18, 25, 33, 35, 57, 61, 102, 113, 125, 147, 195–6; see also space-time
spheres 99–100, 101, 102, 104–5, 148, 154, 181, 189
Spivak, Gayatri 98
Stalker 37, 131–2

Steyerl, Hito 79, 81
striated space 99, 122, 139
subjectivity 33, 35, 51, 84, 137, 147, 149, 161, 184, 186, 188, 189, 196
subversive practice 7, 30, 39, 51, 122, 128, 130
symbolic meaning 22, 54, 61, 76, 80, 148, 190

tactic 6, 31, 39, 120–22, 128, 129, 133, 173, 183
technology 56, 101, 134, 137, 154, 161, 173, 181
temporality 5, 7, 24, 32, 34, 117, 181, 183
Terraswarm 103
territory 8, 20, 51, 58, 78, 93–7, 98, 102, 126; see also bio-territory
ticks 8, 101, 102–3, 104, 105
time
    cyclical 18, 39, 196
    rhythmic 7, 15, 18, 39, 166
topological
    approach 8, 25, 115, 125, 126, 197
    connections 9, 120, 141, 147–8, 162
    culture 34, 40n24
    deformations 51, 149, 161; see also spatial deformation
    object 25, 85
    spaces 7, 19–21, 22, 113, 147, 155, 181, 189
    surface 20–21, 22
topology 19–20, 22, 76, 160
tracing relations 21, 60–61, 62, 84, 116, 131, 132–4, 142, 161, 184
trajectories 31, 96–7, 133, 154, 161, 186
trans-local relations 2, 6, 54, 56–7, 131, 133, 148, 172, 174, 180, 189, 196
trans-localities 8, 10n2, 35, 59, 60–61, 125, 147
transnational 5, 10n3, 97

von Uexküll, Jakob 102
umwelt 93, 98, 101–2, 104
Unnayan 141
urban practice 36, 37

value systems 22, 33, 54, 61, 63n14, 76, 115, 147–8, 197
Verran, Helen 22, 115
visibility 37, 38, 75

walking
  as everyday act 31–2
  as mapping 122, 128–32, 133, 142,
    155, 161
  as urban practice 9, 35, 93, 105, 150,
    154

wandering 9, 128; *see also* walking
Weizman, Eyal 95
Winichakul, Thongchai 78
Wise, J. MacGregor 57

Yaneva, Albena 115